BORN 1900

Julius Hay

BORN 1900

Memoirs

Translated from the original German
and abridged by
J. A. Underwood

With a Foreword by
Arthur Koestler

A Library Press Book

Open Court, La Salle, Illinois

© Christian Wegner Verlag GmbH Reinbek bei Hamburg 1971
Translation © Hutchinson & Co. (Publishers) Ltd 1974

First printed in the United States in 1975 by Library Press, La Salle,
Illinois 61301.

ISBN 0-912050-53-5

Set in Monotype Ehrhardt

To the girl in blue

Contents

8

9

Foreword

by Arthur Koestler

On the third day of the Hungarian revolution of 1956, 'some farm wagons drew up in front of the Writers' Union. They brought gifts of food: bread, lard, live geese, whole carcasses of pork – in the midst of the starving city. These peasants had come seeking the writers out: it was for them that the otherwise hardly open-handed villagers had donated all these delicacies. Peasants and writers!...' (see pp. 331–2).

It is a fact – which sounds strange if not incredible to Western ears – that the most dramatic popular uprising in post-war history had been initiated by a handful of writers: novelists, playwrights, journalists, literary critics. Several factors contributed to this apparent paradox. One is the fundamental difference between the role played by intellectuals in Western democracies on the one hand, and in the various despotisms, past and present, in Central and Eastern Europe on the other. The *Concise Oxford Dictionary* defines the term 'intelligentsia' as 'the part of a nation (esp. the Russian) that aspires to independent thinking'.* Where there is freedom of speech, everybody can 'think independently' to his heart's content, and there is no particular virtue attached to it; nor are intellectuals held in high esteem. But where opinions are regimented, whether it be Tsarist Russia or the Hungary of 1956, every independent voice, if it succeeds in making itself heard, carries an explosive potential. Hence the deep, reverberating echoes of a Pasternak, a Solzhenitsyn – or

---

* *C.O.D.*, third edition (1934). In the fourth edition (1950) the words in brackets have been omitted.

of the voice of the Hungarian Writers' Union during that Budapest summer full of hope and promise.

There had been a Thaw – one of those periodic Thaws which precede a new Ice Age. Stalin was dead, and his successor had denounced him as a criminal maniac; Rákosi – Hungary's little Stalin – had been demoted; some of his victims were released from jail, others, who had been hanged, were posthumously rehabilitated. The air was full of great expectations – as if after a terrible drought the first clouds had at long last appeared over the horizon. But those clouds were still thin, diffuse – they needed seeding to condense and yield their vital moisture. There was no legal opposition party to fulfil that task, no independent trade union, no free Press. There were only two organizations of the intelligentsia, harmless in appearance, tolerated by the regime as a safety valve, which were allowed to indulge in a certain amount of 'independent thinking' – within the framework of Communist ideology. One was the Writers' Union and their weekly *Literary Journal*, the other the 'Petöfi Circle' of students and academics. Between them – perhaps to their own surprise – they provided the required seeding which triggered the cloudburst. What started as a monologue of disgruntled littérateurs became within a few weeks a dialogue with the nation which brought first the workers, then the kolkhoz peasants into the revolutionary camp. Hence the bread, pigs and geese which the rustics brought to the Writers' Union as a token of their common fight against an intolerably repressive regime.

It was a glorious episode in the history of the European intelligentsia, which, unavoidably, ended in a bloodbath. One of the major actors in the tragedy was Julius Hay, Hungary's most prominent playwright, and a devoted Communist who had proudly carried his Party card since the first Hungarian Commune of 1919, without ever getting tarnished by the corrosive atmosphere of intrigue, denunciation and sycophancy which dominated Stalin's brave new world. His immunity against corruption was derived from a kind of sleep-walking innocence, a complete lack of personal ambition – except the one, guiding passion to see his plays produced by a perfect cast, under a perfect director. He was at eighteen, and still is at seventy-three, the romantic type of revolutionary who would have felt more at home in the last century – on the barricades of 1848 – than being 'Born 1900'. This dreamy aloofness seems to have protected him not only against the perversions of Party life, but also against the more savage forms of persecution by the twin monsters of Gestapo and GPU. He survived the beginning of the Nazi regime in Berlin, the Great Purge of the thirties in Moscow, and Rákosi's terror years in Budapest, rather like a fire-walker unscathed – until the unavoidable fate of a romantic revolutionary born 1900 caught up with him at the age of fifty-seven. He was arrested, together with other writers who had taken an active part in the revolution, and after a secret trial – a farce performed behind closed doors to save some appearance of legality – was sentenced to six years of prison and confiscation of all his possessions. It was, by Eastern standards, still a mild sentence – what saved Hay, and other writers, from the gallows was a storm of international protests, with signatories ranging from conservatives to left-wingers, including eminent European Communists.

Hay's principal crime was a literary creation – Comrade Kucsera, a satire on the jackbooted Party boss,

the bureaucrat as wielder of power, as exploiter of our society . . .

I really do not like Comrade Kucsera – and I have my reasons. Nor does Comrade Kucsera have any liking for me. There's a reason for that too . . .

Kucsera is the great mistake of our History. Kucsera is the know-nothing by conviction and passion, who looks down on us from the pedestal of his ignorance and clings fanatically to the fallacious principle of the permanent sharpening of the class struggle . . .

There is no room in History for both Kucsera and us. We have to choose: either Kucsera or humanity. In Kucsera's eyes a lie is not a lie, murder not murder, law not law, and man not human . . .

This incendiary article, under the headline 'Why don't I like Comrade Kucsera?' was published in the *Literary Journal* on 6 October 1956, on the day when the bones of László Rajk – the former hero of the Party, hanged by Rákosi in 1949, now rehabilitated – were disinterred and reinterred again after a solemn state funeral. (See pp. 306–7.) Literally overnight, 'Comrade Kucsera' became a household word like Scrooge or Tartuffe, a national symbol for the little Neros who ruled the country. 'When the demonstrating masses filled the streets of Budapest on 23 October, many of their banners read, "Down with the Kucseras!" ' Rarely has a writer been offered such proof of the power of his pen.

The glory was shortlived. Less than a fortnight later the Russian tanks returned to Budapest and crushed the revolution under their tracks – Kucsera's juggernauts had the last word. But the last voice of the dying revolution, a strangled cry for help heard all over the world, was Julius Hay's. On the morning of 4 November, while the tanks rumbled into the capital, he and his wife rushed to the radio station in the Parliament building, which was not yet occupied by the Russians, and sent out a touchingly quixotic appeal to rouse the conscience of the world (see p. 333):

To all writers of the world, to all scientists, academics and leaders of cultural life: Help us! Time is short. You know the facts. We do not have to explain them! Help the Hungarian people! Help the Hungarian writers, scientists, workers, peasants and intellectuals! Help! Help! Help!

Then Julius and Eva Hay went home and waited. They could still have found a way to cross the Austrian border as tens of thousands did. Instead, Hay decided to stay and share the fate of his country – hoping against hope that the fall of the curtain was not final, that it would rise again for the second act with a happy finale which inaugurated the programme of the revolution, the utopia of 'Communism with a human face'. That too may be called a quixotic gesture – but without that gaunt knight and his avatars, the world would be even poorer than it is.

* * *

Julius Hay's dramatic oeuvre consists of about twenty plays written over forty years. There are collected editions in Hungarian and German, but so far only one play (*The Horse*) has appeared in English translation. It was one of *Three Eastern European Plays* (Penguin, 1970) and in his introduction Martin Esslin writes: 'Hay shows himself a master of the scrupulously constructed,

16

brilliantly carpentered "well-made play". He is a consummate craftsman in the manner of Ibsen, Hauptmann and Shaw . . .'

I am not alone therefore in considering him to be one of the outstanding dramatists of our time; yet it would be pointless to attempt a critical evaluation, referring to works which are not available to the reader. I hope that the long overdue translations of at least the major historical dramas will be published soon; and I am confident that they will have an impact similar to the belated discovery by the West of Bertolt Brecht – Julius Hay's only rival of comparable stature among playwrights of the European left.

Meanwhile the philosophy which is implicit in his plays, and is based on his experience of the past and his hopes for the future, is expressed in this autobiography with restraint and his own special brand of wry humour.

Prelude

Concerning Saul and Paul – Who is Staff
Sergeant Németh's boss? – Introducing my
constant companion

MY father died one summer day in 1934. I was unable to escort him to the grave because I was in prison in Vienna at the time. As a dangerous Communist.

My mother died one autumn day in 1958. I was prevented from attending her funeral by the fact that I was serving a term in a Budapest jail. As a dangerous anti-Communist.

Was Dr Berger, superintendent of political police in Vienna, telling the truth when he described me as a convinced Communist? Absolutely.

Was Comrade Justice Vida right in calling me an intellectual fomenter of the Hungarian Revolution of 1956 and sentencing me as an enemy of the Communist regime to six years behind bars? Unquestionably.

Between 1934 and 1958 lay a period of twenty-four years – more often than not the whole of a man's productive life. In my case they just sufficed to get me from one prison to another. On two entirely contradictory and mutually incompatible charges, moreover, and by such roundabout ways as could never be traced on any mere map.

Did *I* change so fundamentally during the course of those years? Did the world around me undergo so radical a transformation as to turn me into the opposite of what I had been before? Did my opinions, my aims, my very being somehow veer right round through one hundred and eighty degrees? Had white sheep become black and black sheep white?

Friends and acquaintances still ask me about the secret of those twenty-four years, years that – so at least it would appear – turned a Saul into a Paul or a Paul into a Saul, depending on who is asking the question.

There is of course no point to a record of this kind unless it sticks as close to the pure truth as it is possible for a man to make it do. I want to take the term 'memoirs' quite literally and only record things that spring spontaneously to memory. If there are things I have forgotten over the course of the years, then let them stay forgotten.

I have never kept a diary and hardly ever made notes; what little I did jot down here and there I have lost, right down to the last scrap of paper. I have made no use of newspapers, books or archive material of any kind. I had rather run the risk of making the odd mistake than trespass beyond the bounds of memory.

Once, on a journey from Moscow to Alma Ata in 1941, I carefully noted down in a little book – because I had a particular reason for regarding them as noteworthy – the names of the stations and the times of arrival and departure. A year later, when I wanted to refer to them, I found the pages blank. My Moscow pencil – wartime standard – had been so constituted that no trace of its passage remained.

Staff Sergeant Németh served in the special wing of the Budapest Reception Prison in which only condemned men awaiting execution and political detainees of my particular category were housed. He had been serving there since the First World War, when he had lost an eye in action. Occasionally – and it was a matter of complete indifference to him who was listening – he would start to talk about himself. His one and only theme was the high regard in which he was held by his commanding officer. This commanding officer, however, was a somewhat timeless figure, and Staff Sergeant Németh was no longer quite clear in his mind as to who exactly his commanding officer had been at any one time – His Excellency X, perhaps, or was it Comrade Y? And he could not have cared less where the people whom he regaled with his saga of subordination came from or where they were bound. Or whether they were always the same people or different each time. One thing he knew for certain: anyone occupying a cell on the ground floor was for the gallows early next morning. But whether the prisoners up on our floor were headed for the punishment cells or whether we were headed for the discharge cells was something he neither knew nor had any desire to know. Why should he? All he had to remember was how many of us there were; everything else was irrelevant and not worth thinking about.

We inmates of the special wing had neither Staff Sergeant Németh's experience nor his wisdom. We could see that the paths of our lives had repeatedly cut across the broad highway of world history, and we could not help wondering whether we ourselves had been steering a tortuous course or whether history had made such violent zigzags that, willy-nilly, our paths had kept crossing its own.

As I embark upon these memoirs at the age of almost seventy, it is with the intention – among others – of tracking down an answer to this question: will I, somewhere along the meandering line of my narrative, stumble across some Damascus road where as a result of a spectacular volte-face I became a different person? Or will I, despite the evidence of that abrupt reversal, be unable to pin down either a place or a time at which I switched directions?

Prisons change their masters fairly frequently nowadays. They change their inmates even more frequently. And the reason why the lock snaps shut behind you becomes more obscure each time. Whether my jailer-in-chief be His Excellency X or Comrade Y, the air I breathe is the same jail air, and peering at me through the peep-hole is Staff Sergeant Németh's single, age-dimmed eye.

Inevitably, the reader will sometimes get the feeling he is in prison himself. In one prison or another. Nor can I make any absolute promise that I shall be able to tell him at any one time exactly whose prisoner he is.

Rigidly as I have adhered to the strictest truth, my book still bears a certain resemblance to an adventure story. In every proper adventure story, hot on the hero's heels there is a travelling companion who sees to it that things stay adventurous, even at points where the stream of adventure threatens to dry up. In my case this companion's name is The Twentieth Century.

Born in the same year, the century and I have always been, and continue to be, year for year the same age. When the century – let's say – was ten years old, ten tiny candles were lighted on little J.H.'s birthday cake.* In fact we can abbreviate his name to J.H. 10. And now, when the old man under discussion must be referred to as J.H. 70, the twentieth century too is seventy years old.

I and the century, then, have marched side by side, even if one or the other of us has occasionally been a little out of step. And whatever the reader may think of this century of ours it will be signing its name – as the accused signs his statement – on every page of this book.

* *Jahrhundert*, 'century' in the language in which Julius Hay wrote his book, has of course the same initials as himself (Translator).

Part One

I

Three architects talk shop – Many plans go awry –
Banzai! – *Cucumbers and tallow candles –*
Breughel in Hungary

SHALL I tell you about young J.H. 14, who on a railway journey
between Cegléd and Abony (both in Hungary, about seventeen
kilometres apart) was dragged unwittingly by his constant or
inconstant travelling companion, the twentieth century, into the
most ghastly adventure conceivable and – in company with his
entire generation – more gambled with than any chip that was
ever tossed on a casino table?

He was a pupil at the Cegléd grammar school. The school year
1913–14 being at an end, the occasion was celebrated with an
excursion of several days' duration to what was then the south-
eastern tip of Hungary. The party descended the Danube as far
as the Iron Gate, that is to say as far as the frontier between
the Austro-Hungarian Empire and the Kingdom of Romania.

The excursion ended back in Cegléd and from there I travelled
alone to Abony. In the second-class compartment in which with a
wordless greeting to the other passengers I took a corner seat,
there were two gentlemen from Budapest whose destination was
the same as my own. After a few minutes' indiscreet eaves-
dropping and skilful decipherment of luggage-labels I was in
possession not only of the two gentlemen's names but also of the
fact that one of them – Mr Szegö – was an architect, and the
other – Mr Kis – a master builder.

School excursions call for a swaggering toilet. My own,
swaggering enough in my eyes, was doubtless unkempt in the
eyes of those who shared the compartment with me. But how shall
a fourteen-year-old just back from seeing and thereby making his

25

own the most splendidly remote reaches of his fatherland – how shall he publish his conquests except by means of dirty shoes and a dusty raincoat?

As, gazing down from the position of moral and patriotic superiority conferred upon me by my truly filthy shoes and my unbrushed raincoat, I saw Mr Kis (or was it Mr Szegö?) impatiently pull out his watch for the third time and look out of the window in search of the twin towers of Abony, I plucked up my courage, sprang open my pocket-watch (which had already earned me the respect of my schoolfellows during the excursion), and said, not without some emphasis, 'We shall be in Abony in fifteen and a half minutes from now.'

'How do you know we're going to Abony?' asked Mr Szegö (or was it Mr Kis?). 'The train goes on past there.'

Young J.H. 14 was of a shy and awkward nature (they tell me J.H. 70 is still the same). This time, however, he was properly launched (they tell me it happens to J.H. 70 too on occasion) and replied with an unnecessary volume of sound, 'Because the gentlemen are coming to see my father.'

'Who is your father, then?'

With a sudden lapse into shyness I spoke my father's name much too quietly. Even so it was not without its effect.

'The engineer?'

Feeling pretty secure now under the protection of my father's engineering diploma, dating as it did from the last century, I pointed to one of the drawings that the gentlemen had spread out before them.

'I drew that.'

It was a neatly executed ground-plan, on a scale of one to a hundred, of our house in Abony, with a series of projected alterations and modernizations sketched in.

'Did you really draw this yourself?' The gentlemen – who were also fairly young and not entirely sure of themselves – had begun to address me in the polite form of the second person, as they would have a grown-up.

'Yes.'

'But daddy gave you a hand?'

The idea of my father helping me with my drawing made me

laugh. He had long since lost all taste for the petty manual operations which his profession involved. Even to imagine him taking the compasses and T-square from my hand and beginning to draw himself was completely beyond me.

Thanks to the colossal admiration of the two gentlemen (and very likely of my mother as well) my neat little piece of work began to strike me as a quite extraordinary achievement. Rarely have I felt so utterly confident of myself and my abilities as I did at that moment.

The three of us began to talk shop. Among the subjects covered was the exact course of my future career. After passing my school-leaving examination I intended to matriculate in the Budapest School of Technology's faculty of architecture. Four years later J.H. 21 (only 21) would receive his diploma. One like my father had, and like my older brothers would have before long – all from the same university but each one from a different faculty. (For my younger brother there were no faculties left, but then he was only seven at the time.)

The two gentlemen offered me a job in their firm, which I could take up once I had my diploma and had spent two years studying abroad. I accepted their offer in all seriousness.

A well-ordered future in a well-ordered age. It was the very career that my parents had mapped out for me. Anything more reassuring it would be difficult to imagine.

Then we reached Abony, and had to alight.

A man with a flaxen Franz-Joseph beard and wearing the uniform of a railway official, complete with arm-band to show that he was on duty, emerged from the cloud of steam issuing from the locomotive and approached my two companions.

'Do the gentlemen happen to have any fresh news from Sarajevo?'

'Which Sarajevo would that be?' Mr Szegö, smiling gaily, clearly suspected a case of mistaken identity.

'Do you mean .. ? Good God! In that case, gentlemen, it is my sad duty to have to inform you that the Archduke and his wife have been assassinated by Serbs.'

J.H. 14 was not the only one who failed to grasp in that moment the full significance of the agonizing, odious, absurd, and hopeless adventure into which my travelling companion, the twentieth century, had just dragged us. Not one single detail of those beautiful and precise plans could henceforth become reality. I did not become an architect, nor did I ever receive a diploma either from that university or from any other. No drawing-board awaited me in the office of the two gentlemen. Instead I became intimately acquainted with the insides of numerous prison cells.

If I were to tell you everything that happened and that failed to happen from that moment on in consequence of the capricious game that my inseparable companion, the twentieth century, had begun to play with me, it would fill a book. In fact it is going to. This book.

I wanted to make some pertinent remark but nothing occurred to me. It was not that I was upset or deeply moved or anything like that. I simply did not know what one said when the heir to the throne was assassinated.

After a protracted silence Mr Kis said, half to himself, 'I'm an officer in the reserve, actually . . .'

The railway official: 'Railwaymen will probably be exempt . . .'

Mr Szegö, after a further long pause: 'But you surely don't think that a war . . . ? In the twentieth century . . . !'

It was not my first encounter with war. As a four- and five-year-old I used to rush around brandishing a little white flag with a large red spot in the middle and shouting, '*Banzai!*' The game was the Russo-Japanese War and I was a Jap. We all wanted to be Japs then. The Japanese were victorious enough at Liaojang and Tsushima, but in Abony they carried all before them.

Where Hungarian children got this unequivocal repudiation of Russian soldiery from in the early years of this century I cannot exactly say. The origins of the feeling probably lay back in 1848 and 1849. At the time when I was beginning to take notice of such things as personal relationships, that is to say a good half-century after the Russians had intervened to crush the great Hungarian revolution against the Habsburgs, the wounds were still smarting. One still saw the occasional old man in a thread-bare, tobacco-coloured uniform, wearing the red cap of Kossuth's citizen army, the Honvéd, with an arm missing or with a wooden leg, decently begging or perhaps employed as a park attendant or in some such capacity. These men were inexhaustible sources of reminiscences, depicting the historical role of the Tsar's army of intervention in ghastly detail, yet on the whole sticking pretty closely to the truth. So transparent and unmistakable a role as 'gendarme of Europe' it required no training in politics to understand.

What was surprising, though, was which details in particular of these retrospective accounts did most to stoke the fires of national feeling. I remember one aged, aged woman who practised the indispensable trade of going from farm to farm making capons of the superfluous cocks. At the time of the Russian intervention she had been a young and – by her own account – very pretty girl, and she would often whisper tales of goings-on that at that time passed my understanding. But even on grown-ups the effect was equivocal. Perhaps they lacked the imagination to picture the witch-like old crone before them as a sixteen-year-old girl, and to tremble for her virginity.

There was nothing equivocal, however, about their indignation when the woman related that the Russians had eaten raw cucumbers. In Hungary, or at least in my part of it, cucumbers are only eaten in the pickled state. People who simply plucked and ate them were clearly capable of anything. According to another version the Russian soldiers had eaten tallow candles. There was no distinguishing between probable and improbable in reports of this kind.

This traditional antipathy towards the Russians, whom we twentieth-century Hungarians held responsible – not entirely without justification – for the political and economic subjection in which our country was held, was combined in the case of the more sophisticated kind of Hungarian intellectual with a predilection for progressive Russian literature. In the circle in which I grew up Tolstoy, Dostoievsky, and Chekhov were among the authors most widely read. Gorky was someone everybody knew at least by name. One was able at any rate to draw a distinction: one was delighted at the sinking of the Russian warship *Petropavlovsk* but one mourned deeply the fact that the anti-war painter Vereschagin, who had been on board in order to record on canvas the horrors of war, should have been among the dead.

When in 1917 we heard that the long-awaited Russian Revolution had at last arrived, that the Tsar was overthrown and democracy was victorious, our natural reaction was, 'Quite right too – no more than we expected of you.'

At that time, though, the hatred was almost always bound up with historical memories and abstractions. Once the Russians entered our lives as living people – for prisoners-of-war began to be sent to the village to bolster the dwindling labour force – we found ourselves prepared from the bottom of our hearts to forgive them more and more – the intervention, the violence, the cucumbers, the tallow candles – simply and solely as a result of the shattering and hope-inspiring recognition on our part that they were people too.

If the Hungarian had inherited from the previous century an aversion to Russians, a whole series of earlier centuries had given him a solid tradition of hatred of the Germans. Of the actual causes of the war we were ignorant, nor were we in the habit of inquiring into such things. But about one thing every Hungarian was clear in his mind: the interests of Germany and Austria-Hungary were by no means identical, while those of the two principal parts of the Monarchy, the Kingdom of Hungary and the Austrian Empire, were downright incompatible.

Real hatred was something the people of Hungary felt only for Serbs. It was the hatred of a guilty conscience. Hungarian farmers, particularly pig-farmers – and not only the wealthy ones but also the middling wealthy – had an interest in the suppression of Serbian agriculture. Hungarians therefore had a tendency to believe anything bad of the Serbs and to sing old soldier songs expressive of their hatred. In fact they were almost prepared to go so far as to mourn the most unpopular couple in Hungarian history upon the latter's assassination in Sarajevo.

Montenegro and its King Nikita belonged, in our imagination, primarily to the world of operetta. Croatia was a kind of autonomous portion of Hungary. Bosnia and Herzegovina had been formally annexed in 1908 and were regarded as being the common property of Austria and Hungary, Dalmatia we considered Hungarian in theory but Austrian in practice, and as for the other parts of what is now Yugoslavia, such was our national conceit that we were barely even aware of them. There was occasional mention of Russian influence among the Yugoslav peoples as being a vaguely disturbing and even insulting factor.

For young and old alike, therefore, it was a big surprise to find that the war had become such a serious business.

We children spent the time making vast quantities of cigarettes, filling the cheapest papers with positively the lowest grade of tobacco. We took the full packets along to the station and there assisted the ladies of the locality to supply thousands of transit troops with something to smoke. German troop transports started passing through our station as early as the autumn of 1914 for it lay on one of the main lines of communication with the eastern front. We gradually became accustomed to the outward appearance of German soldiers, and custom did something to mitigate our dislike. Everything the newspapers had talked about in order to win people's hearts for the great ally – his strength, his might, his organization – had served only to feed people's animosity. The things we found to laugh at, on the other hand, created a certain feeling of sympathy.

And we found plenty to laugh at. The little round caps without a peak that the German soldiers wore would have suited children better than grown men. Their half-length boots looked as if they were only half-finished. Then there was the fact that the Germans were too thin, often being incredibly tall with a correspondingly narrow build. They also had protruding Adam's apples and an unusually high proportion of them wore spectacles, had squeaky voices, and were ungainly in their movements. And one day they betrayed a further shortcoming that made them even more ridiculous in our eyes and contributed towards dissolving that great, abstract hatred: they could not take their wine.

Szolnok station was incapable of dealing with the steady stream of troop transports without considerable delays. Trains used to be held up for hours at a stretch between stations or at smaller country halts.

31

Was permission granted, I wonder, or was there just no stopping them? Anyway, one day the entire complement of several
carriages decided to leg it to the nearest village for a friendly call.

Our Abony was an overgrown village that had never quite
succeeded in becoming a town. Such villages are characteristic
of the Great Hungarian Plain. At that time it numbered seventeen
thousand inhabitants but with the exception of an extremely
modest centre – and even that was without mains water and
drainage – every street and every corner of every street looked as
if it belonged to some God-forsaken hamlet.

Your Hungarian – every inch a generous host – gave his visitor
a cheerful welcome. 'Wife, give the poor lad a glass of the new
wine.' 'Let the unfortunate fellow drink.' 'Another glass won't
do him any harm.'

But the Germans, used to beer, did not get on with our new
wine at all. They gulped it down like water instead of rolling it
round the tongue in the approved fashion and holding it up
thoughtfully against the light to judge the progress of clarifica-
tion. They simply tossed it back and held out their glasses for
more.

The Hungarian host kept his guest company, savouring his
own wine slowly and with much smacking of the lips. Imbibed
with a proper restraint, it remained his friend.

Within the space of half an hour the whole landscape was
transformed. The three-and-a-half-kilometre stretch of road
between the station and the centre of the village was suddenly
full of drunken Germans. They strayed off into the fields, stag-
gered about, keeled over, and fell asleep. They tried laboriously
to get to their feet again, leaned against one another for support,
and collapsed in a heap. They swore at one another and then
burst into tears or brayed with helpless laughter. They puked
over themselves and each other, dropped their trousers, crawled
about on all fours, and rolled in the ditches. As far as the eye
could reach, Abony was metamorphosed into a painting by
Breughel.

The host shrugged his shoulders with a kindly grin. Of course,
if a fellow can't drink, he first has to learn.

From the station came the despairing, panicky shriek of the

waiting engine. From a radius of several kilometres came an answering chorus of snores, farts, belches, and groans.

Did the train steam off empty or did it wait there, blocking the line, until one by one the German soldiers slowly trickled back? I don't remember.

But from that afternoon on it was crystal clear to the Hungarian peasant that the Germans were going to lose this war.

As the war progressed, however, the first naively enthusiastic desire for victory gradually evaporated. When one saw one's older friends disappear from their school desks into the army, when one knew how soon one's own turn would come – for there was no end to the nightmare in sight – when one noticed how every week more and more of one's schoolfellows wore the mourning crape on their arms, when one witnessed at first hand how children who had thought of nothing but play the day before were turned overnight by the war into their families' breadwinners, and how young people, overtaxed by this burden, sank into apathy, or a gloomy seriousness, or a cocky omniscience, or a cheerless practicality, or an unhealthy boredom – when one had all this before one's eyes the question whether kings and generals would conquer or be conquered was of secondary importance.

We, the children of that time, played savage games; we had the twentieth century for a playmate.

2

A well-balanced account – Taming the wild waters – Question: Are women grateful?

FATHER'S salary as manager and chief engineer of the Gerje and Perje Flood-Control Company cannot have been very high. (Gerje and Perje, incidentally, were not two gentlemen but two streams by means of which Father had brought a section of the refractory Tisza valley under control.) The private commissions for engineering jobs that came his way from time to time were not particularly rewarding financially. So occasionally my father would borrow small amounts from my grandfather, which he would then pay back with painstaking exactitude.

Although Father had five brothers and sisters, the family fortune remained concentrated right up until 1909 in one hand, a hand as spindly as a mummy's, threaded with blue-black veins, covered with grizzled hairs, and stinking of the cheapest pipe-tobacco its owner – my grandfather – could buy.

Again until 1909 I had daily to cross the road to my grandparents' house opposite and kiss that hand. Had it not been for this unappetizing but compulsory expression of affection I might even have been fond of the gnarled little old fellow. Even so I had more time for him than for my grandmother, despite that lovely smell of freshly baked cakes that always wafted into the room with her.

When one sets out to relate the story of one's own life one finds oneself telling an almost endless tale of other people's deaths. Of all the close relations that peopled the Abony of my childhood only one – apart from myself – is alive as I write these words: my sister Juliska. She is ten years older than I. Before I reach the

34

last page of this book, Juliska will have her eightieth birthday behind her. When my hare-brained travelling companion, the twentieth century, first met her she was already a well-brought-up schoolgirl in a black pinafore and with her hair done up in a short, thin, ash-blonde pigtail, on her way to school with her dark-haired sister Irene, who was a year older than herself. Irene died at the age of forty-five.

First, then, I must tell you about my grandfather's death.

Grandfather was a short, thin, silent, pipe-smoking, old, rich, Jewish Hungarian. For further information about his and his family's origins I refer you to Chief Rabbi Dr Vajda's learned book, *Az abonyi zsidók története.* The book is written in Hungarian and its title means 'History of the Abony Jews'. The author's name has a Hungarian ring as well although back in the days of Kaiser Joseph II, when the Hungarian Jews received their surnames, the Austrian officials will certainly have seen to it that his ancestors too were issued with a suitably foreign-sounding appellation.

But there in the middle of the Great Hungarian Plain large populations of non-Hungarian extraction were engaged in a silent and unremitting process of merging with their Hungarian environment.

Curious that a nation so small numerically as the Hungarian should possess such a large capacity for assimilation. Moreover it is a capacity they enjoy making use of. Many nations look askance at people who shrug off their own national characteristics and adopt the idiom of the majority. The changing of surnames to make them sound indigenous is regarded in many countries with mistrust. Hungarians, particularly around the turn of the century, took it entirely as a matter of course that families that lived in Hungary and had inherited foreign-sounding names from their ancestors should exchange these for names that lay more comfortably on Hungarian tongues.

When I and the century were still children this process of assimilation was going ahead at a particularly rapid rate, helped by the fact that the lowland Jews were extremely liberal from the religious point of view and had for generations practised only a token observance of the old orthodox forms. Even when they were devout, their religious devotion went hand in hand with national feeling.

I remember the Abony station-master, Mr Vámos; he was a devout synagogue-goer, but on the white shroud and accompanying headgear that were the required dress for particularly festive occasions in the life of the synagogue he had had embroidered – it was beautifully done in gold thread – the emblem of the Hungarian State Railways. (Mr Vámos, by the way, did not die in his white shroud with the gold-embroidered winged wheel. He died in a gas-chamber in Auschwitz.)

At the time I am talking of, then, the majority of the Jews living in the Hungarian lowlands regarded themselves not as Hungarian Jews but as Jewish Hungarians.

But in 1918 the Austro-Hungarian Monarchy collapsed. The boundaries of our country – boundaries we had only recently believed to be so sacrosanct and untouchable – shrank overnight. All the evil and baseness that lay dormant in man this convulsion unleashed upon my contemporaries. Including anti-Semitism. Thousands of hungry and homeless Hungarians retreated in streams towards the middle of the country. Hunger begat envy, and envy begat a jealous exclusiveness. Was the non-Magyar to be accepted as Magyar when shortage of land, shortage of the necessaries of existence, sometimes even shortage of a roof over one's head, made life a bitter struggle?

What was to happen fifteen and twenty years later was another story entirely; in the shadow of the Auschwitz crematoria it would be nonsense to talk of assimilation.

Grandfather Miska was, as I said, a wealthy man. At least, what was considered wealthy at the time. Nowadays he would hardly even qualify as 'comfortable'. He owned land and stock and houses. Houses in Abony and an elegant apartment-house in Budapest, in which he had his own second residence.

Once a year, in autumn, Grandfather and Grandmother would climb into the closed carriage with glass windows that was reserved exclusively for this purpose, and that the staff referred to grandly as 'the coach'. My bachelor uncle Gyula and my old maiden aunt Emmi, brother and sister to my father, followed in an open carriage. The luggage went on a cart. The cook and one kitchen-maid had been sent on ahead, and the parlour-maid rode beside the driver of the 'coach'. Thus they proceeded to the station on the first leg of the journey to winter quarters in Nádor Square in Budapest. In spring the process was reversed and the party returned by the same route to the summer residence in Abony. In both residences the unmarried brother and sister occupied a modest room apiece. The house in Szolnok Street, Abony, was a solid and spacious affair that looked as if it had been built to last for ever. (The Second World War left not one single brick standing on another.)

Attached to the house were a disproportionately small and unlovely garden, a stable for three pairs of horses, a coach-house, a kitchen wing, a bath-house, and a three-storey barn. The barn contained mostly wheat – good, hard durum wheat – because that is what a landowner in the Great Hungarian Plain grows for preference. Grandfather also had some flocks of sheep. When the sheep were shorn the wool was stuffed into enormous sacks and these too were stored in the barn.

One day in 1909 the wool was delivered as usual. Grandfather – aged ninety-three – had some years before given up his old habit of standing by the scales throughout the weighing. These days he had a wooden stool brought from one of the servants' rooms. He entered everything in a little note-book item by item in his tiny, rounded hand.

He then went up to his room, settled himself on the black leather sofa, arranged his spectacles with some ceremony on his nose, and added up all the items. Looking up at the clock that hung ticking away and striking the quarter-hours from the wall above his head, he pulled his fat, gold repeater from his pocket, checked it against the clock, found the comparison satisfactory, climbed on to the sofa, wound the three weights up to the top with the little handle, sat down again, filled his long-stemmed cherry-wood pipe with tobacco, lit it, carefully got it going, closed his eyes, and died.

Inquisitive sons and grandsons of course wanted to know whether in the final hour of his existence the old man had still been able to add up as well as before. They checked that note-book page by page and did not find a single mistake.

I am his grandson – one of thirteen. I have more than once had to cover half the distance to death and then after all received a reprieve for the second half. On not one of those occasions would my death have borne any resemblance to my grandfather's. None of his peace, none of his impeccable adding-up . . . And not a shred of a hope of eternal repose . . .

The heirs forgathered at our house to decide upon the most judicious distribution of the inheritance. At the grand family banquet that ensued, a young serving-girl, having smashed forty-two china plates with a single clumsy movement, was not even told off. The rest of the staff drew the unanimous conclusion that the inheritance had turned out to be even larger than expected.

Father would not accept that this put our family economy on an entirely different footing. He refused, for example, to give up his job as an engineer. His paternal admonitions were few and far between, but one of them was to the effect that agriculture was a chancy business and that the only guarantee of a solid liveli-hood was a diploma. He was delighted when the first member of the family – my older brother Max – collected his diploma in chemical engineering and specialized in agricultural chemistry. (Seek him not, the quiet, unlovely Max. He met his end in Bergen-Belsen, while his wife and small daughter were killed in Auschwitz.)

My second oldest brother Bandi took his diploma exam and went to work in one of the biggest factories in Budapest (and when, thirty-two years later, his work and his life both came to an end, he was still in the same factory, though by then in a managerial position).

It was only my younger brother Kari that no one expected to become an engineer. His artistic gift already appeared to be beyond question when he was only five or six. (Him too you will no longer find among the living. He lies in Buda cemetery, under one of those standard gravestones with which the Communist Party furnishes the graves of its former partisans of the middle rank. He contracted a heart disease in the fascist death-camp at Bor and died of it after a long and painful illness in 1961.)

How my father came to attach such importance to the engineering profession I do not know. Perhaps his going to university was the upshot of a fierce struggle with his father, who placed the same exclusive faith in agriculture as my father was to do in technical know-how and a certificate to show for it. There was a time when my father had to be out of the house day and night often for weeks on end. On horseback in the early years and later in a britzka with two enormous wheels, he would dash hither and thither along the Gerje and the Perje, always on the spot to do battle with the wild waters that flowed down the flat valley of the moody River Tisza. He spent the nights under canvas, and lived during the week on the chunk of salami that he took with him; the dam supervisor's wife baked his bread.

My father had *one* great passion, and that was music. He played the cello. Was he a true artist or merely a gifted amateur? Again I cannot say. In his younger days he played in large Budapest orchestras that were still under the spell of Franz Liszt. He also appeared as a soloist, mostly in churches. Having no interest whatsoever in matters of religion, he was utterly indifferent to which particular faith those churches adhered to. His cello paid its respects to each and every God – or to none at all. In Abony he had a trio and organized musical evenings once or twice a week. They played mainly Mozart and Haydn.

I remember him coming home from Budapest on one occasion. I may have been six or seven years old at the time. He had been to a concert the previous evening and had heard a young cellist. 'Chaps like us ought never to pick up a bow again. No one should dare even to attempt the cello after that young man ...' 'That young man' was a Spaniard, and his name was Pablo Casals.

Now, looking back on that scene, I realize that that taciturn man with his impeccable outward calm was capable of experiencing deep emotion without betraying the slightest sign. A great deal of it undoubtedly escaped me, owing to the fact that he was not more communicative. Or would I have had to meet him halfway? But how could I have done – I who was his son and had inherited from him that selfsame characteristic?

Politically he struck me as conservative, though one could only go by the newspapers he read. I never once heard him discuss politics or attempt to bring anyone round to his point of view. Not even when his sons – Kari and myself – took a political direction that was alien to his nature. At first I respected him deeply for it. Later I was less generous and put it down to a certain inertia on his part. Today I am convinced that in the very depths of his heart he was so dissatisfied with his own life that he made a point of never trying to show others the way.

My parents' marriage was considered exemplary. Even after the arrival of the fifth or sixth child, when little nervous tiffs and my mother's migraine-like headaches had already begun to be the order of the day, the legends of the last century lived on – legends of a violent passion, of my mother's parents' refusal to give their daughter to a man fifteen or sixteen years her senior, of the engineer's threat to abduct his chosen, and finally of love's unqualified triumph. The legends lived on, and came to my ears by way of the kitchen.

My mother did not give the impression of being cut out to weather the storms of history. She was sensitive, demanding, and of a playful nature. Yet she was among those who managed to hold out longest under the shattering strains to come.

In 1944 she just missed deportation. Consigned to the Budapest ghetto, she came out of it alive – at seventy-five. And lived for another fifteen years, almost reaching her ninetieth birthday.

My mother was a short woman, but her rotundity, clad in the fashions of the turn of the century, gave her a truly imposing presence. She read a great deal – Hungarian, German, and French – but most of the books were from the lending library; she never wanted to build up a library of her own. She subscribed to the Parisian magazine *L'Illustration*, which carried a supplement in which a complete play was printed, with photographs of the Paris production. I used to stare at those pictures for hours and hours, dreaming of God knows what non-existent plays.

My mother was fond of retailing her experiences in an interesting and – when the company was right – often over-colourful manner, a fact which earned her the secret scorn of her more soberly and objectively inclined daughters.

Religion was a point of honour with her, but *only* a point of honour. She fasted rigorously on Yom Kippur so that no one might say she was a free-thinker for convenience's sake. All other religious rules and regulations, particularly those pertaining to the household, she openly and pretty consistently disregarded.

Her great problem in her younger years was her weight. When I was a small child I often used to help her dress. The lacing-up of her corset called for both strength and skill. For some reason this was a service for which I particularly enjoyed receiving her praise. On more than one occasion she turned to me with a smile I did not understand and said, 'Women will be grateful to you for that.'

Women were *not* grateful. They discarded the corset, and my generation had to readjust its ideas en route.

The war against overweight was a long and bitter one, yet in her old age it turned out to have been superfluous after all. By 1944 my mother had lost so much weight that her daughter Juliska, who was no taller than she, could pack her exhausted body on her back and carry her into the ghetto.

Yes, indeed – my generation has often had to readjust its ideas. Often and without success.

3

Flowers to topple tyrants – Good-bye architec-
ture – A discussion in the Váci-utca

HOLLYHOCKS, masses and masses of hollyhocks . . .

It was something of a mystery to me why at eleven o'clock of an ordinary October morning a man dressed half in uniform and half in civvies should be striding across the Abony marketplace strewing far and wide, with improbably sweeping gestures more suitable to a Greek god than a shell-shocked Hungarian infantry-man, enormous quantities of white hollyhocks.

My brother Bandi was then twenty-five; I was eighteen. Bandi had just spent several weeks in a Budapest military hospital after having been hit by a shell fragment, and he was now on three days' home leave before he had to return to his mounted artillery regiment on the eastern front. I had taken a few days off from the School of Technology, as I often did.

Bandi was in the middle of an affair with an assistant radiologist called Hedda, an extremely attractive girl who kept up a wide-ranging interest in young men while – so Abony rumour had it – officially sleeping with her elderly boss. I went with him to the coffee-house where Hedda usually left the little notes by means of which they organized their evening rendezvous. He said he would only be a minute but in fact he was in there for some time.

Meanwhile Mrs Neruzsil from the laundry appeared with a huge basketful of the white hollyhocks with which she usually spent that time towards the end of October making wreaths for All Saints' and All Souls'. She was immediately surrounded by a crowd of people and in no time at all had sold every last flower in her basket. Everyone now had at least one flower either in his hand or stuck into his army cap, and still I had no idea why.

42

A lorry came roaring past from the direction of Szolnok and disappeared without stopping down the road towards Cegléd and Budapest, chock-full of soldiers brandishing white hollyhocks and shouting something unintelligible.

There was an element of the unreal about Bandi too, as there was about everything that morning in Abony marketplace. He emerged from the coffee-house wearing the by now inevitable hollyhock stuck into the front of his officer's cap where the rosette with the king's monogram had been. The rosette was no longer there; it had been cut off. The two gold stars to right and left that indicated the rank of lieutenant were no longer there either. A few twisted ends of black thread outlined the bare patches.

That day every ranking and non-commissioned officer in Hungary had been demoted by the masses; they were all just plain soldiers, with no right to issue and no desire to receive orders.

'If you want to know,' Bandi told me in an over-loud and unreasonably aggressive voice, 'it's revolution, that's what it is! See those white hollyhocks? Well, anyone wearing one of those is for the revolution! And no more stars on our collars! Do you understand? No more little silver and gold stars . . .' He burst out laughing and threw himself into a tango step. 'And maybe . . . maybe I won't even have to go back to the front!'

By this time I too had a white hollyhock in my buttonhole, though I could not have said who had put it there.

That was the first revolution at whose birth I was present. And how many more were to come?

That same evening (or was it one of the following evenings?) Count Tisza, the dictator who for years had enjoyed almost unlimited power, was assassinated. A party of unknown soldiers – so we read – had ferreted him out and shot him where he stood.

Unknown soldiers . . . So the unknown soldier had become a factor in politics. The man over whose mortal remains – discreet object of some discreet diplomatic ceremonial – all governments were later to erect gravestones, once stormed and rampaged around threateningly in the flesh, on foot or in the back of a lorry, with a loaded rifle in his hands, hand-grenades at his waist, and a white hollyhock in his cap or buttonhole.

No blood-bath, no St Bartholomew's Day Massacre followed Tisza's death. Instead there came a moment of calm, settled enough to be capable of providing a sensible solution to the most pressing problems of many peoples.

But history was not sensible. The men who made it were even less so. They all seized the first available opportunity to take a wrong turning, and their successors have proved incapable of making good their mistakes.

That evening my father shut himself up alone in his room and played the cello for hours and hours.

Had the world continued to be as stable as it had been – or had seemed to be – four years before, I should have accepted the university as it was and patiently made allowance for everything I felt was wrong with it. Now that everything was suddenly on the move, however, we soon became aware of how meaningless and irrelevant our university studies were.

The Váci-utca in Budapest was renowned as being the finest and most fashionable shopping street in the country, indeed in any country – east of Vienna. It and a part of the Danube embankment together formed a most attractive promenade. After crossing the Kossuth-Lajos-utca, the Váci-utca continued as a quiet residential street, and at number forty there was a small pension belonging to a couple called Palkovits. A not unfriendly little room in the Pension Palkovits was my home at the time the hollyhocks revolution began. (Many years later this same pension was to play a momentous role in my life.)

Beautiful women, magnificent horses, famous people, the finest goods in the shop windows – even in the fourth year of the war the Váci-utca refused to give in. Or was giving in so discreetly that one hardly noticed it. Perhaps the beautiful women were a little worn – not with love but with the cares and irritations of everyday existence. Most of the carriages were drawn by discharged military horses, and the solid celebrities of pre-war years had largely been replaced by *nouveaux riches* and nine days' wonders. Until the day of the hollyhocks.

On that first night of the revolution the centre of Budapest was trying to sham dead. The streets were deserted and almost with-out light. It was drizzling. A carpet of wilting, soiled, and trampled hollyhocks lay underfoot. My steps echoed and re-echoed in apparent emptiness. In the pension I found the door of my room locked. Three pairs of shoes stood outside – one pair of men's shoes and two pairs of ladies' shoes.

Mr Palkovits came hurrying from the kitchen. 'My dear fellow, but you said you'd be away for three or four days.'

'The room remains mine even in my absence.'

'Well, yes, but . . .'

'Whose are these shoes?' I demanded aggressively, if not too intelligently.

Mr Palkovits was a good forty. The jacket of his uniform, with the two pairs of stars of a first lieutenant still in place, was only half buttoned up. He paused for a moment before announcing with some solemnity, 'Those shoes belong to three refugees.'

His words having failed to produce the effect anticipated, he went on rather crossly to explain that the shoes were the property of refugees from Eszék in Croatia, relations of his who had turned up unexpectedly after a perilous journey and had asked to be taken in. With a full complement on his books he had had to put them in my room. I must now make do with a temporary solution.

For the moment I was less interested in the problem of a temporary solution than in the fact that people were fleeing from Croatia. Why?

Mr Palkovits became more and more worked up as he explained between weighty imprecations how the national minorities were everywhere up in arms. Entire regiments of Croatian and Slavonian soldiers had scandalously deserted the front and instead of going back to barracks had camped in their thousands in the forest, calling themselves the 'Green Cadres'.

'Bravo!' I cried, and in no time at all the kitchen of the Pension Palkovits was the scene of an impassioned set-to on the subject of the nationalities question in Hungary.

Mrs Palkovits, an attractive blonde with an enigmatic smile, came in wearing a dressing-gown over her nightdress. She in-formed me in a whisper that for the rest of the night I could have the maid's room, that in two days' time her husband had to report back on duty, and that then a more permanent solution would surely offer itself; if I would forgive the inconvenience, she added, and be sympathetic towards the unfortunate refugees, I should not regret it in the long run. All this was accompanied by a smile that did indeed promise rich rewards and by that misty look with which as an eighteen-year-old in an unsettled time I was becoming gradually familiar.

Having long since ceased to regard the Kingdom of Hungary as an indivisible entity and the paradise of its subject peoples, I found the nationalities question a constant source of concern and anxiety. I had accidentally come across the book written on the subject by that outstanding expert on Hungarian affairs, Oszkár Jászi, and had read it avidly. Little by little I had become aware of the diabolical architecture of the prison in which Austria-Hungary kept its national minorities and in which Hungary, itself a passive prisoner, was at the same time a cruel jailer. I had looked for and discovered other books and obtained an increasingly clear picture of the appalling contrasts that made life in that monstrous political system such hell.

The solution to the whole intricate complex of problems was summed up by the one word 'federation'. Complete national, cultural, and linguistic freedom for all nations and national groups from the greatest to the smallest coupled with a free and voluntary union of the peoples thus liberated. The Switzerland of Eastern Europe – that was what Hungary must become, and this federation must solve its problems in free collaboration with an Austria similarly reorganized on a federal basis.

No task seemed to J.H. 18 more urgent on that night of the hollyhocks, in the midst of the uprising (of which, however, the only perceptible evidence was the occasional lorry roaring past and the very occasional sound of a shot) than to win Mr Palkovits round to the federalist system as the basis of the Hungary of the future. It puzzled and annoyed me that an other-wise intelligent man, instead of welcoming the truth with open arms, should so obstinately and arrogantly resist it.

The first lieutenant – in civilian life an insurance executive – although himself either Serbian or Croatian by origin, clung grimly to the sovereign authority of the Hungarian nation over all national minorities within the historical frontiers of the kingdom. He described to me in gruesomely imaginative detail the retribution that should be wrought upon the mutinous subject nations. He would rather, he said, make unlimited concessions to Austria than recognize the rights of the minority peoples.

Meanwhile Mrs Palkovits had removed her slippers in order not to wake boarders or refugees with the clopping of her heels, crept into my room to collect my things, and brought them down to the kitchen. Among them were my books, and on top of the pile of books lay a number of pamphlets by Karl Marx that the Socialist Publishing House had just brought out. In Tisza's heyday they could never have been published so openly.

Palkovits pounced on them. 'So that's it! That's what's behind all this!'

The kitchen was unheated and Mrs Palkovits drew her husband's army greatcoat over her shoulders as she stayed to watch the struggle. Her smile, almost mocking by now, was both amused and provocative.

'So that's the nigger in the woodpile, is it?' shouted Palkovits, beginning to lose his temper. 'That's what you're trying to get at, is it? That's why you want to louse up our monarchy with all kinds of Slovaks, Romanians, Croats, Serbs, Czechs, Slovenes, Bosnians, Ruthenians, and God knows what! Don't give me any of your socialism, young man! The Russians can have it if they like. And Mr Trotsky! And Mr Lenin! We Hungarians are gentlemen. You won't catch us eating out of the same pot as a rabble of gipsies. Nor passing our women round, either. You ought to be ashamed of yourself, young man!'

The blonde gave a little giggle and pulled coat and dressing-gown more snugly round her with a movement that began by leaving her transparent nightdress exposed for the space of several emphatic seconds.

I was confused. The version of socialism that I had come across in my reading of Marx and Engels and in the popular pamphlets was very different from the one expounded by Palkovits. I tried to explain that what I mainly looked to socialism for was perpetual peace. After all, war – as I maintained as insistently as he trotted

47

out his tales of free love and the victualling of entire city blocks
from a single field-kitchen – was purely and simply the result of
economic crises, which in turn were the result of the capitalist
pursuit of profit.

'But that's human nature. Turn and turn about! What do you
propose to do about that, young man?'

'Expropriate the expropriators.'

'What does that mean?'

'Make it impossible for anyone to exploit other people.'

'Your old man included?'

'In so far as he is an expropriator, my father included. Everyone! The lot of them!'

'A fine son you are! And how do you intend to set about it?'

'The revolution.'

'And where's your revolution going to leave *me*, eh? Strung
up somewhere?'

'But Mr Palkovits, I don't want to . . . I mean, there'll be no
need to . . . No, but surely you see . . .'

'I don't bloody see anything! Murderous bloody mob!'

'But a federal system . . .'

'You're not shoving me in with a lot of Walachs and Polacks!
I'll take the first knife I can lay hands on and I'll have the balls
off the first bugger that . . .'

'Shame on you, Sándor! What a way to talk! He didn't mean it
like that at all, did you – you didn't mean it like that at all?'

'Yes, that's exactly how I meant it!'

'You're a socialist, then?'

'Yes!'

'Not the Russian kind, though, are you?'

'Yes I am!'

There I was improvising. I had never before said, and it had
never even occurred to me to think, that I was a socialist of 'the
Russian kind' – a Bolshevik, as the newspapers of the period
called them. But having said it I stuck by it. As time went on the
word assumed more and more meaning for me, and it was a
meaning I liked more and more. To put an end to war for ever
by removing its causes. To make work a pleasure. To give to each
according to his needs. And so on and so forth – all the things that

48

should make mankind irrevocably happy, including the equality of all nations. (Mr P.: 'I'd sooner strangle my family with my own bare hands . . .' Mrs P., after a barely perceptible scream: 'Shame on you, Sándor! Come – surely you didn't mean that?' Mr P.: 'I meant exactly that.' J.H. 18: 'And so did I!')

Mr Palkovits turned to go, but then came back with a polite smile on his face. He formally gave me notice to leave, clicked his heels, and quit the room.

Whereupon his young wife repeated the performance with the coat and the dressing-gown, but even more slowly this time, even more blatantly, and with a smile that made the eighteen-year-old almost regret his precipitancy.

'Do you know what you are?' she said. 'You're a fool. You're not only a fool – you're a spoilsport.'

And that was the end of the discussion in the Váci-utca.

4

*The Battle of the Suspension Bridge – The
republic and the republicans – Assez! Assez! –
The rectangle of darkness, and how to become
a writer*

THERE was one demonstration after another in those days –
students, workers, soldiers. One evening a procession of demonstrators wanted to cross the Suspension Bridge from Pest to
Buda. It was a toll-bridge, and we none of us thought of refusing
to pay the small sum that had been demanded of users since the
bridge's erection. In such a crowd as we were, however, it was
simply impossible to fish into one's pocket for change, pay, get a
little metal ticket, and toss this into the bin on the Buda side of
the bridge. Those of us at the front – and J.H. 18 was up there
this time – were unable to stop. And in finding we could not,
found we did not want to.

The old man who issued the metal tickets was in tears of
despair. We had no right to put his world out of joint, he pleaded.
In vain. Before us was the vacuum of the empty bridge, behind
us the pressure of the throng. For a moment we saw the old man
still, his back to the parapet, helpless in his despair. Then we saw
nothing more. We just marched on, and on, and on.

And then something happened that no one had thought possible. None of us had ever been in the immediate vicinity of that
sharp, stomach-turning noise before. It was a second or two
before we realized that those flashing lights were gun muzzles
and that those whistling noises were the bullets we had read so
much about. The police . . ! The police had opened fire . . !

Soldiers, workers, and students stumbled, fell, and bled. Men, women, youths – we could not tell how many, and even afterwards we never learned the exact toll we paid for that night.

The front rows tried to retreat. Impossible. The pressure from behind was irresistible. There was only one way out: forwards. And already the police had scattered – put to flight by an unarmed crowd.

Later we christened it 'The Battle of the Suspension Bridge'.

There was a 'Storming of the Castle' too. That time we were met on one side by Bosnian soldiers wearing the field-grey fez who did not understand one word of the slogans we were shouting at them. Even so they did not open fire. Or was it that no one dared give the order? We were stopped, beaten bloody, and dispersed by mounted police, who went at us with the flats of their swords. They were Hungarians and understood what we were saying. The words, that is. Not the meaning. They were policemen.

And so it went on for ten days. And after ten days Karl von Habsburg, by the grace of God Emperor of Austria and Apostolic King of Hungary, King of Bohemia, Dalmatia, Croatia, Slavonia, Galicia, Lodomeria, and Illyria; King of Jerusalem, etc.; Archduke of Austria; Grand Duke of Tuscany and Cracow; Duke of Lothringia, Salzburg, Styria, Carinthia, Carniola, and Bucovina; Grand Duke of Transylvania; Margrave of Moravia; Duke of Upper and Lower Silesia, of Modena, Parma, Piacenza, and Guastalla, of Auschwitz and Zator, of Teschen, Friaul, Ragusa, and Zara; Prince-Count of Habsburg and the Tyrol, of Kyburg, Görz, and Gradiska; Prince of Trento and Bressanone; Margrave of Upper and Lower Lusatia, and in Istria; Count of Hohenems, Feldkirch, Bregenz, Sonnenberg, etc.; Lord of Trieste, Cattaro, and over the Windisch March; Grand Voivode of Serbia, etc., etc., abdicated.

Which made Hungary a republic.

The men who created this brand-new republic were no improvisers. They had spent their whole lives in bitter conflict with the Hungarian oligarchy and the Habsburg overlords. To some extent in Parliament but to a greater extent outside it they had battled with no other weapon than the pen against Count Tisza and all that made the monarchy odious. They formed a more competent government than Hungary had ever had in its whole existence. And this government was not allowed to govern.

A decisive criterion as far as I was concerned was the fact that Oszkár Jászi, the great expert on national questions, was given a Ministry of Nationalities with the unambiguous programme of turning Hungary into a federal republic in which each national group should seek its happiness on the basis of its own language, its own culture, and its own traditions and in which all should find their common good together.

Count Mihály Károlyi was the ideal prime minister and later president for the young republic. He was a sincere and genuine democrat – one, moreover, who knew what democracy was or might have been. An unshakable opponent of war, he represented an ideal that, had it been followed, might have spared a threatened humanity much suffering.

One morning the cry went up, 'To Károlyi's palace!' It was still early in those ten (or was it eleven?) days that turned a kingdom into a republic. What we were actually after in Károlyi's palace was something no one thought to ask – ourselves least of all. It was a time when doors stood open; people just went in and came out again if they did not stay inside.

At that period several thousand Hungarian youths were temporarily – and from a distance – in love with Count Károlyi's young wife, *née* Katinka, Countess Andrássy. She had become a figure-head for us, a symbol of the golden future, a guardian angel amid the bloody menace of war. It was a wonderful thing to idolize one's own happiness in the person of a woman of such radiant youth, for she was hardly a year or two older than I was myself.

While J.H. 18 was lost in contemplation of the lovely and utterly captivating countess, and while the countess listened enraptured to the words of her husband, her husband, a tall, good-looking man in his forties, proceeded to address the people from the great balcony of his ancestral palace. What about? It was difficult to tell. Károlyi had a very bad speech defect. But he spoke with courage and conviction, and in time one got used to it.

Assez! Assez!

Of all the enemy armies that had beaten Germany together with her unfortunate allies, the closest to the Hungarian capital at that time were the French, who had penetrated deep into south-eastern Europe. This fact filled the new Hungarian government under Károlyi with high hopes. Hungary no longer felt herself to be a part of the collapsed Monarchy but a country that had just cut loose from a dreadful past; she saw herself as the young republic that was prepared to throw herself with the deepest sympathy and trust into the arms of her elder sister, the glorious French republic.

Whenever this malevolent century has not quite felt up to spreading sufficient mischief on its own, it has called upon the services of a general. Franchet d'Esperey was the name of the French general to whom Károlyi looked forward to baring his soul and enthusiastically expounding all the new republic's beautiful plans including the highly propitious federal system.

'*Assez! Assez!*' shouted Franchet d'Esperey after the first sentence. He was not interested in any republic, in any federation of nationalities, in any 'Switzerland of Eastern Europe'; he would hear nothing of the old, wicked Hungary's having ceased to exist and of the new Hungary that wished to enter upon its inheritance in the heart of Europe.

'*Assez! Assez!*' A general wants to conquer and have the conquered at his feet. He is not interested in giving liberated nations a helping hand; he wants beaten peoples he can tread underfoot. No wise, far-reaching concern for the future inhabits the general's soul, only the intoxication of present victory.

'*Assez! Assez!*' Under such circumstances the republic was able to last only a few more weeks. What came afterwards was the desperate experiment of a different kind of life in a new political system – a soviet republic.

There was a demonstration in Gisella Square one evening, outside the offices of the Radical Party. The street-lighting was off and the moon was not doing much better. J.H. 18 began the evening down in the street with everyone else, chanting, 'Long live the republic!'

Suddenly from one corner of the square there came the cry,

'Long live the soviet republic!' Although clearly neither un-planned nor unrehearsed, it was feeble and was soon drowned. It had come from the newly-founded Communist Party.

Then we heard a name repeated over and over again: 'Béla Kun! Béla Kun!'

Did one, I wonder, already know that evening who Béla Kun was? I think the picture that the majority of us had of him was far from clear. One had heard that this short, slight man with the face of a cunning frog had been a humble provincial social security official before the war, that he had been taken prisoner by the Russians, had become Lenin's right-hand man for Hungarian affairs, and had now returned to Hungary as head of the Hungarian Communists – a somewhat mysterious force – with a staff that was a completely unknown quantity.

Some young Bourgeois-Radicals took me inside the building with them. There was a large open window from which someone had just finished addressing the crowd below. He stepped down and the window was left vacant. There were no more speakers. Down below, however, the crowd was still thronging the square. It was dangerous to leave them unoccupied. There was some discussion in the room as to what was to be done, but it got no further than that.

'You talk to them for a bit!' somebody said to me, giving me a push in the direction of the window. Obviously he had mistaken me for someone else. Or had he? Had fate singled me out for something that a moment before had never even occurred to me? The stranger hurried away and appeared to take no further interest either in me or in the window. But he had planted a flea in my ear.

How about it? A riproaring speech about something or other and I'm a famous man. Maybe my speech will be printed in the papers tomorrow. One pace forward, one thundering sentence, and I'm a politician. A man who with his voice alone holds sway over the revolutionary masses. At eighteen . . . The dark rectangle of the window drew me like a magnet.

Are there people, you ask, who become politicians in that way? Undoubtedly. I did not.

In front of the window there was a kind of podium, which made it possible for the speaker to be seen by the crowd below. I climbed it step by step. Outside there was another rectangle, enlarged and distorted, thrown by the light from the window on the heads of the people thronging the square. Framed by that rectangle was the dark figure of a giant, growing step by step – my shadow.

Did I not manage to produce a sound? Or did I speak, but in so feeble a voice that I could not be heard? Did I say nothing, frightened by my own shadow? Or was it just that I could not hear what I was saying? I do not know. I felt hoarse. Or my throat was tied in a knot. Or something. And I could not for the life of me think of anything to say.

It was not until many years later that I did at last find a roundabout way to the ear of the masses. And a very different way it was, too!

Step by step I descended from the podium. I was terrified I should be the laughing-stock of the room. But nothing happened. My bold venture had passed completely unnoticed. And that was the end of my one and only attempt at a career in politics. Although the dark rectangle of an open window has more than once invited me to make another.

I went off home in a filthy mood, 'home' being no longer in the Váci-utca but in the Honvéd-utca, where Professor Vas, who lived alone with a housekeeper, rented me a room in order to avoid having any foreigners billeted on him.

No sooner was I in my room than I opened a drawer and pulled out a sheaf of closely-written manuscript. And in a trice everything around me had disappeared and was forgotten; nothing remained but that stack of paper.

It was a novel I had begun that summer, the summer of 1918, when I was still in love with Bella . . .

(Seek it not, that first manuscript of mine, nor the two novels that followed it. There came a time when books were burned. There came a time when people, whole peoples, were burned. The literary first-fruits of a nineteen-year-old youth were not exempt.)

5

Congratulations! – Two model cadres – The last
Marxist – Professor Vas starts asking questions

BEFORE President Károlyi gave up the struggle and he and
Countess Katinka fled across the Austrian border with forged
passports, he did something truly great, or rather something
that would have struck us as great had not our feeling for great
deeds been badly blunted.

In February 1919 Károlyi and his government passed the law
for the partition of the large landed estates among the landless,
and began immediately to put it into practice. The head of state
himself had his own estates expropriated – the Károlyis owned
land on a mammoth scale – and proceeded without further ado
to portion them out among the land-hungry people.

His time, however, was too short. Not many days later he was
already on foreign soil, beginning his begging-tour in search of
asylum. One country after another refused for one reason or
another to accept him on a permanent basis. Rich people are
welcome everywhere. Poor people too – sometimes. But there is
something sinister about rich people who have voluntarily made
themselves poor, and no one welcomes them. History made
Károlyi a tragically superfluous figure, the more so since his
successors at Hungary's crippled helm – Béla Kun and his men –
proved to be in no hurry whatever to pursue his policy and to
continue with the redistribution of the land.

The partition of the Károlyi estates began and ended in the
village of Kálkápolna. This act, initiated with simple ceremony,
became a symbol, a legend; had the camera not recorded it one
might have thought it had been a dream, a wish-fulfilment
dream of the have-nots.

Congratulations!

But what I could not begin to understand was why under Béla Kun the partition of the land should have been delayed and delayed, until it lost all momentum and passed into oblivion.

That aside, however, the soviet revolution made its presence felt in many ways. On 21 March 1919, following the conclusion of a secret agreement between a number of Social Democrats of Károlyi's toppled government and the recently founded Communist Party, the revolution was simply proclaimed without a shot being fired. Moreover a broad cross-section of the population supported it as being the only possible way to save Hungary.

The Communists, and the Social Democrats who had entered into an alliance with them, were prepared – and to begin with looked able – to protect Hungary from the destructive fury of the generals and politicians of the Entente (*Assez! Assez!*) and to abide by a policy of federalism, now unfortunately losing more and more of its definition. A beaten and heavily bled Hungary with a defeated army and a fierce yearning for peace had, if she was to survive, to show some fight; in pursuance of the iron law of revolutionary strategy she must switch to the offensive.

Only Communists with two years' Russian experience behind them and the few Social Democrats who had also adopted Lenin and Trotsky as their models – trade-unionists who saw the worker masses with very different eyes from even the most sympathetically inclined bourgeois – only they were able to muster sufficient dogged recklessness to contemplate, in such a situation, the prospect of fighting on.

How abruptly the swing to Communism made its appearance in Hungarian politics and how much more the leadership was hurled into it than won over to it is manifest from the very place where the pact was concluded, namely the Budapest Reception Prison.

Only the day before Béla Kun and the rest of the Communists had been rounded up by the police and, in the best police tradition of the Hungarian Monarchy, beaten to a pulp – just in case.

(I bet Staff Sergeant Németh was there too – still young, still enjoying the sight of both eyes, and as handy with his fists as with his gun-butt. Twenty-four hours later the same police force became a 'Red Guard' and Németh and his colleagues 'Red

Guards'. A further one hundred and thirty-three days later they were the police again. Their function, however, was, and remained, the same throughout.)

On 21 March 1919 I was confined to my room at Professor Vas's by a mild case of tonsillitis. My sister Juliska had come over – she was living nearby – with some home-made remedy or other. It was she who went to open the door when Szivessy rang.

Szivessy was a fellow-student at the university and we had become good friends; in fact he might have become my best friend for life had not various shifts of fate repeatedly conspired to keep us apart, the last of them being his premature death. We did at all events spend an important slice of our lives together, and it began in that moment when he stepped into Professor Vas's flat, gave Juliska a polite greeting, and yelled to me from the hall, 'The soviet republic's been proclaimed!'

Happy and excited, I yelled back, 'Congratulations!'

Whereupon we shook hands at length and with manly firmness.

Juliska was confused. 'Is that the same as the dictatorship of the proletariat?'

'Yes!'

'Oh my God . . !'

But the two nineteen-year-olds wished the dictatorship of the proletariat a hearty welcome.

I was determined to do my bit for the cause and first thing the next morning (who cared about a touch of tonsillitis!) I went along to the Ministry of Education in the Hold-utca to ask for a job. To my surprise I found a large crowd outside the main entrance of the Ministry (actually it was already a 'People's Commissariat', having been renamed on the Russian model), burning with industry and waiting to be admitted. It was an inspiring new beginning.

People wanted to be on the payroll of the new state and to be issued with ration-cards, and it was not only because one had somehow to live but also because it was proof that one belonged, that one was accepted by the new order as being a useful person.

Two model cadres

Your real Budapester – and such I was attempting to become, although I was always a bit of a country cousin and still am – never waits outside a main entrance for long; he wastes no time in finding suitable side entrances.

The young man who not many minutes later was my boss in the People's Commissariat was called Boros. He was slim, fair, and good-looking. His assistant, and the person who looked after my work, was a medical student by the name of Mitzi Rothbart, a slight, sensible, and very charming girl with whom – though she was not exactly beautiful – I should in the normal course of events inevitably have fallen in love, had she not succeeded in parrying all my timid advances with a mixture of cool, impersonal interest and an almost motherly readiness to help. Conversation between us was so utterly lacking in private content that I cannot even remember whether she was married at that time or not. At any rate she was or later became the life-long and most estimable companion of the Hungarian-Yugoslav writer Ervin Sinkó.

I was employed by the People's Commissariat as a young-worker propagandist. It was my first regular job and it gave me a feeling of being solidly integrated in human society. I was entrusted with the middle portion of two Budapest districts, V and VI, districts that actually contained more schoolchildren than young workers. Initially my job was simply to organize a kind of club at which young people should come together to nourish themselves with Marxist ideology. Our club-room was half of a vacant café; the other half housed the cartographical institute of 'Kogutowicz and Sons'. I can remember having some stirring discussions with the younger Kogutowicz; what I cannot remember is what they were about.

At the age of nineteen, then, I took upon myself the Marxist education of my club-members. On one occasion I assumed a similar burden in respect of the theories of Sigmund Freud, which I was studying with great attention at the time. My Freudian lecture, however, was a success only in terms of the laughter it occasioned, and after it one or two of the older girls stopped visiting the club.

Born 1900

My keenest and most reliable assistants were the Fazekas
sisters, who lived in the Sziget-utca. Elisabeth was perhaps a year
younger than myself and was just coming up to her school-leaving
exam. She was nothing special to look at but she was extraordinarily serious about her revolutionary vocation. She was also
a very courageous girl. When we were trying to go underground
after the overthrow of the soviet revolution I was once detailed
to deliver a highly confidential parcel to a comrade who was in
hiding aboard a Danube steamer. I took Elisabeth along to help.
We had to pass through several areas that were positively stiff
with police and detectives, which was an extremely perilous
undertaking. We made it, however, and the sailor comrade was
very pleased to get the parcel. I think there was money in it.

The Party made us each a present of a boiled sweet, with the
remark that in Vienna one could buy as many of them as one had
money for. We sucked the sweets with dreamy enjoyment and
tried to imagine a city where one could just go into a shop and
buy such things.

Elisabeth made the revolution her life-long profession. I did
not see her again until sixteen years later, in Moscow. She was
married then to a man called Ernö Gerö, who played an important
part in the Communist movement and indeed in the history of
Hungary. For many years he was 'No. 2' (after Mátyás Rákosi)
in the Hungarian Communist Party, and for a time he was even
'No. 1'. He also had a very important top-ranking job in the
Soviet Army. Both he and his wife took part in the Spanish Civil
War, he on some extremely high-powered secret Soviet mission.
Apparently Elisabeth showed great bravery there too, as she was
to do again in the Second World War, serving at the front for a
long time and marching into Hungary in officer's uniform in
1945 with the Soviet Army.

Elisabeth was frantically jealous regarding her Ernö. I was
walking down Gorky Street in Moscow with her one day when
she suddenly started screaming abuse at a boy who was coming
towards us from the other direction, breaking off only to tell me,
'He had that one by a Pole!' Back in Budapest in 1945 the
ascetic-looking 'No. 2' apparently began an affair with the woman
doctor who was treating his eye complaint.

60

Gerö himself was one of the few professional politicians I ever met who took an interest in literature, and in his dealings with me he was almost cordial.

And yet, and yet . . . If I could still curse in the way my ancestors no doubt could, one of my most resounding curses would be for Ernö Gerö, 'No. 2' (and occasional 'No. 1') in Communist Hungary, for all his crimes (and they were incessant) against his country, against humanity, and against socialism, but most especially for those committed in 1956, the year of the Hungarian Revolution.

Elisabeth made sporadic attempts to immortalize our shared adventure on the Danube steamer – which she came to see in a progressively more heroic perspective – in the form of a poem, a form for which she had not the slightest talent. Her talents in the field of historical science were likewise completely non-existent. Gerö, however, was Gerö, and his wife had set her heart on having the chair of history at Budapest University. And when she got her chair, of course Gerö's doctor had to have her clinic too.

Anna, two or three years younger than her sister, was also prettier. She survived the war in Hungary. After it, being Gerö's sister-in-law, she was appointed head of a large state publishing house. Her ambitions extending to authorship, she began to write children's verse, which she arranged for the state to print and, when printed, for the state to praise.

When Elisabeth died after the Hungarian Revolution at the age of more than sixty, Gerö, by then both physically and politically impotent, up and married Anna.

These two 'cadres' – the Fazekas sisters – our young-worker propagandist J.H. 19 succeeded in the space of 133 days in educating for Communism.

'Private property has made us so stupid and narrow-minded that a thing is not ours till we possess it . . .'

I cannot claim that J.H. 19 – who was a little too hungry, among other things, to concentrate on new and strange ideas – understood everything that was said in the overcrowded lecture-room of the university that evening by a short, slightly built man with a sharp profile and a huge red moustache. But that sentence – a quotation from Marx – caught and held the nineteen-year-old's attention for a while, and the remarks that the lecturer appended to it struck him as being clear and of manifest truth.

'In place of all the physical and mental senses, therefore,' the Marx quotation went on, 'we have the simple alienation of all those senses, namely the sense of possession . . .'

In the Fischer Restaurant opposite the Vig Theatre, J.H. 19 was thinking concurrently, they still had barley broth; it would only have meant queuing for another half-hour. Otherwise there was nothing to be had in the entire city but boiled pumpkin.

The lecturer spoke clearly and possibly a shade dogmatically. J.H. 19 continued to take in a bit here and there and to miss other bits. Pity he couldn't have got a better place, he thought. But he had only got in at all by pleading that, since he worked in the People's Commissariat for Education, the lecturer that evening, Comrade Georg Lukács, was *his* People's Commissar.

The young professor with the red Nietzsche moustache was taking pains to keep his vast audience's attention. He wanted to make his listeners think. Think. Think and understand. In order to be able to think further. Is there any other guarantee of freedom? '. . . Man, reduced to the absolute poverty that in the capitalist order is henceforth his, must bring his mighty inner wealth forth from within himself . . .'

The tired, burning eyes often stayed closed for minutes on end. Why, J.H. 19 wondered, had the girl who was pressed so tightly against him in the crowd suddenly become so warm and soft? She had fallen asleep . . . Grinding her teeth the while . . . Grinding on nothing . . . In the Fischer Restaurant, J.H. 19 remembered, there was one waitress who, if you smiled at her nicely, could turn two bread-stamps into three with nimble snips of her scissors . . .

Professor Georg Lukács, the People's Commissar with the fiery Nietzsche moustache, was thirty-four years old. Now, as J.H. 70 writes these words, Georg Lukács is already eighty-five. The Nietzsche moustache he shaved off many decades ago. He now has a thick crop of snowy white hair, at the back perhaps a shade too long . . . Many people call him the last of the Marxists. He does not want to be the last of the Marxists and I, his friend, have no wish to call him that either. Far better call him the *first* of the new school of Marxists – if, that is, we ever manage at last to give the word a *new meaning* . . .

The smoke of those wretched ersatz cigarettes – the lecturer was puffing away for ten men himself – made one's eyes smart and drank the tear glands dry.

'Liberation of the personality . . .' That was what the People's Commissar with the bright red Nietzsche moustache was fighting for . . . and that was what, clean-shaven and with wrinkles furrowing his face, he would still be fighting for half a century later.*

And would the world, in that time, come even a step closer to his goals?

Before the First of May my landlord, Professor Vas, informed me through his housekeeper that he wished to discuss an important question with me.

I was familiar with Professor Vas's questions. On one occasion he had stood me a cup of ersatz tea and a saccharin tablet for the privilege of being able to conduct a little informal research into the probable social standing of the scholastic profession under Communism. My answer had apparently satisfied him, otherwise he would not have lain in wait for me on another occasion as I passed with a bucket of water in each hand (for some time we had had to carry our water up in buckets from the ground floor) in order to ask in a whisper whether he, who practised a useful profession, did not have more chance of being recognized by the soviet republic as his ninety-year-old aunt's heir than his brother, who was a bank manager, in other words a bourgeois *par excellence*.

On this occasion, however, his voice was severe; he was calling me to account. Was it true, he demanded, that Béla Kun, leader of the Communist Party, theoretically foreign minister but in fact head of the new government of a country that was dying of hunger, had sent consignments of food to Russia in payment for the miserable red paper hangings with which he was having the city decorated for the First of May?

* And as he continued to do until his death in 1971 (Translator).

Flabbergasted, I stammered out – truthfully – that I knew nothing about it.

'Oh yes you do, comrade. You know all about it. You're just not allowed to say so.'

As I beat a hasty retreat he flung a further question after me.

'And why does your Béla Kun not go on with the partition of the estates of the aristocrats and bourgeois that was begun by Károlyi?'

To which, badly shaken, I could only repeat, 'I don't know.'

6

'Not ours till we possess it ...' – Teddy and the 'Lenin Boys' – Sári Fedák dances the csárdás – *A May (and an August) to remember*

WHY *did* Béla Kun not go on with the redistribution of the land begun by Károlyi?

The question left me no peace, and at times it positively tormented me. Although not once during those 133 days did it occur to me to doubt that Béla Kun's policy was right and in the people's best interests. I *wanted* to believe that it was so, and I succeeded. At nineteen I succeeded easily. In later years, later decades, it became more difficult. Even so I went on succeeding for a long time. Not believing was for a long time an even greater strain. But the failure to understand and the inability to justify – these tormented me already in those early years.

The land question, the 'to have or not to have?' question, was the chief subject of discussion on hundreds and thousands of large and not so large farms all over Hungary during the revolutionary period. Nowhere were such discussions followed up by redistribution, and always the same reason was given: lest the production of the most essential foodstuffs be brought to a standstill.

My father's estate too was declared forfeit and socialized. They took the news calmly in Abony, or at least they appeared to. The usual cure for all ills in our family – silence – was in this case applied with more than the usual thoroughness. Not only on my parents' side but also on my own.

Yet the formality of socialization failed to quench the people's thirst for land. The land now belonged to the state, and the Hungarian peasant was very far from identifying himself with the state. He wanted to *have* his little plot; he wanted to *possess* it. But smallholding is insufficiently productive. So the large and medium-sized agricultural estates were left as they were, and the partition process begun by Károlyi was deliberately forgotten.

The nationalized farms were in the main run by so-called production commissars. In our case this office was filled by a Mr Sztrányai, an estate-management graduate who had for years filled the same office in my father's employ to their complete mutual satisfaction.

From the point of view of the agricultural worker, then, nothing had changed. Not even in appearance. The decree to the effect that the produce of the land no longer belonged to the previous owner but to an imaginary entity called 'the state' meant as good as nothing to the man who had never owned anything. Even the majority of the land-owners accepted the fact with a shrug of the shoulders. They saw themselves as in any case surrounded by insoluble problems. One more or less – what difference did it make?

And they sat down to wait for the catastrophe.

The tragic contradiction was patently obvious. As long as the peasant's land was not his *property* he felt no inducement to defend it, to cultivate it to the best of his strength and ability, and if need be to make superhuman sacrifices for it. No *collective* ownership – not at least at the present stage of human evolution – can replace this supreme feeling of individual possession.

Here lay the roots of the inevitable collapse.

Mr Homoki worked for the railways and often travelled between Abony and Budapest. Every trip he visited Juliska and her husband Elek, bringing letters and also food. He tended to be somewhat reserved in my presence, but I did learn from him that the Reds had been giving my father a very bad time, confiscating every last grain of seed-corn, slaughtering the milch cows, ruining one tractor and taking the other away, and squeezing him for large amounts of money into the bargain. The fact that the estate did not even belong to my father any more was in our case too beside the point.

This state of affairs continued until the big flood scare. Then, however, Homoki went on, the Reds were completely and utterly dependent on the services of Engineer Hay. The peasants were not worried about the flood at all; in fact they did not give a damn about anything, firstly because the whole thing went against the grain with them anyway and secondly because they were doing better barter trade with the towns than they had ever done in their lives. The land-owners had of course been dispossessed, but the production commissars were only waiting for the collapse to come so that they could hand the estates back to their former proprietors.

So the Reds came to my father and told him he must help keep the flood water in check. Father showed them into his office, bade them sit down, and asked Mother to offer the guests raspberry juice, this being a time of prohibition. Calmly my father told them that there was no question of 'must'. On the contrary, it was none of his business to interfere, since the danger zone lay outside the area covered by the Gerje and Perje Company.

Among the Reds was one old man who knew the area and could reel off the names of the villages and impoverished districts that were in danger. Surely one could not leave them in the lurch?

Whereupon my father answered that things were exactly as the old man had described them. His guests should therefore go to the devil, but in half an hour there should be a carriage with two good horses and an experienced driver at his door. What he did (said my father) he did simply and solely because his diploma made it his duty to do it.

Homoki told us how Engineer Hay, sixty-three years of age, had spent four days and four nights on the threatened dam. When the people saw him up there they came and did everything he told them to do, just as they had in earlier years when there had been danger of flooding. With the exception of two villages that had to be evacuated, my father and his helpers succeeded in keeping the water back. It was not until much later that my mother learned – and even then not from Father – that the dam they had saved had been under intermittent fire from the Romanian artillery.

After that the Reds treated Father with respect, but they did

67

not have many more days to go, and who knew who would succeed them?

Busy though I was with meetings and briefing sessions at the People's Commissariat, and with my work at the club, I often liked to go round to my sister Juliska's and sit for an hour or so with her, her husband Elek – who as a solicitor found there was not much he could do with himself at that period – and their six-year-old son Laci.

I arrived, we sat around in silence, and I went away again. This kind of visit was not unusual in our family, yet none of us would have been willing to forgo it. The only noisy, lively one was little Laci. He used to play 'Lenin Boys', scorching around in imaginary cars, firing make-believe machine-guns, and sporting a fictitious black-leather jacket and cap.

His parents can hardly have been pleased at the fact that their son chose to model his game on precisely the most ferocious representatives of the 'Red Terror'. But they were intelligent enough to appreciate that for a boy of his age it was inevitable that the most dynamic element in his environment held the greatest attraction; they were also prudent enough never to say a word against these special commandos of the dreaded Commissar of the Interior, Tibor Szamuely, not even when Laci was the only person within earshot and certainly not when I was.

For some reason or other Elek wanted the child to play with an enormous, battered old teddy-bear, but Laci was already too old for that.

'Let Teddy play too,' Elek would insist. 'Teddy likes to play so much. You must always let Teddy play.'

In the end, as a favour to his parents, Laci enrolled the teddy-bear among his 'Lenin Boys' so that the dear old thing could go hunting *burshujs* too.

Was it the 'Red Terror' that reigned in Hungary during those days? I must confess that I seldom asked myself the question and was never able to give a reliable answer. One got one's information from two opposing quarters, neither of which was interested in the truth. The murderous havoc that the 'Lenin Boys' in their martial-looking black-leather jackets, black-leather

caps, and cartridge-belts wrought in Count Batthyány's confiscated palace and in the cellar of the Britannia Hotel was hardly
evidence of irenic intentions – that was clear. Likewise beyond
question was the fact that the People's Commissar of the Interior,
Tibor Szamuely, did not go tearing about Russian-style in an
armoured car just for fun. There was also the story of the two
brothers – I think they were journalists – who had been thrown
into the Danube from the middle of a bridge in Budapest by Red
sailors. (According to another version, which may have been put
about deliberately, the case had been devoid of political content
and had merely been the upshot of a homosexual tiff.) Even the
harvest was not brought in without bloodshed that year.

Once some little posters went up with the information that a
number of plunderers had been caught red-handed and were to
be publicly shot in front of the Parliament Building. When I next
walked past there I saw them putting up enormous wooden panels
to catch the stray bullets, and I hurried on my way so as not to
hear the shooting.

The rebellion of the army-college cadets and the sailors of the
Danube gunboats against the soviet government also gave the
Communists occasion for a kind of retaliation that openly called
itself a 'Red Terror'. (It was said, however, that Béla Kun granted
the mutinous students – they were originally to have been
hanged in the middle of the city – a pardon on the quiet, perhaps
with a view to a pardon for himself one day, should it ever come
to that.)

Elek turned to me abruptly and said, 'If Sári Fedák dances for
you I'll eat my hat.'

Sári Fedák, by far the most popular actress in Hungary, was
said to have promised the Kun government that she would appear
on one of the lorries that were to serve as open-air stages for the
forthcoming First of May celebrations.

'An actress has to make her living and for that she needs
applause. Fedák is not going to gamble with her popularity for
your sakes.'

Elek was wrong. Sári Fedák actually *danced* on that lorry on
the First of May and it did her popularity no harm at all. Just as

69

she danced with even greater fervour for the Fascists some twenty years later, for which the Communists punished her after the Second World War with a three-year prison term and a professional ban for life. And when she died at a ripe old age she was escorted to the grave by several tens of thousands of people, each of whom silently threw a rose into her grave. (What dictator can presume to pilot the people's affections – whether merited or not – by violent means?)

And it was a real First of May. The entire city was out in the streets. Everyone, as I remember, got his lost hopes back on loan for that day.

The streets and squares of the city presented a curious sight. All statues that might have served as reminders of a distasteful past had been concealed by means of gigantic red globes made of wood and covered with the red paper canvas that Professor Vas had mentioned. There were masses of those globes, all exactly identical. Equally numerous and equally undifferentiated were the heads of Marx and Engels that had been executed on a simply enormous scale in plaster and canvas and stood out glaringly white amid the red decorations. The Millennium Memorial had been disguised as a red obelisk and in front of it stood a colossal white-plaster Marx bringing worker and peasant together in brotherly unity. The same group was to be seen at several other points too. And then there were the red triumphal arches and the countless, countless red flags. There was something oddly clumsy about the whole thing, nothing that could be called taste; perhaps it was that that gave an impression of sincerity.

A procession formed up in the Andrássy-ut – lorry after lorry full of happy or at least happy-looking people. Organized workers recalled once-forbidden May Day parades and enjoyed the freedom to march in rank and file and sing the old fighting songs. But the majority formed a shapeless mass that surged hither and thither in no particular order and with no particular memories, savouring the moment, oblivious of the morrow. Crowds came streaming out of the side-streets – grown-ups who had not had a good time for years, children who had yet to learn what a good time was. They beamed with joy to see the most popular actors and actresses in the land dancing the *csárdás* on the backs of lorries. Earnest-looking gentlemen – the greatest poets and writers in the land – waited on the lorries for their turn to read aloud from their works. What did it matter whether anybody understood them?

For a while there was even a kind of beer to be had, and a few artificial sweets.

Giant posters covered the walls with Red Army soldiers – cubist, expressionist, enthusiastic, and inspiring – swinging along to the legend, 'Red Army, Forward March!' We had heard that next day the staffs of all factories were to be mobilized for the front. My brother Bandi, still a student, had been called up again. He had been promoted too. But since officer ranks had been abolished the autumn before, the commission had been addressed to 'Former Second Lieutenant Hay', who thus became 'Former First Lieutenant Hay'. We saw nothing funny about it that First of May.

J.H. 19 was everywhere and nowhere and thinking about his manuscript, then at the typist's.

The end of the soviet revolution – in Hungary it was known simply as 'the Commune' – came in the simplest fashion for me. Towards the end of July Mitzi Rothbart sent me to Debrecen to set up young-worker propaganda for them on the basis of our experiences in Budapest. There was not a great deal I could do because the people there had their own ideas about young-worker propaganda and were not going to let themselves be dictated to from the capital. After a few days I had no choice but to take the train back to Budapest.

Arriving in Szolnok after a slow and difficult journey on the roofs of trucks and in guard's vans I learned that the whole way from Debrecen I had been just in front of the advancing Royal Romanian Army, which was driving the defeated Hungarian Red divisions before it.

Whereas the Communist troops on the Romanian front were beaten in straight combat, the resistance of those fighting on the northern front in Slovakia was broken more by political means. Clemenceau himself is supposed to have written the letter that, with its intimations of a peaceful solution, persuaded Béla Kun

71

to retreat. But when a revolutionary army voluntarily retreats, its fate is sealed.

At the People's Commissariat in the Hold-utca someone whispered in my ear that I should unobtrusively make my way to a particular room. I found a number of young people, most of whom were doing the same job as I was but in other districts, and two men in leather jackets who did not work in our department. One of them I vaguely knew; he was subsequently executed by the Romanians. Silence reigned in the room and I gathered we were waiting for more people to arrive.

At last one of the leather-jacketed men began to speak. The dictatorship of the proletariat, he told us, was facing a terrible crisis; the military assistance expected from Russia had still not materialized, and the Romanians were already at Szolnok. Béla Kun let Clemenceau order him about and had pulled the Red Army out of Slovakia. The farmers were trying to starve the capital out, the Communist uprising that our comrades had promised in Vienna was apparently not going to take place, and no world revolution was in sight. What was to be done? If our leaders wavered, then we, the youth, must be all the more determined.

The other man in the leather jacket got up and asked whether we ought not perhaps to follow a more liberal course. Supposing – he suggested – we put a slightly looser interpretation on our Bolshevik principles for a while in order to please Clemenceau but not of course displease Lenin and Bukharin. (The same Bukharin as Lenin was then calling the darling of the Party Stalin, in 1938, ordered to be tried and shot.)

A young man by the name of Rudas took the floor. I knew a number of Rudas brothers in the Party. There were – and possibly still are – certain families that played an outstanding role in the life of the Communist Party; in the Hungarian Party we had the Rudas, Szamuely, Szántó, and Rákosi brothers, the Andics sisters, the Blühs (mother and daughters), and several others. In fact it often looked as if these families constituted the backbone of the Party. One of the most important – though of course rarely articulated – questions in the political life of the Communist

Parties is always: *who* is going to exercise *in practice* the dictatorship that *in theory* is the proletariat's? Personal relationships and
friendships as well as nepotism play a large part in the way this
question is answered at any given time. Anyone who wants to
get on in the Party has to know his way around within those
relationships.

Rudas spoke with great passion, if little volume; often his voice
was barely audible. He rejected compromise of any kind and
declared that the Communist youth should seize power itself
rather than go along with any shady deal concluded by the
Party's aged leaders.

We all agreed, and when one of the men in leather jackets
asked who shared Comrade Rudas's opinion everyone present
raised his or her hand. Immediately the two men's expressions
changed as they explained that they had wanted to test our loyalty
to principle and were now reassured.

A silent pantomime accompanied these speeches for and
against. During the compromise proposals a short, slightly
crippled youth named Jakab pulled a revolver from his pocket
and aimed it at the speaker in the leather jacket. A girl of little
more than eighteen, whose name was Lonci and who had attracted
my attention long before this by her positively angelic beauty and
pretty way of dressing, restored the balance by drawing – with
impeccable calm – a small ladies' revolver decorated with mother
of pearl, and silently aiming it at Jakab.

'Put them away!' said a stocky, red-haired youth called Zoli
Móor eventually. (Zoli is now a grandfather on a kibbutz in
Israel.) And after a brief hesitation Jakab and Lonci both put
their weapons away at the same time.

The two men in leather jackets soon passed out of my life
completely. At the time I found nothing particularly remarkable
about this incident. It was not until later that I began with
increasing alarm to recall it.

On 1 August the police, having played the part of 'Red Guard'
for more than four months, reappeared on the streets wearing
their old police caps with striking red-white-and-green cockades.
Béla Kun and his People's Commissars had fled to Austria,

most of them with the intention of continuing to Russia. Only Tibor Szamuely was caught at the frontier and killed. And within a few days Hungary was the scene of the 'White Terror'.

I was able to collect my novel at last from the typing bureau. On the way back I was surprised to hear music. Military music. The *Marseillaise*.

I felt quite dizzy, not just from general physical weakness and exhaustion and the hunger that a nineteen-year-old found particularly hard to bear; for the space of one unguarded moment all my shattered hopes were resurrected. But only to be shattered again – this time for good.

Trotting down the Andrássy-ut from the direction of the city park were mounted soldiers carrying long lances such as we did not have in the Hungarian Army, with little triangular red-green-and-blue flags on them. Romanians. Budapest was in the process of being occupied. Occupied by the Royal Romanian Army.

So much for the federation of peoples as the grand solution to the nationalities question! We had fetched up with the most primitive kind of revenge. *Assez! Assez!*

Professor Vas gave me notice to quit in the same tone of voice and with the same emotion as Mr Palkovits had done the autumn before.

I threw all my things into my two cases and got out of his flat in a hurry. On the stairs I bumped into a young fellow who looked like a schoolboy and who happened to be asking for me. He brought a letter – for there was no post at this time – from my friend Szivessy, who had been living at his mother's in Szeged for some time. Szeged was under French occupation, he wrote, supplies were good, there was no danger, and one was certainly better off than under the Romanians. He said I should come immediately and we would work out something together for the future.

I realized that the word 'future' had been missing from my vocabulary for the last few days.

Once again the streets were in the process of altering their appearance within a matter of minutes. I saw the caretaker and his family together with all the assistant caretakers and the few remaining maids standing with buckets and brushes amid piles and puddles of filth. Of the huge and splendid posters that had so recently covered the walls only a few shreds now remained: 'PROL . . . OF . . . NITE . . . ED ARM . . . MARCH!'

The Romanian general had issued strict orders that the entire past was to be obliterated on the instant. And how often and from how many different quarters have we had that same order since then!

There was time for a quick call on Juliska and Elek. They were both very much in favour of my going to Szeged. On no account should I show my face in Abony, they said; a number of raw youngsters like me had already been nabbed and deported, and had not been heard from since.

Laci had given up playing 'Lenin Boys'. They had not even had to tell him not to. The child had automatically ceased to be influenced as soon as the dynamic element had disappeared.

The teddy-bear, centre of interest for the last time in its life, lay on the table with its stomach slit open. Beside it was a by no means impressive pile of jewellery and foreign bank-notes. Nor did it occur to anyone now to sew Teddy up again.

'And have you had permission from the Party to move your sphere of activities to Szeged?'

The young man by whom I was unexpectedly and for the first time in my life – though not by any means the last – interrogated thus was called Zádor. He was tall and thin, with close-cropped hair, and hardly older than I was.

'Party discipline,' he amplified.

Such an obligation had never occurred to me before. It now emerged that apart from the authorities I had always known I was henceforth subject to another kind of dependence: dependence upon the Party.

My initial reaction to this discovery was not one of joy. I did not want this new tie; the old ties were already hateful to me. The first thing that occurred to me was that I had never officially – who bothered about papers in March 1919? – joined the

75

Communist Party. Maybe I was not even a member. But before I had had time to give expression to the thought I realized I could not take advantage of a neglected formality. There were hard times ahead, and for that very reason I could not duck out. And then – it was a great feeling to belong to a powerful international organization that was sooner or later to usher in the much talked-of world revolution.

Zádor suggested I spend the night with him in Budafok – that is to say in the vacant house in the middle of the vineyards in which he and a number of other Communists were temporarily in residence, unbeknown to the police. Forbát was due there too today, he told me, because a big theoretical attack by the Bakuninists was imminent which he had to repulse. Forbát could give me permission for my journey in the event of the Party's approving my decision. Vera would be there as well; she was going to read from Kollontai's book *The Way of Love*.

There were a number of things J.H. 19 did not understand. He did not know who Forbát was, nor how Forbát could give or withhold permission for him to travel to Szeged; he did not know why a lot of Communists who were not registered with the police thought they were better off in a vacant house in Budafok than anywhere else; he did not know who the Bakuninists were whose theoretical attack had to be repulsed; and he had never heard of either Vera or Kollontai. But the way of love interested him at all events and the excitement of an unknown world had an irresistible attraction.

One got to Budafok by means of a suburban train that was invariably overcrowded. Zádor did not even attempt to find room inside the train but swung himself up on the end of the last carriage with one foot on a part of the bogie attachment and the other in the air. He invited me to do the same and I complied with alacrity, despite my being handicapped by a travelling-bag.

Before the train pulled out a plain, dark-haired girl took up a position at the end of the running-board. It was a while before I realized that she was one of the Bakuninists. The minute the train started she and Zádor struck up a preliminary discussion.

As the wheels clattered on at a middling pace over the worn rails, and the old, loose sleepers flicked past beneath our swaying behinds, and the breeze threatened to whip the then still obligatory hats from the heads of the disputants, the girl set forth in precise terms the nature of the sacred right and duty of youth in the given historical epoch. The sacred right and duty of youth in the given historical epoch was: to abolish the state. Zádor's view on the other hand was that youth must first take over the state and subsequently build it up into an entirely new kind of authority.

The girl called for Bakunin's anti-authoritarian collectivism, Zádor for Communism. Youth must fight immediately for the unqualified freedom of the individual, said the girl. Freedom in what sense? Freedom in the political, legal, economic, and sexual sense.

No! Only when the state had been seized and made all-powerful could the human personality be politically, legally, economically, and sexually liberated. That was what constituted the sacred right and duty of youth in the given historical epoch.

The engagement with the main body of the Bakuninist anarchists ended satisfactorily. Forbát, who – two or three years older than myself – listened sternly to my report of my projected journey to Szeged and as sternly granted me permission to undertake it, debated like a master and afterwards slept with the plain, dark-haired Bakuninist.

Vera, at twenty-five the oldest person present, tallish, pretty, big-boned, and blonde, translated the Russian Bolshevik Alexandra Kollontai's work extempore from the English. She had brought along a jar of imitation honey, which we all polished off together, and afterwards she slept with me.

That was the first time it was permitted me to stay in bed with a woman until the next morning. We had no bed linen, but that did not bother us.

Part Two

7

Plans for the future – One thing Auntie would
not have been good at *– The plucky little*
interpreter

'THE future . . .' In French-occupied Szeged, Szivessy and I
talked of nothing but the future.

Szivessy was about my age, about my height (around five foot
nine inches), and like me had been liable for military service in
the last year of the war but had not been called up – probably not
so much on account of his health, which was in fact good, as out
of a somewhat belated concern that there should be a few youngsters left over to fill the gaps in the intellectual professions.

Szivessy always spent the vacations with his mother, and he
had left for Szeged shortly after the manly handshake with which
on 21 March we had welcomed Béla Kun's soviet government as
a guarantee of a better future. Szivessy wanted to be an architect
and was in fact extremely gifted, but the way from Szeged to the
architectural schools of Western Europe and to his great hero,
the French-Swiss Le Corbusier, was a long and uncertain one.
Initially, because of visa, exchange, and other problems, the only
possibility was Germany. And since at the time I had no clear
plans for the future myself, he came to the same decision on my
behalf as well.

My case was simpler because I was never so totally wrapped
up in architecture as he was. Having heard that in Germany it
was easier to get into a top art school to study stage design, I was
not at all sure whether I did not in fact prefer this compromise to
my original intention.

So together we planned our journey, and my parents heaved a
sigh of relief because the campaign of reprisals against all who had

had anything to do with the soviet revolution in Hungary, or could somehow – justly or unjustly – be connected with it, was becoming bloodier and more fanatical every day. Small, armed bands of professional officers had taken advantage of the complete collapse of authority in Hungary to carry out a private war of revenge against the Communists. Or people they suspected of being Communists. Or people they happened to want to be rid of for one reason or another. Or simply the Jews. Or just anyone they thought they could squeeze for money.

I learnt from Mr Homoki, the railwayman, who visited me in Szeged and brought me enough money to support my not exactly modest life-style at the Kass Hotel, that one of these groups had set up its headquarters in an abandoned house in the Vigyázó Gardens, a large private park near Abony that had been the scene of much of my love affair with Bella (and hence of my first novel). The once-peaceful gardens were now loud with the victims' cries of pain. I had known already that things were grim and that in the Britannia Hotel in Budapest, for example, the Whites were simply continuing what the Reds had begun – only with even more brutal savagery. But I was surprised and alarmed to hear of such extremes of anarchy and violence in the immediate vicinity of my home.

Mr Homoki, however, was able to assure me that nothing of the kind had occurred in the village itself. The Romanians had shot or hanged a few people right at the beginning, he said, but since then life in Abony had been pretty safe. Apart from keeping Mr Bandi a prisoner-of-war in Arad Castle until Miss Edith had gone and got him out, the Romanians had left my father more or less alone, if very much the poorer for all the money they had extracted from him in war assessments.

Partly for moral reasons and partly because he was afraid it might distress me, Mr Homoki was reluctant to tell me the story of my brother Bandi and our cousin Edith. I had to coax it out of him.

Bandi – seven years older than I – serving in the Red Army as a 'former first lieutenant', had been taken prisoner by the Romanians and locked up in Arad Castle. My father had done everything in his power to buy him out, but all his efforts had failed.

Then one day cousin Edith threw some things into a suitcase and set out for the station, saying that she was going to get Bandi out. No one took her seriously.

A few days later a huge car flying the Romanian flag drew up in front of our house in Abony and out climbed Edith – with Bandi behind her.

'However did you do it?' asked my mother, tears of happiness in her eyes and a note of naive admiration in her voice.

'Let's just say I don't think you could have done it, Auntie.'

Meanwhile the manuscript of my first novel refused to lie idle in my suitcase. It came via Szivessy into the hands of the very fine poet Gyula Juhász, who liked it so much he wanted to show it to the top man in Hungarian literary criticism, Ernö Osváth. Unfortunately he had recently fallen out with Osváth and was not on speaking terms with him. Juhász, however, fell out with everybody, and out of his vast experience of not being on speaking terms with people he had evolved a system of getting round himself and contriving nevertheless to give others a helping hand. He wrote me a note to the literary historian Soma Braun in Budapest, and after an adventurous journey through occupied Hungary with suspect papers I found Braun during his 'hours' at the Vigszinház Café. (Braun was killed in a so-called labour camp during the Second World War.) Braun went to the telephone and came back in a few minutes with the information that Osváth would see me that same day – not at the New York Café, not at the Korona Café either, but, since he was ill, at his flat in the Izabella-utca.

The door was opened by Osváth's daughter, a dark-haired girl with large and disturbingly beautiful consumptive eyes. She was seriously ill and had not long to live. (Osváth's friends all knew that he would not survive his daughter's death, and when it came he did in fact commit suicide.)

Osváth was the organizing spirit behind the *Nyugat* movement. *Nyugat* ('The West'), a literary monthly founded in 1908, was more than just a magazine; it was the embodiment of a nation's will to fight for a better future, to build a Hungary that belonged to Europe, a Hungary in which human beings enjoyed human rights, a Hungary that subjected none of its nationalities and was itself not in subjection, a Hungary that should not be bogged down in antiquated economic forms and medieval political structures, a Hungary, finally, in which one could speak, write, and print the truth. *Nyugat* did not stand alone but formed the nucleus of a number of associations and magazines (occasionally tolerated, more often suppressed) with the same or approximately the same programme. The leading role in this struggle is something every generation of Hungarian writers has inherited from its forbears and bequeathed to its successors, a process that still continues today and will certainly continue tomorrow as well.

Osváth wrote little himself. He tended to direct things orally, in a voice that was more like a whisper. Sometimes he just nodded, or else he shook his head. My novel got the nod. Not immediately; two weeks later when I went back to see him as arranged. The moment could not have been less favourable. It was the day before Szivessy and I were due to leave for Vienna. My passport was burning in my pocket, and my ears were ringing with 'The future . . . the future . . . the future . . .' As long as Osváth praised my novel I was able to concentrate, but when he turned to criticizing certain points of detail I began to feel that the whole episode was a boring waste of time.

He ended with a word of praise for my dialogue, which he said would sound astonishingly good on the stage. As he was saying this, father and daughter exchanged nods. I inferred that they had been discussing my dialogue between themselves.

Here my patience gave way completely. At a time when I ought to have experienced the deepest gratitude I was almost rude. What right had this literary potentate to discuss my dialogue style with a half-grown girl?

'Is my novel suitable for publication?' I asked – I fear somewhat brusquely.

'It would be a useful thing to publish,' replied Osváth after a pause.

This was too vague for me. 'Then please will you publish it in *Nyugat*?' I said.

'In *Nyugat*?'

All the colour had drained from his lined and furrowed face. He looked unenthusiastically up at me, at the stacks of manuscripts that burdened his desk, and then at the latest copy of *Nyugat*, which lay before him. It was already several months old, consisted of only a few pages, and was printed on yellow wartime paper. There was no knowing when the next issue could come out. Finally he looked across at his daughter, whose own eyes were on the floor.

And J.H. 19 had neither the will nor the wits to understand that in those few moments Osváth was bearing to the grave everything he had lived for: Hungary, great literature, *Nyugat*, Europe, humanity. And his child.

As I stood up to go he said again, prompted by a glance from his daughter, 'Yes, your dialogue – very suitable for the stage.'

In the autumn of 1919 a poor family of the suburb of Szeged-Rókus was caught red-handed stealing fuel from a depot. The case came under French jurisdiction. The people's sympathies were with the thieves.

One Dr Székely was appointed by the court to defend the accused, and he brought along his twenty-year-old niece Margit P., who spoke excellent French (she even gave lessons), to act as interpreter.

The French military judges were divided in their opinions. Some of them wanted to make an example and execute at least the father of the family. Others were for showing mercy and humanity in the form of very mild sentences. So it looked as if the skill and eloquence of defending counsel were going to play a decisive part in tipping the scales of justice.

The proceedings were about to get under way when it occurred to one of the judges that French law did not admit as counsel anyone who did not speak French. Dr Székely introduced his young interpreter, but it was discovered that, superb as her French was, she did not possess the formal qualifications of a court interpreter. The presiding judge found the answer to that one: French law might not allow Mademoiselle to interpret but it allowed anyone – i.e. her included – to defend an accused before a court. Did Mademoiselle undertake to defend the accused herself? She did.

I have never discovered whether the conduct of that trial was juridically impeccable or not. The fact is that it turned into a highly amusing oral examination in the French language. For hour after hour the judges subjected their pretty victim to a series of searching and intricate legal questions, and then had her make her plea for the defence. And each well-phrased answer, each amusing mistranslation of legal technicalities improved the chances of the poor defendants, who eventually got off with light sentences for what could after all hardly be called a weighty offence. By Szeged standards this was a major occasion, and for weeks afterwards the plucky little interpreter was the talk of the town.

When J.H. 19 heard the story he could not wait to meet its intriguing heroine – a wish that was fulfilled that same afternoon as he and Szivessy came across Margit P. out walking with some friends. Szivessy (who had of course known her since the cradle) introduced me, and Margit took the opportunity to invite us both to her birthday party the following Wednesday.

At the party things took a most satisfactory course and by the second hour Margit and I were already exchanging kisses in the cloakroom. As a kissing companion she was not unlike Bella, though she showed less inclination to fall apart. I was proud of the fact that of all the girls at the party I should have found favour with the very one who had shown such pluck and adroitness in the defence of the oppressed and exploited. Moreover Margit turned out to be a well-read, quick-witted, and lively girl who spoke the delightful local dialect (as was usual even among the better families in Szeged), had been abroad several times with her uncle (I had not been abroad once), and was convinced of my architectural gifts from the very first moment of our acquaintance. The next day she read my novel and said that she was jealous of the heroine.

Szivessy laughed at me for taking Margit, her kisses, her pluck before the French court-martial, and her feeling of social responsibility so seriously. Like all young men who do not have much luck with women, he took a disillusioned view of the female sex. He told me in unambiguous terms exactly *what* the French officers had wanted of their impromptu defence counsel, and added that our provincial girls were too stupid even for *that*. They only made themselves look interesting for as long as it took for someone to up and marry them. After that they stopped taking the trouble to think, be intelligent, educated, and enterprising, and nurture feelings of social responsibility. They even forgot their foreign languages in a couple of years.

His advice to me was to tip her up on the divan next time we were alone and give her the one thing she needed. Otherwise she would only work herself up with me during the day in order to have something to do alone at night. But if I attended to her peace of mind in the only proper way I should soon see what remained of all her splendid qualities.

Margit, however, was the first girl of whom I had wanted something more than Szivessy so unequivocally urged me to take.

Be that as it may, J.H. 19 left Szeged secretly engaged to Margit P.; J.H. 20, 21, and 22 confirmed his promise on numerous occasions; J.H. 23 took Margit to wife; and their marriage lasted for nearly seven years. He was J.H. 29 before he managed to slip the tie.

8

'You've done the sets, now write the play!' —
The new dicky-bird — *How I failed to get to*
Königsberg

PROFESSOR ALEXANDER BARANOWSKI of the Dresden
Academy of Arts and Crafts cannot have been too displeased
with my work or he would never have sent me to Professor
Linnebach, chief designer for the Dresden State Playhouse, with
the recommendation that he take me on as an apprentice in his
technically ultra-modern theatre.

Between the academy and the theatre my days were full and
happy. I have never for a moment regretted that I did not become
an architect, and my parents were quite happy with my new
choice of profession since everyone assured them that stage
design was an altogether serious and occasionally even lucrative
activity. In fact only a part of my work was of any immediate
use to the theatre (and my salary was little more than symbolic).
Most of what I did was for the benefit of my own education and
consisted of designing all the sets for entire plays that of course
did not figure in the theatre's current repertory.

I was also allowed to hang around behind the scenes during
the evening performances and watch the whole magical process.
Some plays I knew *only* from behind, as it were. I saw only what
the audience did *not* see; for me the actors were only there when
from the house's point of view they were absent. I was free to let
my fancy roam as I wondered what transformations their fates
and characters might have undergone in the periods they spent
out of my sight. I gradually got into the habit of working out
entire non-existent plays, rather as I had done as a child before
the photographs in Mother's theatre magazines. Occasionally I

was given a complimentary ticket or I got hold of an acting script, and then I was able to check my imaginary play against the real one. And once or twice, I must admit, the play I had puzzled out for myself struck me as being better or at any rate more interesting than the one the author had written. But it was not often that I indulged in such complacency, and when I did it went no further than myself.

What used to thrill me most about that world behind the scenes was the way the actors changed into their parts and then afterwards changed back again into their everyday selves. In the no-man's-land between private life and dramatic life no two actors behave the same, and there were not a few who in that split second of time made a quite unforgettable impression on me.

After a year in Dresden Szivessy and I both moved on to Berlin. On the basis of my Dresden work I was accepted for Professor César Klein's class in the college attached to the National Museum of Arts and Crafts in the Prinz-Albrecht-Strasse. (The building subsequently got a nasty reputation when it was appropriated by the Gestapo.) At that time it was the best college for stage design in the whole of Germany.

César Klein made it clear to me in various subtle ways that he regarded his Dresden colleagues' opinion of my work as rather extravagant. In fact he let almost two years go by before he really praised anything of mine. But one or two of the sets I designed for non-existent, half-worked-out, half-dreamt-up plays caught his eye from the very beginning.

'Do you ever try *writing* the plays you design these sets for?'
'No.'

'Pity. There's real tension here. These things have style. They know where they're going. One can *feel* the clash of forces. There's something happening here. Pity we never discover what. Why don't you try your hand at a play?'

There we were again. Shades of Osváth. So I should write plays. And I did in fact begin to wonder occasionally whether I should not take up my writing again and write something that had tension and style and that knew where it was going. A work in which one could feel the clash of forces. A work in which something happened – and one actually found out what. But I was still thinking in terms of novels rather than of plays, and even there I had no coherent plans. My only systematic work went into my sets, with a bit of commercial work on the side – book jackets, posters, illustrations, and so on.

Professor Linnebach had a brother in Berlin. They were both fair, had little pointed beards, and altogether bore a striking resemblance to one another. Moreover the brother occupied the same position in the Berlin Opera House as Professor Linnebach occupied in the Dresden State Playhouse. Both men were real professionals at their job.

One day in 1922 – the Opera House was closed for holidays at the time – the Berlin Linnebach summoned me urgently to his office. He had just received word very unexpectedly that there was to be a big public ceremony in the Opera House on the morning of the day after next – the third anniversary of the Weimar Constitution and the first time the celebrations were to be held in Berlin. The stage had to be decorated for the occasion with a special set to publicize the new national coat of arms (valid as from the day of the ceremony).

'Here – they've sent us a drawing of the new dicky-bird.'

He had no one available at the moment who could design the set in such short order. The materials were there and the scene painters were there, and his brother, he said, had sworn blind that I, J.H. 22, was just the man for this kind of imaginative job. The republic would pay me for my time and trouble. He (Linnebach) had a train to catch – good-bye!

It was clear that he personally attached no very great importance either to the new coat of arms or to the new republic. But I was for two whole days undisputed master of the Berlin Opera House! There would be no one to supervise my design, and I should be in sole charge of its execution. The first people who would see my décor would be the members of the government, the diplomatic corps, the President ... And what if it didn't work? Oh well, plenty of things didn't work in those days.

But it *did* work. And they liked it. In front in the middle was a rostrum with the German eagle painted on it in the proper heraldic colours. And behind, shimmering in translucent gold against a mysterious background of incorporeal black, reaching right up into the flies and extending over the whole width of the stage, there was the 'new dicky-bird' again. Linnebach did in fact get back at the last minute and he expressed his approval. Admittedly I had to lead Chancellor Wirth on stage by the hand because all the paint was still sopping wet and I did not want him to get any on his clothes, but nobody noticed. Before and after the Chancellor's speech Leo Blech conducted Beethoven.

Some two weeks later I received a letter asking me to call on the 'National Art Curator' at such and such a time. At the end of a long, deserted corridor in I have forgotten which ministry I found a door that bore that title. In a small room beyond it sat a young man who informed me that he was the National Art Curator. The fact that I was J.H. appeared to surprise him.

He told me that they needed an experienced stage designer at Königsberg in Prussia. He had seen my work at the Opera House and Linnebach had assured him that I had done the design and supervised its execution entirely on my own. Did I have any objection to his putting my name forward for the Königsberg job?

J.H. 22: 'None whatever! I should love the job, especially as I am thinking of getting married.'

National Art Curator: 'I hardly think Königsberg will be thinking in terms of the kind of salary one could support a family on.'

J.H. 22: 'For a great objective I am prepared to make any sacrifice. And so is my fiancée.'

A few days later Königsberg replied that they did not take foreigners.

My brief Königsberg dreams reminded me for a moment that there was such a thing as politics. Back in Hungary absolutely everything had reminded me of revolution and counter-revolution, of those interminable discussions, of violence and bloodshed, of the smart of defeat, and of the swift resurrection of youthful hopes. Then, when I had crossed the border, new perspectives had appeared, or rather the old ones had disappeared.

The machine-guns crackled once more on the streets of Germany for a few days early in 1920 – in Dresden, too, where I was living at the time. That was the Kapp Putsch, and it prompted me to inquire into what was happening in this country in which I was now living and for the time being wanted to go on living. In the Hungarian 'Commune' we had heard virtually nothing of the soviet revolution in Bavaria. It was a foregone conclusion that I should have sided with the Communists Liebknecht and Rosa Luxemburg when – at least a year after the event – I learned the details of their assassination.

On the whole, however, it struck me that on the plane of world history there was nothing very much going on. And I experienced this apparent uneventfulness as something pleasant. Had anyone asked J.H. 22 about his political convictions he would have answered, 'I'm a revolutionary. I'm a Communist.' That, after all, was the reason why he had gone into exile in 1919 and why he was still in exile in 1922. Similarly he would have said, and did in fact say, 'I am engaged to Margit P. of Szeged.'

And if someone had one day brought me the news, 'The world revolution has broken out!' I should have replied, 'Congratulations!' and my answer would have been no less sincere than it had been on 21 March 1919. But no one did bring me the news, and the world revolution gently slid off my agenda. My political convictions became swathed in a kind of mist that rounded off all the corners and made it tricky to judge distances.

What much older, cleverer, and more experienced people, what indeed political geniuses had failed to notice, J.H. 22 could of course hardly be expected to notice either, namely that the world revolution was off. No, it had not been delayed, nor was it approaching from another direction; it was simply not coming.

And even if the world had not yet completely grasped the fact, it was beginning to draw certain conclusions. Conclusions whose novelty on the plane of world history lay in the fact that no such novelty had occurred or was to be expected. One part of the world, a part that had looked forward to the new age with a longing that turned out to have been vain, was now searching feverishly for a substitute for the world revolution that should provide those committed to revolution as a career with a goal in life and a reason for pursuing it. Meanwhile the others, those who feared the world revolution, tried with trembling hands to bolt and bar the door, unaware of the fact that there was no one around at the time who could have hoped to burst it open.

As for myself, I saw that the world was gradually calming down. My exile reached its end. At the end of 1923 I went back to Hungary and married Margit P.

9

The musical landlord – A student and his wife –
Flight from inflation – Transports of a young
father – Kari – 'And the shark has pearly teeth,
dear'

WE gradually lost all awareness of day and night. Our bodies were apart for no more than seconds at a time. It made me happier than I had ever been before to know that Margit was mine not just for a matter of hours, not just for a matter of days, but – as I thought – for ever. My malevolent companion the twentieth century has knocked the bottom out of my life on repeated occasions; when from time to time it offered some compensation in the form of a fleeting feeling of relative stability, my joy knew no bounds.

Had my world remained as it had been before Sarajevo I should have known what I must do and what I might look forward to. And had my father attempted at any time during our long engagement to convince me of the senselessness of my marriage to Margit, I believe he would have succeeded. But he was not even convinced himself. Who knew – perhaps these scatter-brained youngsters were right after all. His modesty, too, inhibited him from discussing the subject of love. Besides, the remnant of Hungary that remained after the armistice was flooded with out-of-work intellectuals. A diploma was no guarantee against poverty any more. So he was glad that one of his sons at least was marrying the niece of a wealthy man (Margit's uncle's rope and sack factory in Szeged was doing very well at the time). For the same reason everyone approved of the young couple's decision to begin their married life in Berlin. In Hungary our prospects

94

were hardly rosy, whereas Germany was a go-ahead country, a Western country, a country where justice prevailed. An artistic country, too, in which sincere and gifted young people had a chance of getting on.

Margit, though, went abroad with mixed feelings.

In a house on the Kaiserdamm we rented two rooms with bath and use of kitchen from a very pleasant, portly old gentleman whom we subsequently discovered to be a retired singer – a discovery we owed to the fact that he gave singing lessons all day and every day. But at the time even that did not bother us. Our world ended at the edge of the bed.

The trouble started the first time we found ourselves with an hour to spare between embraces. There were plenty of things we could have discussed and quite a number that we ought to have discussed. Back in the early days of our engagement we had had the feeling that it was our airing our important problems that made the world go round. We tried to resurrect the old subjects. Hopeless. They held no further interest for us. I talked about my artistic ideas, about the cultural problems of our day and age, about the short- and long-term prospects of the human race – topics with which J.H. 19 had been able to awaken in Margit the liveliest interest. I analysed the Treaty of Rapallo between Russia and Germany, discussed the so rashly scuttled solution of the nationalities problem on a federal basis, commented on our country's unfitness for survival as crippled by the Treaty of Trianon – a subject to which every Hungarian inevitably found himself returning over and over again at various levels during those years. Margit would reply with a yawn, a shrug of the shoulders, a vacant stare, a cloud of smoke from her cigarette . . . and then turn to harping on *her* pet theme in one of its thousand variations – namely her own social position as she felt it ought to have been in consequence of our marriage, and as it in fact most unfairly was or looked like becoming. My micro-success in Dresden, the two sketches of mine that had been reproduced in a book on modern stage design, an exhibition of designs in Munich that earned some praise, an unimportant competition in which I won second prize, the recognition given me by the Linnebach brothers, the interest shown in me by the National Art Curator – all these things represented in her eyes the tumultuous start of a career whose continuation was now being unjustly delayed. She began by blaming the whole world for the fact that these insignificant achievements remained without sequel. She ended by putting all the blame on me.

The worst of it was that people like us *had* no definable social position in the Germany of that time. In fact the very social order itself defied definition. We were sub-tenants, foreigners, and, if not exactly indigent, pretty poorly off. I was in fact still a student, though one who appeared with increasing infrequency at his place of study. She was a student's wife. Things did begin to look up at one point: on a sudden inspiration I drew a series of Boccaccio illustrations that César Klein said was one of the best things I had ever done. But all attempts to find a publisher proved fruitless. The times were just not right.

Meanwhile Germany's post-war inflation was beginning to take on alarming proportions, and the situation was not improved by my truly boundless ineptitude in money matters. There was nothing for it but to pack our bags and retreat in disorder to Hungary, where we stayed for the next few years, living on a modest allowance from Margit's uncle and my father. The fact that we had originally come back only for a holiday visit was gently forgotten.

My brother-in-law Miklós Halmi, sixteen years older than myself, promised to take me under his wing. And if anyone knew his way about in the tangled maze of the Hungarian economy at that time it was Miklós Halmi. The hardworking, literate, witty, well-brought-up, but penniless son of our doctor in Abony, he had sought and somewhat surprisingly won the hand of my sister Irene in 1912 and carried her off with him to Szabadka in the southern part of Hungary, where he shortly became managing director of the Southern Bank. The people who tended to refer to him as 'jumped up' at this point little dreamed that the career of this slight young man with the clever face and the charming smile had hardly even begun.

Among the many plans of the Károlyi government that the victor brushed aside in the autumn of 1918 with an '*Assez!*

Assez!' was a new and up-to-date financial policy to replace the antiquated system that had accompanied the Austro-Hungarian Monarchy to its downfall. It made his victory look more victorious, of course, but it left Europe with a broken backbone, a prey to every unhealthy influence. And there was no shortage of unhealthy influences. In the resultant financial chaos, as I say, Miklós Halmi found his way about better than anyone – better, at any rate, than the experts of the Allied Control Commission who were calling the tune in Budapest. He left Serbian-occupied Szabadka in secret and moved to the capital, where he became overnight one of the biggest beneficiaries of the whole imbroglio. I was told that this move alone spelt ruin for certain of his Szabadka friends who had helped to launch him on his career. But if he had worried his head about such as them he would never have become the legendary figure in Budapest financial circles that he did become.

Making promises was Halmi's great passion. He spared himself no pains and balked at no sacrifice in his search for people in whom a promise would raise high and fervent hopes. Then, having promised, he would break his promise, and look on as those people were quite literally cast down, and smile his charming smile. I used to wonder just what he must have suffered in his youth in the way of scorn, mistrust, and abuse from people richer and more powerful than himself to make him so frankly and passionately malicious. To me he promised everything, as was his wont. But – and actually I should say this with a certain pride – he rarely got a chance to break his promise: I quit first.

Not that I was lacking in either ability or enthusiasm. In fact I made various attempts, mostly at Halmi's suggestion but sometimes entirely on my own initiative, to become a useful citizen. Occasionally I even managed to earn a bit of money. But nothing ever lasted. The only activity for which I seemed to have any staying power was the apparently quite unpromising one of writing my second novel. Moreover, as I came to write 'The End' on the last page of the manuscript I was not surprised to discover that I already had the plan of a third novel in my head.

I had of course to steal the time I spent on my novels. I got into the habit – which I have retained to this day – of writing in little blue exercise books that I could quickly slip into a pocket out of sight. Nor of course did my novels earn us any money. (They never will, either. I left them in Abony – for me the very symbol of peace and security – and they were destroyed down to the last scrap of paper when my older brother Max and his family were dragged off to the gas-chamber in 1944.)

From time to time, though, I did manage to earn something with my pen. The sums involved were tiny, but what mattered to me was the fact that someone was prepared to pay money for my work. It was a kind of confirmation. Articles, book reviews, and the very occasional short story of mine were published in various Hungarian magazines not only in Hungary but also in Romania, Yugoslavia, and Czechoslovakia – countries that the Treaty of Trianon had provided with large Hungarian minorities. (At that time the traditional Hungarian cultural centres in the areas amputated from Hungary by the Treaty were in greater or lesser degree allowed to flourish. It was not until 1945 that the governments installed by the Kremlin, in a mockery of their own loudly proclaimed principles, virtually severed those minorities' cultural contacts.)

Little by little I became a not entirely unknown figure on the fringe of progressive Hungarian literature, although my chief profession remained, as before, various branches of commercial and applied art. To arrive at this dubious result my prodigal travelling companion, the twentieth century, had needed to run almost a quarter of its course.

Must I call my twenties wasted years, then? Certainly not! How can you call any time wasted in which a human being is born? In October 1925 Margit bore me a son – Peter. Peter was a quite exceptionally beautiful and attractive child. It was impossible not to fall for him at first sight. There was no resisting the radiance of his affection. I was exactly like any other twenty-five-year-old father. I doted on my son. But as for feeling a sense of responsibility for him . . . No – that was something I only really felt for the present and future contents of my little blue exercise books. And when in the autumn of 1929 I gave my four-year-old son a kiss – 'Daddy's just off to Berlin, Peter' – I had no idea that, apart from two very brief visits to Hungary, I should be away for sixteen years. Even less did I suspect that I should return to find my son a Roman Catholic priest.

The late twenties were also the years in which my youngest brother Kari (Károly-László, seven years younger than I) began to play an important part in my life. Towards the end of the twenties, no doubt influenced by the fact that his elder brother had been an active participant in the soviet revolution of 1919, Kari started going around in Budapest with a crowd of young people some of whom were secret Communists and all of whom were to a greater or lesser degree in sympathy with the Communist underground. The environment in which this group lived was very different from that in which I had joined the Communists ten years before. Admiral Horthy's tyrannical system was by this time firmly established. Many essential features of the Fascist and Nazi systems of the thirties were tried out on a smaller scale in the Hungary of the twenties. Including the merciless persecution of dissidents, particularly Communist dissidents.

The fact that the victors in the First World War had demolished the Austro-Hungarian Monarchy – long ripe for demolition – *without* effectively providing its once subject peoples with security, respecting their national interests, and safeguarding their human rights had given rise to a fundamentally new political situation. Europe's eastern flank was left unprotected – or rather protected solely by the fact that Russia, whose expansionist tendencies were still essentially intact, was for the time being in a severely weakened condition. An internal strengthening of Russian might, a reinforcement of her political and military apparatus must inevitably mean that the exposed flank would sooner or later fall a prey to Russian ambitions. And Russia *was* quietly, consistently, and by no means slowly becoming stronger; the balance of power was shifting steadily in her favour. One day the scales were going to have to tip.

However, since the political system currently obtaining in Russia was of *revolutionary origin* the victors overlooked the Russian empire's traditional and now revolutionarily new urge to expand. They succumbed to the conviction that Europe was threatened only by an *ideology*, and saw in *dissidence* the only danger. A hastily modernized political police force began to wage permanent war on boys and girls who, had they been allowed to think their ideas through without interference from outside, might well have arrived at quite different results. Instead the muddle-headed were martyred and their minds driven into the shallows of romanticism on the one hand and rigid Party discipline on the other. The attacks of the oppressors were no less dilettantish than the counter-attacks of the oppressed, but still it was a matter of life and death. The underground fighters were few in number and their successes insignificant, yet there were many people who saw each of those successes as a promise. They were hunted down, dragged before courts of injustice, condemned, slung into jail for years, handed over to the hangman, or quietly left to die. Their ranks were riddled with informers. The theme of revolution wove a halo round their heads that was often visible to none but themselves but that was *there* and was a source of inspiration to many who sought a way out of their insoluble confusion.

Something about Kari and his young friends made me like to be in their company. Was I perhaps trying to repair the connection broken off ten years before, trying as it were to renew contact with my own younger self? It is possible. I even tried to fall in love with a girl – a very beautiful redhead – but found myself unable to whip up the emotions I should have cherished so dearly once aroused.

And then I began to feel homesick for the city I had left, especially after I had made the acquaintance of Brecht and Weill's *The Threepenny Opera*. The songs were like a personal greeting from Berlin to me. A greeting – and a reproach for my infidelity.

As I remember, the following things all occurred at the same time, though I expect in reality they merely came in rapid succession.

J.H. 29 decided to go back to Berlin as soon as somehow possible and suggested to Margit that she follow in a short while with the child and that they begin a new life there. He could not give any very clear picture of that new life at first but he intended, apart from the monthly allowance from home, to live by his pen. When he put it to Margit that she help support the family by making use of her knowledge of the French language she looked at him as if this was the first she had heard of its existence.

He put down his brush and his pencil in the firm resolve to give up painting and drawing for good, despite the fact that he had scored a few nice successes recently, whereas with his writing he had hardly got anywhere.

Having reckoned himself a Communist since the heroic days of March 1919 he found that there were now all kinds of formalities and that he did not in fact possess a Party card. He determined to look into the matter as soon as he was in Berlin.

And the fourth thing was this: J.H. 29 suddenly thought of four plays all at once – and so clearly and in such detail that with three of them practically all he had to do was to write them down (the fourth requiring some historical research). He must have been working away at those plays unconsciously for years while he was drawing and painting and writing his novels and generally doing his level best to disregard the advice of Osváth and César Klein and others that he should write for the stage. Why had he tried to disregard it, anyway? Perhaps because he was scared of the decision that must inevitably set his life on a new and unfamiliar course.

IO

The secret of the little blue exercise books – An audience with royalty – All hell breaks loose

FOR me, then, there was no longer a shadow of a doubt. I had found my one proper job in life: I *had* to write plays. Nor was I lacking in the conviction that I *could* write plays. As to *why* I wanted to write plays, I was also quite clear about that: to change the existing social order. Whether such a change was necessary seemed every bit as unquestionable to J.H. 30 as it had to J.H. 19 when he decided to stake his all on a new Hungary, a new Europe, a new humanity.

I wrote the three plays that had come to me just like that at a tremendous pace partly before leaving Budapest and partly in Berlin, and I immediately began collecting the historical material for the fourth. The little blue exercise books began to pile up. And I was not even aware of the fact that I still regarded the working hours I put in on them more or less as stolen time.

I knew from my Dresden days that German theatres drew their contemporary repertoire from the big publishing houses, which all ran special theatre departments for the purpose, so when my three plays were finished and typed, off they went. I got the first batch back ('We sincerely regret . . .') on a Thursday. The second arrived on the Friday. And so it went on, with me in regular receipt of one or two parcels a week.

It was on a Saturday in the autumn of 1931 that the white postcard from the S. Fischer Verlag in Berlin arrived. I was invited to meet Dr Konrad Maril, head of the theatre department. I managed to survive until the Monday, when I treated myself to a two-minute taxi ride to the firm's offices in the Bülow-Strasse. Dr Maril, a quiet, friendly, and – as I felt then and was later able to confirm – extremely competent man in his fifties, informed me without any particular preamble that the house of S. Fischer was prepared to take on my plays. He took me slowly through the form of contract, explaining everything as if to a child, either because he had immediately divined my haziness in business matters or because he treated all his authors like that just in case, and said that my contract could be ready for signature next day at the same time. Was that all right with me and did I wish for an advance? I replied to the first question with a swift if barely audible 'yes' and suggested in answer to the second the sum of five hundred marks. He agreed with a smile. (I found out later that I should have asked for at least two thousand.)

Next day, however, there was a telephone call from his secretary: Would I please not come today – Dr Maril would be in touch again in a few days' time. Aha, I thought, there's another dream that didn't come true, and from that moment on I turned my whole attention to my fourth, historical play about Emperor Sigismund and John Hus that was to make a name for itself the following year under the title *God, Emperor, and Peasant.*

But he did get in touch again, and this time I was ushered into the presence of a bald-headed old gentleman – how weird to think that as I write this I am almost as old as Sami Fischer was then – who was bent over a desk eating a bowl of soup with an egg in it and who took absolutely no notice of our entrance (I was accompanied on this awesome occasion by Dr Maril and by the junior head of the firm, Dr Bermann Fischer).

His soup finished, he wiped his mouth, put down his napkin (whereupon a secretary removed his breakfast tray in a trice), swivelled round to face us, and motioned me into an enormous armchair.

'They tell me you have written one or two good plays,' he began in a voice feeble with age. 'Last night I read your manuscripts, and now I wonder if you would be so kind as to tell me what, in your opinion, is good about them.'

I've had it, I thought. How do you answer a question like that? I have a tendency to stutter at the best of times. Trying my hardest not to sound presumptuous, I attempted to analyse what

I had meant to put across in my three plays while leaving open the question of how far I might have succeeded.

The little old man leaned imperceptibly closer. The junior head, his son-in-law, noticing the movement, came over to stand behind me and said quietly, 'Mr Fischer can't hear you – you must speak louder.'

Suffering the tortures of the damned, I had to repeat my whole speech virtually at the top of my voice. The little but grand old man listened with a serious, thoughtful expression on his face. From time to time I caught a mocking glint in the corner of his eye. At last I thought I could decently stop. There was a silence. (An angel passed, as they say – but who knew whether it was my good or evil angel?)

For a fraction of a second a grin flitted across the old man's features. Then he spoke – so quietly that this time I had to lean right forward to catch what he said.

'When George Bernard Shaw was sitting in that chair I asked him the same question.' Pause. 'His answer was wittier.' Pause. 'A great deal wittier . . .'

Failed! Here I was, talking with the mightiest king of that continent called Literature, and I had failed. By my own stupidity. Simply and solely by my own hopeless stupidity.

When we were outside again, however, my two companions looked by no means as disappointed as I felt. In fact they seized me by the hand and congratulated me; the normally restrained Dr Maril even embraced me. I had got it completely wrong. The old man had liked me and liked my manuscripts . . .

A quarter of an hour later the contract was signed and the five hundred marks in my pocket, and less than a fortnight later one of my plays, *The New Paradise*, was on the repertoire of Reinhardt's Deutsche Theater in Berlin for the 1931–2 season. The artistic director of the theatre and one of the most important German producers of the period, Heinz Hilpert, wanted to produce the play himself, which meant that I should be making my début in my new and now permanent profession with the whole weight of his tremendous artistic authority behind me.

How about that, then, I thought to myself, and only a few years ago the lad was walking around with his tail between his legs because the National Art Curator could not get him a job as a stage designer in Königsberg!

I ought perhaps at this point – as a sort of seventieth-birthday present to myself – to depart from my original intention and continue this story as it *might* have continued, indeed as it inevitably *must* have continued had my contrary companion the twentieth century not made such a mess of everything.

I have sworn, however, to stick to the truth and leave day-dreaming aside. So this book is not going to be a success story. Actually, though, I find this sticking to the truth – even in its less palatable forms – more fun.

I had thought that the clearest confirmation of membership of my new profession would be when someone paid money for my work. There is another, even clearer form of confirmation, however, and I was lucky enough to receive it: I had a play *stolen*.

My publisher had sent out the usual duplicated reading scripts to the various theatres, offering first-performance rights. Shortly afterwards we heard through private channels that *The New Paradise* had been produced in Riga – without permission and without even publisher or author having been officially informed. Lithuania not being a member of the Berne Convention, all Dr Maril's efforts to legalize the première and collect a bit of money for me – and for the firm – proved fruitless. But I was as happy as a sandboy. No one steals what is of no value, and I now felt I was fully qualified professionally.

It was on the day of the Riga première that I repeated my suggestion to Margit that she should join me in Berlin. I must admit I breathed a sigh of relief when she stuck to her refusal.

Meanwhile Hilpert's Berlin première was postponed by his move to the Volksbühne, but he made it a condition that he be allowed to take *The New Paradise* with him, and the delay meant that my première would fall into the most favourable period of the season, so I was quite happy about that too. How should I have known how little time was left to me for these first performances and world premières and all the rest of it? I was soon to learn.

I finished my Emperor Sigismund play in the spring of 1932. This was something very different from my previous work. No more of that half-unconscious leaving things to chance. Hours of careful research, comparison of different variants, and ruthless cutting of scenes that not long before had seemed to me particularly successful, were the laborious prelude to the final text. During the whole time I was secretly living in the Middle Ages. I say 'secretly' because I still could not bear anyone knowing what I was working on while I was working on it.

Again it was Reinhardt's Deutsche Theater that secured the first-performance rights for Berlin, and the première of *God, Emperor, and Peasant* was set for December 1932, a date that became the target of much excited anticipation.

The foremost actors in Germany were interested in the part of Emperor Sigismund, but my publisher was not prepared to compromise even for the sake of the most brilliant names. I got goose-pimples when I heard that the great Alexander Moissi had been refused the part because he did not fit *my* idea of the character. In Breslau, where another production was in rehearsal, I saw the actor playing János Hunyadi weeping in the wings because he had heard that the author was displeased with his performance. Personally I felt like joining him. I began to have anxious thoughts about the gods of Greek tragedy and their habit of mercilessly punishing human presumption. Loyalty to one's own work, however, was apparently not something the gods considered punishable, and I got not only the best cast available in Berlin at that time but just about the best cast imaginable. (And virtually concurrently another superb cast under Hilpert was playing *The New Paradise* at the Volksbühne.)

As an occasion the first night was right up to the usual Reinhardt standard. The producer's pretty, ash-blonde wife explained to me in rapid whispers exactly who was there in the audience, for I knew hardly anyone myself. She was proud of the fact that there was such a full complement of important people present. Who would have thought that a play would stimulate that amount of interest in a time of such political tension?

Before the curtain went up we saw Alfred Kerr standing down in front on one side, facing the audience – the king of the critics showing himself to his people. On the other side the opposition assembled under the leadership of Herbert Ihering. It was already common knowledge that this time Ihering would be writing *for* and Kerr *against* the new author.

During the first few minutes of the play the audience was disturbingly cool. We felt this very clearly up in the box and my companion made some mildly reproachful remark about historical plays in general. Then, abruptly, the whole atmosphere changed; the stage as it were overran the auditorium. Applause dispelled the young author's agonizing stage-fright. And the gods did not protest. No – the gods of the drama were well-disposed toward me and gave me their blessing. It was hell that protested.

When they brought me the news after the third performance that a group of young people had objected to the portrayal of the Pope on religious grounds and had kicked up such a row that the cast had hardly been able to get through the play, I immediately had my doubts about this version of the story. Admittedly my political outlook was simple and naive but the experiences of my youth had not entirely failed to implant in me the seeds of a sense of reality. I found it hard to believe that young Christians should find anything to object to in the artistic representation of a medieval anti-pope whom the Church itself had rejected at the time.

On the fourth evening – which was quieter, but not without its disturbances – the truth came out: the rowdies were Nazis, SA men in civilian clothes, their Catholic slogans imperfectly memorized. And next day the Hitlerites – at that time still not yet officially masters of the country – put themselves openly, through the columns of their press, at the head of the barracking hooligans. All pretence of a religious protest was dropped.

The official evening paper of the National Socialist Party declared: 'This is what it comes down to, then – an attempt to misrepresent the primal origins of the history of the German people. And no one will deny that J.H. is an expert at robbing people of illusions.'

According to well-informed sources these lines were from the pen of the editor-in-chief of *Angriff* in person – Dr Joseph

Goebbels. The name was already a household word in Germany.

I had a few minutes to grasp the fact that I had landed in the middle of a political battlefield that extended far beyond my own personal horizon. I felt pretty much alone, and curiously enough it was a not unpleasant feeling. I was not aware of a need to go and ask a lot of people for their advice.

I wanted to do something, and I wanted to decide for myself what.

I I

All about MASch – Start of a round trip – The
God, Emperor, and Peasant *Affair – A call*
from afar

NOT that I was so alone. In fact anyone involved in a battle
could think himself lucky to have half as much sympathy behind
him as I had. There was one group of people in particular who
had known me for two years and who were glad to have an opportunity of feeling proud of one of their number – my MASch
colleagues.

On my return to Berlin in 1929 I had found out that anyone
who wanted to join the German Communist Party had only to
fill in a form and get two people to sign it. He soon got his Party
card, had to stick in his stamps every month and do some Party
work in a basic organization also known as a Party cell. And of
course he must accept Party discipline.

In my case, however, since I already had a Party 'history', the
process was very much more elaborate. The illegal Party in
Budapest and the Comintern in Moscow must first be asked
about me. As a veteran of 1919 I found all this much too stiff and
formal. I wanted to be a member of an international revolutionary
organization and create a new world in place of a world gone
rotten. And now it was all as cold and hyper-organized as if it
had been a part of that hateful world. It all seemed very different
from that brilliant First of May when Sári Fedák had danced on
the back of a lorry.

To keep me busy in the meantime I was advised to go along
to the Marxistische Arbeiterschule (Marxist Workers' College,
known by its initials as MASch), where I could extend my

knowledge of Marxism and at the same time make myself useful to the college's principal.

Strange as it may seem today the college was open to anyone who wished to attend it; its job was to propagate the Marxist ideology at as high a level as possible even among people who were not professionally concerned with and involved in it. Moreover this entirely Communist institution was expanding at such a rate – to keep pace with an ever-expanding demand – that at the end of 1932, not six months before Hitler's rise to power, it was able and indeed obliged to look around for larger premises.

As soon as I set foot in the place I felt thoroughly at home there. I toted chairs, worked out timetables, collected money, got hold of lecturers, and filled in as teacher myself when necessary; I even designed posters for the college, almost harking back to the profession I had dropped for ever. And whenever I had a break I would retire into a quiet corner and out would come one of my little blue exercise books.

The principal of the college was called Johann Schmidt, or rather, that is what he called himself, and one was even inclined to believe him as long as he kept his mouth shut. His unmistakable accent was more in tune with his real name: László Radványi, born in Budapest.

Hungarians are often accused of clannishness; once one of them gets his foot in the door, so it is said, you soon have the whole caboodle. An example often quoted is Sir Alexander Korda, who, as a Hungarian working with a staff riddled with Hungarians, created the British film industry. Johann Schmidt collected Hungarians around him too, but they were not the sort who were after a career. On the contrary, he could always find countrymen of his who were prepared to make any sacrifice and who took no thought for their own future in helping him build up the college.

Although there was nothing illegal about the work according to the laws in force at the time, it was not without its hazards. If a foreigner was caught doing it, for example, he could be slung out of the country. Especially if, like me, he had no wish to forgo the more militant activities of a Communist. I was often out demonstrating on the streets, or doing picket duty with an enormous placard. Consequently I did not at first use my own name at MASch but called myself Stefan – Stefan Faber.

There were so many courses on at the same time that one never got to know anything like all the lecturers personally, and it was typical of Radványi's exemplary discretion (or genius for conspiracy) that I saw the lectures of Georg and Gertrud Keller announced week after week after week, even taking the handbills to the printer myself or correcting the proofs, and did not learn until years later that the two 'Kellers' were Georg Lukács and his wife. (The big red Nietzsche moustache, incidentally, was already a thing of the past.)

By the time *God, Emperor, and Peasant* was premièred, 'Stefan Faber' too was a thing of the past. My picture began to appear in the papers and my MASch colleagues learned my real name. And, as I said, they were delighted at the chance of fêting one of their number.

I was particularly closely associated with the MASch Agitprop troupe. Agitprop troupes (Agitation and Propaganda) were a typical phenomenon of the period. The idea is supposed to have come from the Soviet Union although I never saw anything of the kind while I was there. They probably dated from an earlier epoch; many things about the arts in that country – and not just the arts, either – had taken an unexpected turn in an astonishingly short space of time.

An Agitprop troupe numbered between ten and twenty youths and girls and its repertoire consisted of militant and topical political songs and spoken choruses, with the occasional short sketch. Accompaniment was provided by guitar or accordion. They performed before and at intervals during political meetings, and during election campaigns (Germany was always having elections then), they struck up uninvited in pubs, courtyards, garden restaurants, and so on. Sometimes they fell foul of fists and chair-legs. Sometimes they fell foul of the police – in which case the odd member of the troupe would disappear for a few days or weeks. But often they were given a friendly reception, and if a topical song went over well, if the audience even joined in the chorus at the end, arm in arm and swaying to the beat, and the troupe succeeded in creating and directing a new and different atmosphere, then the players were happy and felt that their existence was justified.

The troupe from which all the others as it were took their cue was 'The Red Mouthpiece', the only Agitprop troupe consisting of professional actors. Its founder, leader, and resident writer was Gustav von Wangenheim; others I remember were Gustav's wife, Inge, Lotte Löbinger, and Heinz Greif, perhaps the most gifted of all the German Communist actors, who died in tragic circumstances in 1946. With several members of this troupe I was to become close friends at a later stage in my life.

Another person I got to know at 'The Red Mouthpiece' was a lanky young worker with soft blond hair who provided musical accompaniments with tremendous ability and infectious enthusiasm. He could play anything from a mouth-organ to a guitar to a concert grand, and he called himself Kurt Funk. It was decades before I discovered his real name. It is Herbert Wehner, and he is now leader of the Social Democratic Party in the West German Bundestag.

He would often disappear from the scene for some time and was undoubtedly engaged in illegal Party work. He too was unemployed (it was gradually becoming the norm) and getting eight marks forty unemployment pay a week. Out of that he had to pay twenty marks a month just for a place to sleep – his between midnight and 8 a.m. One day he left – I think it was for his home town of Dresden – and I did not see him again for several years, when I came across him in Moscow, living in a tiny room in the Lux Hotel and still calling himself Kurt Funk.

I got on well with the Agitproppers and enjoyed their company. I used to sit with them (and yet still somehow alone) in the back rooms of pubs whose landlords were Communists or spying on the Communists or both at once – at any rate they were prepared to let us have a room in which to rehearse the new programme. There I sat, the non-smoker, swathed in clouds of poisonous smoke from the cheapest cigarettes that these cast-offs of an incurably sick social order could still afford or that they contrived to roll themselves from assembled butts, jotting down in my little blue exercise book a few lines of dialogue. Lines about clever Emperor Sigismund who was driven by the unclever forces of history to do the very opposite of what his cleverness commanded, about all of us clever people who in our super-cleverness knew what must be done to spare humanity the most dreadful chapter in its whole history. But the cleverness in us is no use against the stupidity that is also in us; against ourselves we are completely powerless. And what the characters in my plays saw so clearly, I, their author, was a long, long way from seeing.

It was a disturbing and yet at the same time lulling experience to see how all around me millions of people, only months or weeks now from the end, were drugging themselves with theories – or with fragments of theories that did not even make up a whole. Blissfully unconcerned about the day-to-day praxis that was setting those theories at nought, the willing pilgrims came trooping in to the lectures that we had laid on for them and to which the Agitproppers' songs and chants had invited them. They streamed in their thousands to political meetings at which they listened to a string of empty promises and were comforted. In tens of thousands they demonstrated in the streets and got themselves slugged with rubber truncheons. In the most bitter cold hundreds and thousands of them filed in procession past the Communist Party headquarters – a triumph that was already a devastating defeat. Vast masses of people squandered in this way the last spark of their power or will to resist and prepared themselves to commit and be committed to the suicidal crime that was to come.

Suddenly I became aware of how alone I was in a frighteningly foreign world. Alone with my little blue exercise books. Love affairs began and, in the face of external obstacles or for lack of any deeper content, petered out. Or perhaps because a blessed fate preserved me from major catastrophes in this respect. From falling in love with Anna, for example, the gym mistress from Budapest, or with Adrienne, half Hamburg, half darkest Africa . . .

There was a girl in the troupe who, though in her late twenties, looked like a half-grown adolescent. She was short, extremely thin, and had incredibly slender bones (she rarely weighed more than ninety pounds). Because of her mouse-like appearance and

Disney-like movements she was known to one and all as Micky. The glasses she invariably wore (the frames were too big for her but she was always short of either the money to buy a new pair or the time to go along and get one on prescription) made her face even more grotesque. (When I last saw her name – this was several decades later, in the Budapest phone book – I found she had formally adopted 'Micky' as the first part of it. No – Micky is not Hungarian, even if she does live in Budapest now with her daughter and three grandchildren. She is from the Lausitz, not very far from Berlin.)

One evening after an Agitprop rehearsal (this must have been late 1931) I began explaining to Micky what was written in the little blue exercise books. Everything I told her I found she understood and agreed with. I surreptitiously counted the coins in my pocket and invited her for a meal at the Slow Fuse.

The Slow Fuse was a cramped and always crowded pub in the Eislebener-Strasse, if I remember rightly, catering mainly for out-of-work artists. It was called the Slow Fuse after its owner, a vigorous lady with a husky voice, a short back and sides, and a cigar permanently glowing in the corner of her mouth.

I ordered a 'Round Trip'. This was a plate of mixed salad that came with two forks. When we had finished our 'Round Trip', we did not feel like parting just yet. It would have seemed so unnatural, somehow.

We stayed together for fourteen years.

Micky had already been with me for a year when the *God, Emperor, and Peasant* affair blew up. I wanted, as I said, to do something, and I wanted to decide for myself what. Micky stood by me with boundless trust, waiting for me to make up my mind.

This was when the secluded and solitary nature that I had brought with me from Abony, the bell-glass that always and everywhere surrounded me, really did become a burden. I had within a very short space of time to approach a whole series of people with whom I was not personally acquainted. It seemed to me a quite impossible undertaking. Yet when it came to the crunch my incompetence in the mechanics of social intercourse turned out not to be so invincible after all.

The God, Emperor, and Peasant *affair*

I went round from one newspaper and magazine office to another, canvassing support and offering extracts of the play for publication. Every one of them considered my case a matter of public importance. While the death-agony of the Weimar Republic, disguised as a political game played according to democratic rules, pursued its tragi-comic decline into total annihilation and self-destruction there were individuals here and there for whom resistance was as much a matter of course as any other expression of their human existence.

As a result of my visits the major midday papers devoted the whole or part of their centre pages to the fight to keep my play on. *Germania*, the official organ of the Centre Party – the political party of the Roman Catholics in Germany – while admitting to not liking my play, pointed out that what I said in it was true and based on historical events. The *Rote Fahne* ('Red Flag') began by asking, 'What concern is it of ours what our comrades and sympathizers get up to on the bourgeois stage in their spare time?' But in view of the dimensions and ever-increasing intensity of the debate Karl Liebknecht House changed its tune and Friedrich Wolf (I had not met him then but we were later to become good friends) wrote in the Party press, '*God, Emperor, and Peasant* has become a trial of strength. The play must go on being performed. In another theatre! In private halls, if necessary, behind closed doors.'

Wolf was an honest man and I have no doubt at all that he meant well. But I instinctively balked at his suggestion. One does not write in order to be played in private halls and behind closed doors. Nor does one write in order to campaign for a particular political party – even if it is one's own.

Press cuttings about the *God, Emperor, and Peasant* case, both German and foreign (the foreign press and theatre people were almost without exception on my side), continued to pour in until eventually they filled a fair-sized suitcase, but meanwhile the Communist theatre organization – the 'New People's Theatre' or 'Free People's Theatre' or some such name – had pitched in and lost the battle. The general manager of the Deutsches Theater was delighted to have them take the worry off his hands. The 'New People's Theatre', however (or was it the 'Free'?), was not the right kind of set-up for such a delicate operation. They went about it in the clumsiest manner possible, taking unnecessary steps that only gave the police an excuse for intervening, and next day further performances were forbidden.

Morally I regarded myself as the victor and was regarded as such by others. In practical terms I was washed up high and dry. J.H. 32–3 was no longer a beginner who could rely on other people's protection. He had thrown himself wholeheartedly into the fray and for a short time he had been unmistakably on top. Although not even Dr Maril himself was omniscient enough to grasp just how utterly it was all over, neither he nor anyone else could fail to see or sense that things looked bad for Hay. In Germany, at least for a while, the name was quite out of the question.

It was a name at the sound of which every door flew open – and every cash-box slammed shut.

I behaved during this short period of my life with a silliness I had never achieved before and have possibly never equalled since. I hung around aimlessly in Berlin – in the room that Micky and I shared in the Schwäbische-Strasse (and where I sat, doing nothing, while flames consumed the Reichstag building) and in the various pubs frequented by the MASch troupe, or rather those few members of it who had not yet disappeared from the scene. From time to time I would pull out a blue exercise book and write a few lines of my new play *The Barbarian*, while Micky and the other Agitproppers brooded over new programmes for 'after-wards' – i.e. for when this whole senseless Nazi business would be over and the Communists would once more have only the 'Social Fascists' (meaning the Social Democrats) and the 'Polente' (our word for the fuzz) and other familiar enemies to deal with. If anyone asked me how much longer I intended to hang around like this, exposing myself to needless danger, I would answer, 'I'll wait for the elections, anyway.' As if anybody still believed in elections.

In Micky's case it sounded slightly more responsible because at least she was not a foreigner; she had the vote. 'I've got this one vote,' she used to say, 'and I'm not throwing it away for their benefit.'

There really was another general election coming up. It was set for 5 March 1933 if I remember rightly. But in the event of a Communist victory – which as such was still not entirely inconceivable – could one see the Nazis playing by the rules, laying down their weapons, and handing over to the Communists the key positions they had only so recently occupied? (In fact what Hitler would have done in such a case was never put to the test. The spectacle of naked, brute violence, even in those comparatively mild early days, exercised such an irresistible fascination on the voters that the Nazis got their wholesale victory at the polls.)

An Agitprop troupe had a pol-leader, an org-leader, and possibly other leaders as well. (The MASch troupe, numerically a fairly small one, also had its own musician – or should I say mus-leader?)

One evening a comrade from the central committee appeared – after a whole rigmarole of security precautions – in the back room of the pub we were patronizing at the time. He drew Betty, the org-leader, and myself to one side and gravely informed us that we must expel our absent pol-leader, Paul, from our midst. 'He's been getting mixed up with Trotskyites.' What precisely this implied we never discovered. The comrade answered our anxious questions with a few general remarks about vigilance and Party discipline. Betty was appointed provisional pol-leader, and although disturbed at what had happened she was clearly delighted at her appointment.

Then the man pulled out his wallet, turned to me, said nothing for as long as it took his face to assume a suitably solemn expression, then opened his wallet, took out a little black booklet, and handed it to me with the announcement, 'Your Party card, Comrade Faber.'

Undoubtedly my first feeling was one of great joy and happiness. The continuity with 1919 was now really established. At last I *really* belonged to the Party; I was again what I had once been and what I wished to be.

But then, from some unpatrolled area of my being, a totally unexpected anger seized me. I stood there motionless and silent, but my mind was in an uproar. 'So now you come up with it! Tom, Dick, and Harry, who've never done anything, you welcome into the Party with open arms, but me, who did my stint throughout the 133 days of the Hungarian Commune and had done it before and have done it by and large ever since – me you make wait! Why, anyway? Bombast? Bureaucracy? Chicanery? For fear of the senior Party member who might claim some plum job as his due? And why now? Now when through none of your doing my name is known all over the world and could be useful to you for propaganda purposes – is that it? Now that it's getting to be dangerous to own this little black booklet you want to use it to tie me to you – is that the idea?'

I held it before me in a hand trembling with emotion, and for a moment it was in the balance whether I would fling it back in his face or slip it lovingly and reverently into my pocket.

'I came to you in the purity of innocence,' my silent monologue continued. 'Like a young Parsifal I bore the Holy Grail in your midst, only occasionally setting it down for a spell to have my hands free for the girls who crossed my path. I grew up in the war, my companion this wicked, scheming twentieth century. I have learned that man needs redemption. He needs to be redeemed from wholesale slaughter, from hunger, from immorality, from his neighbour's hatred and from hatred of his neighbour, from being exploited and from being driven to exploit in his turn . . . From being sold down the river with cries of "*Assez! Assez!*" . . . From the envy of the poor and from envy of the rich, from distrust of those who speak another language and from their distrust . . . For all this I in my innocence have borne the Grail. For redemption. And I must go on bearing it. I feel a responsibility for man. In my innocence I have taken this responsibility upon myself voluntarily. I cannot and will not leave the Grail by the wayside. I *want* to bear it, even if it should become my Cup of Sorrow . . .'

And while I was thinking all this and keeping quiet about it, and as my face in all likelihood went as red as a beetroot, as white as a sheet, and back to beetroot-red again, I slowly, tenderly, even ceremonially put my new Party card away in my breast pocket.

I received the invitation on the evening of that memorable première. Komját, the expressionist writer and Communist journalist who acted as semi-official representative of the illegal Hungarian Communist Party with the then still legal German Communist Party, hauled me out of the producer's box during the interval – 'Come on – there's someone wants to see you' – and pushed me into the box next door. An elderly, bespectacled, balding man with a sickly pale complexion and a little pointed beard sat there in a suit that was too big for him, as if he had lost a lot of weight recently. Beside him was a no longer young but still extremely beautiful woman.

'Lunacharsky,' was how the People's Commissar from Moscow introduced himself to the young man from Abony. The lady beside him was his wife, the famous Russian actress Rosenelle.

I was well aware of who Lunacharsky was – Lenin's expert on cultural affairs, reformer of the Russian alphabet, and (which is what particularly interested me at the time) author of some magnificent, stirring, expressionist-tinged dramas, one about Cromwell, one about Don Quixote . . .

I could hear that he was praising my play, particularly the two scenes between Emperor and Pope, and I wanted desperately to pay attention to every word, but the stage behind the closed curtains and the odd phrases that floated up from the audience as they discussed the play made it impossible for me to concentrate. Fortunately a long article by him about the première – and its aftermath – appeared in *Isvestia* a few days later and I was able to recover something of what I had missed.

Finally, after a short, awkward pause, he said, 'Would you like to come and visit us? There are interesting things happening in our country. Yes . . . indeed, some very interesting things . . .'

Overjoyed, I nodded an enthusiastic affirmative.

'Good, you're invited . . . Good . . . that's splendid . . . you're invited . . .'

No one could be less sensitive with regard to other people's troubles than a young author on the occasion of his own first

night, yet even I could not help noticing something of the profound and shattering sadness that lay hidden behind the smile
and the words of the People's Commissar from Moscow.

But I was invited. And a day or two later I got a telegram from
Moscow asking for the Russian translation rights.

There we were, then, the two of us, living in our little room in
the Schwäbische-Strasse, both waiting for the other to 'come out
with it'.

One day, I thought, she's going to have to say, 'There's no point
in my staying in Berlin any longer. There's nothing I can do here.
I'm going back to my parents in Finsterwalde.'

To which I would answer, 'All right. I have to leave the
country anyway.'

Whereupon we would both add, 'Just until things clear up.'
Because neither of us doubted that things would in fact 'clear up'.
We had only the haziest notion of how it would happen, the
vaguest picture of a Europe that simply would not stand for such
things going on in its midst, of German civilization that must
inevitably triumph over German barbarism, above all of the
working class, of the world revolution, of an international nation
of working men and women living in love and brotherhood and
destined to utter the word of command at the decisive moment.
Neither of us – none of us – at that time could see all this at all
clearly, but without it the future, already bleak enough, simply
did not bear thinking about.

The day after the election I could wait no longer and, having
talked the matter over with Max Schrecker, the comrade from the
central committee who had issued me with my Party card, I had
to tell Micky, 'I'm leaving the country tomorrow.'

To which Micky, as if it had been the most natural thing in
the world, replied, 'I've already packed our cases.'

I realized to my intense surprise that her words had taken an
enormous weight off my mind.

Without her I wouldn't have lasted a day.

12

One ticket for Mr Brecht – News from home –
In bed with a super-spy – The puppet theatre

I HAD wanted to meet Bertolt Brecht ever since I had first made
the acquaintance of the *Threepenny Opera* songs back in Budapest. I had imagined myself storming back-stage after a performance, shaking the author by the hand, and vowing eternal
friendship. In fact when I did go and see it in Berlin I found every
detail as delightful as ever but the work as a whole left me with a
dissatisfied, 'Is that all?' sort of feeling. It was a magnificent
evening's theatre. I loved the music and I particularly liked the
words of the songs. But the rest of the libretto left me cold. Anyway, I did not go storming back-stage, and when we met soon
afterwards it was quite out of the blue.

It was in the spring of 1932 and I was working on *God, Emperor,
and Peasant*. Micky, when she was not typing for me, was out
visiting prominent and hence prosperous artists and writers in
order to talk them out of as much money as possible for the good
cause of MASch. It was something she was particularly good
at; they all fell for her grotesque appearance.

One evening Micky came home in high spirits.

'Helly Weigel sends her regards.'

I have always had a bad memory for names. 'And who is Helly
Weigel?'

'Actress. Bertolt Brecht's wife.'

'Aha. And how does she know of my existence and of the fact
that I can be sent regards through you?'

'I've just been having coffee with her. I told her about you.
I told her you wrote plays. And what kind of plays.'

'And what did she say to that?'

'She gave a very decent donation for MASch. And she said to tell you that if you want to write plays you ought to go and see Bert. He'll be glad to tell you how it's done. She says it's quite simple.'

I was suddenly as arrogant as only meek people can be when they start to rue their meekness. 'In that case *he'd* better come and see me and *I'll* tell him how *complicated* it is.'

'No, he's not coming – she is.'

'What – here?'

'I warned her it wasn't palatial.'

'What does she want?'

'Your poems.'

'But I haven't got any poems! I've never written any poems!'

'Yes, you have. In fact I had them with me. Accidents will happen. She wants to have them set to music and sing them in public.'

I felt frankly ashamed. 'But they're only try-outs – they're not meant to be recited in public. I can't write poetry.'

'She says he can teach you that too. He likes working with young people who do exactly what he says.'

'When does she want to come?'

'She'll be here in a minute. She just had to get some pickled fish.'

Helene sang my poems – one was against poison-gas warfare and the other rejoiced in the simple title, *The Ballad of Co-operative Production and Individual Expropriation* – at Communist gatherings and one whole summer long they were real hits. It was the beginning and end of my career as a lyric-writer. But through Helene I soon got to know Bert Brecht.

A lot of the time we spent together was passed in silence. He never repeated his offer to take me on as an apprentice, and in fact I would have been worse than useless to him as a pupil. It was not always easy to understand what he was saying when he talked about the theatre. Every now and then I would try to express my disagreement but I suppose I did it very clumsily and was often unclear myself. I cannot remember whether he had already coined the terms 'alienation' and 'alienation effect' at that time but with or without the terms it was always these concepts that formed the core of our discussions.

I wanted a renewal of the drama and so did he, but he wanted to achieve it by the – in my view – much too simple process of incorporating narrative elements. I could not see this leading to any real renewal. And was it really so important to prevent the actor from identifying with his part? Was the dramatic element in theatre a danger threatening the world or at least the literature of the stage? Must the new dramaturgy really be based on this *fear of first-hand experience*? I could never agree. I kept thinking of the shattering moment of transformation of actor into part that I had experienced innumerable times back-stage at the Dresden Playhouse. Was it not sacrilege to interfere with that holy moment, let alone try and do away with it altogether? Were not those the precious seconds for which man had invented this special something he called theatre?

I always felt sad after these discussions. Here was a mind in search of renewal, setting about it in his own sphere on the basis of the 'Thou shalt not' principle. A great writer who kept trying to be a meanie at the same time. One wondered whether he would not sooner or later fall victim to the petty rigidity of party-political considerations.

I was once present at a private performance of Brecht's *The Punitive Measure* before a Party jury and was a silent witness of the ensuing discussion. I considered and still consider *The Punitive Measure* to be one of Brecht's sincerest works, and it was with deep misgivings that I followed that discussion: it seemed to me to be a case of a writer, in order to lend weight and credence to his own *dramaturgical* dogmas, relinquishing his freedom and subordinating his writing to *political* dogmas. I wondered whether this was unavoidable, whether one could tie oneself down to Party dogma and still hope to write great works. Later I learned from my own experience how many limitations Party dogma, with its official and unofficial censorship of information and its subliminal pressures towards subordination of self, can impose on one. Always sufficient to expose the writer to a permanent threat from within. All those works of mine that I no longer like, that I wrote with a nasty taste in my mouth, and that

I should prefer to consign to oblivion suffer precisely from the fact that in the fight against dogma I occasionally went under.

These discussions with Brecht did not affect our friendship, though one did need a sense of humour to take his somewhat boisterous chaffing, as for example on the occasion of the dress rehearsal of my play *The New Paradise*. It was a magnificent production by Heinz Hilpert with a brilliant cast and everyone in the theatre business was there, including Brecht, with Helly and his 'staff'. With growing irritation they were obliged to take cognizance of the fact that the play – which incidentally had been written *before* my first meeting with Brecht – ran very much counter to his theories of the drama. The upshot was that Brecht, Helly, and 'staff' left at the interval. I was so wrapped up in a bad case of dress rehearsal nerves that I did not even see them go.

Next day a slightly embarrassed Micky came to me and said, 'Helly's on the phone. Greetings from Brecht, and would you mind telling him the rest of the play – they didn't stay till the end last night.'

Fortunately I managed to keep my temper. 'Tell her greetings from me too. There's *one* ticket left for tonight's performance. Brecht can go along himself and then he'll be able to tell the others what it's all about. I'm against narrative drama myself.'

How much Micky passed on and how much she kept back is something I never found out.

I forget whether the Brechts travelled to Vienna direct in 1933 or whether like us they first tried to settle in Prague. At any rate we left Berlin by what I subsequently discovered to have been the last train by which people were allowed out of the country without a visa. In Prague neither the ace reporter Egon Erwin Kisch nor the world-famous theatre manager E. F. Burian could get us a residence permit. Czechoslovakia was scared and was turning all refugees away. So it was not long before we met Brecht and Helly again – this time as guests of the charming Austrian authoress Maria Lazar in the Gonzaga-Gasse in Vienna.

The news had just come through from Berlin that Hans Otto, a well-known actor with the National Theatre and a member of the Communist Party, had been arrested by the new secret police, the Gestapo.

In the oppressive silence that followed Brecht's voice asked quietly, 'Do you think they're beating him up?' (The news that Hans Otto had been *killed* by the Gestapo did not come through until the next day.)

Several people answered in the affirmative: prisoners would certainly be beaten and tortured.

'Why?' Brecht asked. 'Just tell me why.'

Stupidly I lost patience with him. How could anyone ask why people beat other people up?

'To cause him pain.'

I regretted my outburst immediately. The sadness of the occasion made it inexcusable.

A long silence. Brecht was thinking hard.

'Yes,' he said at length. 'Just to cause him pain. How ghastly . . .'

A shadow darkened his permanently unshaven face. During that silence he stripped the concepts of beating and torture of all the psychological and philosophical padding in which they had become wrapped. His apparently unnecessary question helped him carry through a bold simplification of his train of thought. That was his secret. A priceless secret. But a dangerous one too. It enabled him to make pronouncements of a grandeur and pithiness equalled by few of his contemporaries. But it also led him into platitudes that served only to bestow an appearance of worth upon a rather bombastic and in any case self-deceiving dramaturgy.

In 1933 I heard from Abony that my father had had a heart attack; it was known that he would never fully recover his health. What should I do? Go to him immediately? Go to my mother's side? It was out of the question. Admiral Horthy's government clearly regarded me as a man who was not to be trusted, and I should never have been allowed out of the country again. In fact I had a stamp in my passport to this effect.

In Austria they were very strict about registering with the

police. They were strict about other things too – unmarried couples were not allowed to register as living in the same room. So Micky and I spent the first part of our time in Vienna in separate and frequently changing quarters.

There were complications. A Hungarian journalist whom I had known since my childhood and whom I shall call Mari Bojtár said we could have her two-roomed flat for a fortnight. It was sweet of her, but she was up to the ears in debt, and we had hardly set foot in the place before we were being dunned from all sides. In the end we reckoned ourselves lucky that the laundry gave us our washing back and did not confiscate it against Mari's debts.

One day somebody gave us yet another 'address'. (An 'address' was a place to sleep – with, if you were lucky, registration possibilities.) This one was in the 9th district, Latschka-Gasse 9, *chez* Friedmann, a room for one, preferably a woman, available as of three days hence for a period of ten days, i.e. as long as the regular tenant was away. Moreover the Friedmanns were comrades.

Three days later Micky and her solitary suitcase duly moved in with Litzi Friedmann. On the fourth day the political police called at the flat and took Litzi away with them. Micky was only asked for her identity card. A further four days later Litzi was restored to liberty, and life in the Friedmann residence resumed its normal course. Micky continued to sleep in the furnished room of the temporarily absent English student. Apparently this had not been Litzi's first brush with the political police, but for the time being there were no repercussions.

Litzi Friedmann, *née* Kohlmann, was twenty-three; married at eighteen, divorced at twenty, she was attractive, in fact *very* attractive, petite, with a nicely rounded, pneumatic, provocative figure and dark-brown hair. She had the kind of femininity that men find hard to resist, and against which a young Englishman who had previously seen her like only from the safe refuge of a Cambridge college never stood a chance. Not that the Englishman had come to Vienna in order to resist the temptations he should encounter there. Not at all. In fact his Cambridge friends had been unanimously of the opinion that it was high time the twenty-two-year-old took a step in the direction of reality, his acquaintanceship with the serious business of life having hitherto been confined to pipe-smoking and theoretical discussion of burning political themes. A colleague with contacts among left-wing politicians had given Kim the address of the Kohlmann-Friedmann family, from whom one could learn so many interesting things about central European and even Eastern European politics.

According to the canons of international spy literature Litzi Friedmann, the lovely Viennese landlady, first gave herself to the Cambridge undergraduate Kim Philby under wintry skies on a carpet of freshly fallen snow. Such an unseasonable escapade is something Litzi's ardent temperament by no means ruled out. In my prosaic way, however, I incline to the view that Litzi chose the five steps from her room to her tenant's room and plumped for the more traditional setting of the bed rather than risk catching a cold in winter. The more so since Litzi felt responsible in this love affair not only for her own soul and her own young body but also, and in fact primarily, for the good of the Party.

It is said that a young Viennese, the first time she has intercourse with an untouched English stripling (of good family, into the bargain), requires to bring great concentration and self-discipline to bear if she is to register complete spiritual and physical success.

A visitor from Budapest confirmed for Litzi what her young partner from Cambridge never began to suspect – that her love was no end in itself. In the best bed in the Kohlmann-Friedmann household, probably the very one in which she had been begotten, Litzi was now sleeping for world history, or rather, to be more precise, for the Third International. As Micky packed her suitcase in Kim Philby's furnished room and I carried it to our new lodgings with Mrs Kranz in the Iglaseegasse, Kim Philby was closeted with Litzi, being recruited for a world-wide spy network.

Amateurs of the literature of espionage are familiar with Philby's story, the story of the master spy who for thirty years held a series of progressively more important posts in the British secret service – and was spying for the Soviets the while.

The man from Budapest who, with Litzi's help, enlisted Philby for this work can hardly have been more than thirty at the time, a small, thin, slightly stooping man, as tailors often are, speaking in a kind of piercing whisper and walking with an irregular gait – in other words a mass of 'special peculiarities' who was yet (or perhaps therefore) not at that time under suspicion by the police. Now everyone in Hungary knows his name – and speaks it with a curse. Even outside Hungary it is not unknown. It is Gábor Péter. After the Second World War he was made a lieutenant-general and placed at the head of Hungary's secret political police, the main prop of the Communist dictator Rákosi's dominion over Hungary and of Stalin's over Rákosi. Now he is none of that any more.

I read in one Philby biography that Gábor Péter had been demoted to the rank of tailor again. The truth is both more and less than that. Not just because he first spent years as a prisoner – if one enjoying preferential treatment – in the very prison he had helped build to house other people. Nor because he was subsequently given a sinecure in the archives of a clothing factory.

In the vast and bloody marionette theatre in which he is, was, and remains a puppet, *this* is now his appointed role. Of the general's trousers with the red stripe down the seam Gábor Péter has been debagged.

For good? Or will his strings be pulled again some time? Who knows? Does Philby know, in his Moscow retirement? Does Litzi know – Litzi who, nearing sixty now but still in great shape, lives in East Berlin and delights in recalling the Philby era? Do any of them know whether and when the skilful puppeteers' dexterous fingers will jerk them into action once again?

It is my belief that anyone who is blind to this dreadful and indefatigable Punch and Judy show of international dimensions is blind to the world as it is today.

13

The light goes out – Vienna, February 1934 –
Red Banner over Floridsdorf – *The door
with no handle*

My next brush with world history began with the light going out
as I was shaving in Mrs Kranz's bathroom.

Everything at Mrs Kranz's was normally in apple-pie order.
Her house was a small two-storeyed villa originally designed for
one family. Its owner was an elderly lady, small in stature but with
a regal bearing, and with the kind of luxuriant growth of snow-
white hair that one found in few places outside Vienna. Mrs
Kranz had nothing to do with politics; we got in touch with her
through an advertisement in the paper.

Behind the villa there was a neglected garden with an enormous
walnut tree in the middle, and Micky and I were allowed to eat
as many nuts as we wanted and were able to. We often had nuts
for lunch and nuts for supper. Our room was tiny but well-
heated, and contained a narrow bed and a short sofa. We were
happier there than words can describe.

When we asked her what was the matter with the light Mrs
Kranz answered in some anxiety and even more embarrassment,
as if *she* had been responsible, 'General strike . . . !'

My books had taught me that a general strike was one of the
preliminaries to the revolution, with only an armed uprising
coming between the two. To be honest, however, the thought
that the long-awaited revolution might in fact be upon us that
day or the next and suddenly occupy the centre of our whole
existence left me distinctly cold. Moreover it bothered me that
the struggle should begin in Austria of all places. Coming from

Germany, we could see the next major revolutionary move only as stemming from the German proletariat.

Which party was at the head of this uprising, anyway? We knew that the Social Democrats had a kind of party army – the *Schutzbund* – with disciplined units and secret weapons dumps that were always being replenished from abroad. How did this tally with the Social Democrats' bitter hatred of the working class about which we Communists had talked so much? It was rather embarrassing to realize, in the middle of these events of global importance, the extent of our ignorance of the most current of current affairs.

In process of mobilization against the *Schutzbund* were the armed forces of the state, inadequate in themselves but amply reinforced by the dogged and bloodthirsty *Heimwehr*, a body recruited from the provinces, bearing a passionate attachment to such very concrete things as minor posts in the civil service, influence, financial increment, houses, and the suppression of the trade unions, and commanded by an extremely insignificant and unscrupulous member of the aristocracy, Prince Starhemberg. And these opposing forces must soon try conclusions in order that a political schemer of supremely diminutive stature both mentally and physically, namely Chancellor Dollfuss (known in Vienna as the Milli-Metternich), might smash his enemies, swindle his friends, and become a Mussolini in his country before Hitler became a Hitler there too.

We were filled with a kind of melancholy defeatism, unable even to toy with the idea of victory. How could one begin to imagine a Europe with, in the middle, an Austria in which the proletariat was going to bear its victorious arms to the very seat of power? Fascist Germany, more and more a reality, was gradually coming to be a part of the picture of Europe. And yet our desire to be somehow involved in the struggle grew stronger by the hour.

The ordeal could hardly have begun less favourably for the *Schutzbund*. Fighting spirit? That was there all right; it chiefly found expression in premature strike action. Discipline? That was there too – in the form of bureaucratic formalism.

As the street fighting went into its second day we young

Vienna, February 1934

Communists who had fled from Germany determined to look for and find our place in events. The directives that at last came through from the leadership of the illegal Austrian Communist Party were extremely vague. The word was that we were to guard against getting too deeply involved with the Social Democrats.

I composed a pamphlet along these somewhat nebulous lines (in content it was probably not particularly original) and Micky reproduced it by the simple method of typing it as many times as possible with nine or ten carbons, mobilizing other people for the job as well.

A rather more perilous undertaking was delivering the finished pamphlets. We loaded them into a taxi and thought our last moment had come when two *Heimwehr* soldiers came up to us. 'Where are you going?' they asked. But their next question was whether they might ride on the running-board since they were going the same way. Our pamphlets thus reached their destination under military escort.

Vienna, after all, is Vienna.

The workers' housing estates were bombarded by artillery from the Hohe Warte. The gaping holes they ripped in the façade of one block, the Karl-Marx-Hof, were put on a postcard and for months afterwards went round the world as a kind of new 'sight' of Austria. The number of men, women, and children killed went into four figures. Special courts condemned people to death without trial, and execution was summary.

Vienna, however, is Vienna. I wanted to cross the Ring one day when it was bristling with machine-guns and told the soldiers that my reason for doing so was that I was always expected in the Café Raimund at this time. They let me through.

When the guns were still again and inhuman reprisals became the order of the day, we Communists at last got some clear directives from our leadership. The immediate aim was the unity of the working class. A series of underground local newspapers was to be founded, serving this aim and speaking the language of all working people. How gladly we Communists would have become a solid prop for the *entire* working class against confusion, bureaucracy, senseless bloodshed, and this squandering of human life. But our thinkers came up with nothing that might have helped

the will become the deed. The way our leadership saw the unifica-
tion of the proletariat was betrayed by the very title of the duplicated newspaper that I as a Party member was required to edit:
Red Banner over Floridsdorf (Floridsdorf being the working-class
district across the Danube from the city of Vienna). This paper,
which in fact consisted mainly of set texts issued by the leadership, I and a number of Communist and Social Democrat
colleagues duly proceeded to produce.

After a couple of weeks it blew up under us. I spent six months
in prison; others spent even longer. There was not one sentence
of that paper that I liked, from the point of view of either content
or style, and I heard Micky and the other people who worked on
it with us say the same. The title alone divided the workers into
two camps – Reds and non-Reds. And even the title was a lie.
Yet I could never have faced myself in the mirror if I had shirked
any part of that senseless and dangerous undertaking or tried to
dodge even a fraction of the price to be paid for it. It was a question of wanting to do something for the cause. There was nothing
meaningful one could do, so one did something meaningless. And
at least one was halfway content with oneself.

Our cleaning-woman was called Mrs Mandel. One day J.H. 34
was sitting in the room he rented from Mrs Kranz when he heard
the following conversation through the closed door.

UNKNOWN MAN: 'Is Mr H. at home?'
MRS MANDEL: 'Who shall I say it is?'
UNKNOWN MAN: 'Just tell me which is his room.'
MRS MANDEL: 'Could I have your name, please?'
UNKNOWN MAN: 'I asked you where Mr H. lived.'
MRS MANDEL: 'And I asked you what name I can say.'
UNKNOWN MAN: 'Get out of my way, you . . !'
MRS MANDEL (very loud): 'Mr H.! There's a detective called
Gruber to see you!'

I love Vienna.
Gruber came and went. He was only from the Aliens' Depart-

ment, wanting to fill in a few details. But we knew very well that the Aliens' Department did not fill in details on its own initiative. Obviously a higher authority, the political police, wanted to know more about us.

Sure enough, early in the morning of the day after next two men came knocking on my door. They let themselves in without waiting for an answer, stayed for over an hour, had a good rummage round the room, and took me with them when they left. 'To settle a few points still outstanding,' was the formula, but when they took you away like that it was usually some time before you got back.

Anyone who joins an illegal political movement soon becomes familiar with a very special kind of suspense – the waiting for one's own arrest. The fear that goes with it is something one quickly gets used to. I do not say 'gets over' – that one can never do. But one learns to live with it; one as it were domesticates it. One may even find oneself worrying when the fateful day is delayed. When is it going to happen to *me*, now that it has already happened to so many others? It's not going to pass me by altogether, is it? Why? Haven't I done enough for the good cause to have earned the hatred of our opponents and qualified for persecution? Have I been looking after 'number one' too much? Have I in my complacency overestimated my own importance? Does the enemy not think I'm important enough? Does that mean I'm equally unimportant as far as our cause is concerned?

This worry gets the better of almost every other critical impulse. Little by little one forgets to ask how far the cause that one holds to be good still in fact is a good cause. One finds sufficient confirmation in the danger to which one is exposing one's life and in the ineluctable approach of that visit by the two (or more) unknown men.

During those years of underground activity one came to know a menace more alarming than any other – the danger of losing the confidence of one's comrades. How often have I withdrawn my confidence from somebody at the bidding of my superiors in the Party? That supposedly aberrant Agitpropper was not the first, nor was he the last. One picks up the art of being suspicious even of oneself. We saw so many comrades fall around us – even back in the underground years – for reasons that were undiscoverable to the naked eye. That one had got mixed up with Trotskyites – hadn't I noticed? No, I needed to be told from *above*, by the Party. Another was tainted with social democracy, the third with pacifism, the fourth with Zionism, the fifth – well, it was not sure, but he might be a police informer. Did I become aware of all this for myself? No. The Party had to apprise me.

And gradually, as a result, I became suffused with a warm and genuine feeling of gratitude towards the Party for the fact that it continually provided me with occasions for sacrifice.

There is no denying (I thought, as the two men accompanied me to the Rossauerlände police prison) that my position is to some extent a privileged one: in Germany, with the Gestapo, I could expect the same fate as the actor Hans Otto met; in Hungary, Horthy's police would torture me by beating the naked soles of my feet with rubber truncheons. I may be a coward but the prospect scares me. Maybe in Vienna, for the time being, I shall be spared such treatment.

And for the space of a few seconds this thought gave rise to a torment of anxiety. By what right did I enjoy such a privileged position? Would it not make the Party look askance at me?

But then I remembered that it was not of my own will that I had come to this country. Max Schrecker in Berlin had given me explicit instructions. The central committee of the Austrian Communist Party had apparently given its approval too. This curtailment of my right to decide my own fate, in favour of an abstract organization that impinged upon my life in the person of various chance representatives, had the effect of restoring my peace of mind, and it was with a feeling approaching solemnity that I heard the cell door slam to behind me. I had reached an important station in my career as a member of the Party.

It was then that I noticed something that I had always known about yet now experienced as a sudden shock – on the inside the door had neither a key nor a handle.

14

Bye-bye, walnut tree – Dr Berger loses interest –
First appearance of my rescuer – Cell-mates –
'In Germany – bang, bang!' – A week to leave
Vienna

WHEN later that same day Micky, from the look-out post behind
Mrs Kranz's over-washed lace curtains where she had been
standing motionless for hours, saw the two men come round the
corner of the street, she slipped on her winter coat (her summer
coat and hat she had on already), picked up the bag she had
carefully packed, ran down the stairs, cut across the back garden –
gathering a few walnuts on the way – and over the fence into a
neighbouring vineyard, came out on the street again through
somebody else's garden gate, and caught a tram going to the
station.
She already had several 'addresses' in Zürich.

On the third or fourth day of my imprisonment I was treated
to the shortest car journey I have ever been on in my life. I was
fetched from my cell by two civilian officials and climbed with
them into the elegant limousine of Dr Berger, chief of political
police in the Republic of Austria. We drove out of the prison
yard through huge iron gates on to the street and into a similar
yard through a pair of equally huge iron gates right next door to
the first.
Dr Berger was a dark-haired man who looked as if he had yet
to pass fifty; irritable but not uncivil, he had a tendency to sink
easily into a state of boredom that was akin to melancholy. There
were two other men present, one of whom fired the occasional

135

abrupt question at me, but I had imagined an interrogation as being a rather less tedious affair.

They asked me a lot about God and the world in general, but one would have needed to be quite exceptionally dense to have failed to notice that all they were interested in was my connection with Litzi Friedmann and Litzi's relations with various other foreigners. Once it had been borne in upon Dr Berger that I was not identical with the man who had come from Budapest and who had probably since gone back there (did he mean Gábor Péter, perhaps?), he lost interest in me to such an extent that he let me be taken back to my cell on foot. The political police's interest in our *Red Banner over Floridsdorf* had really only been incidental.

Before I left the room with my escort he stopped me.

'Just answer me this: what made you become a Communist?'

I pulled myself together for fear of leaving out anything that might persuade the chief of political police of the rightness of my aims and opinions.

'I became a Communist in order that I might assist in making everybody in this world happy; in abolishing war for ever; in securing equal rights for all peoples, whether great or small; in bringing prosperity to the whole of mankind; and in depriving everyone once and for all of the possibility of exploiting others, of oppressing others, and of making others unhappy.'

Dr Berger gave me one of his sad-eyed looks. 'I see. Another Marquis Posa. Take him away.'

I never saw him again.

I was fetched from my cell a second time that day. Waiting for me in the prison office was an elegant and impressive-looking gentleman who introduced himself as Dr Geiringer, lawyer to the Austrian Writers' Union, which body, he informed me, had commissioned him to undertake my defence, subject to my agreement. I was deeply moved, for the organization in question was headed for the most part by writers who were practising Roman Catholics. One could hardly suppose that they were enthusiastic about my *God, Emperor, and Peasant*. Their action implied a feeling of professional solidarity with a colleague that was quite outside the ordinary run of things.

First appearance of my rescuer

Dr Geiringer also brought me warmest personal greetings from Franz Theodor Csokor, greetings that I understood in the sense I was intended to understand them in – as a promise to stand by me and not to relax his efforts for one instant until he had got me out of prison. (Neither of us suspected at the time, incidentally, that the promise was valid for more than this one occasion. But I have needed to be rescued more than once in my life, and more than once he was prepared to do it.)

Franz Theodor Csokor, despite his Hungarian name, was Austrian from tip to toe; in fact he was the perfect example of the Viennese bohemian. Although he was already over fifty then, his greatest years as a militant emigrant and indomitable son of Europe were still ahead of him. A tireless dreamer and writer, he was down-to-earth and practical when it was a case of helping the afflicted. He was never one for sparing himself, and that may be the reason his life was such a long and rich one. At eighty-four he told me, 'People only die out of carelessness.' Not long after that he was 'careless' himself. But of my life he took the greatest care.

After a few weeks the police handed me over to the public prosecutor's department and I was moved to a prison in the Hernals district. It was if possible even filthier than the Rossauer-lände, but in Hernals you got the stink of innumerable slop-pails as well because the antiquated building had never been introduced to the water-closet. I was put into a large room designed for five to six prisoners and currently housing ten to twelve. Its inhabitants had evolved a system whereby the newcomer was obliged to sleep hard by the slop-pail and was able, each time someone went away, to move one plank-bed's width nearer to the window. Since the window was never fully opened the gain was exiguous, but to us it seemed appreciable none the less.

Of my cell-mates I remember particularly two brothers. One was a marriage swindler and used to get a magnificent food parcel at least once a week from one or other of his victims. They remained faithful to him without exception and none of them bore him a grudge; it was his regular girl friend that had reported him. The interesting thing was that he was a short, bald, drab little man, while his brother, who was in for passing counterfeit money, looked just the way you would expect a marriage swindler to look. Then there were a number of hoary sexual criminals, and one young one – a good-looking fellow of about thirty who had just been given two and a half years for seducing a minor. He swore up and down with bitter imprecations that he had not been the seducer at all but the seduced. For men in our position of enforced celibacy his description of the process was perhaps just a little too detailed.

When my examining magistrate (a woman of thirty or so) heard how inadequately I was accommodated she had me transferred to a small, élite cell with two Social Democrat members of parliament who were still awaiting trial in connection with the February uprising. One of them was using the time to compile a dictionary of Austrian criminals' slang. Every Sunday the warders would lock a different professional thief in the cell with us for the day. Professor Werndl would study their argot, noting and classifying their vocabulary and any grammatical peculiarities. The officer in charge of our floor had three sons at school, and the other half of the agreement was that the professor did all their homework every day.

One day – it was 30 June 1934 – this officer opened the door of our cell and announced, 'Gentlemen – in Germany, bang bang!' That was all. But towards evening he brought us a newspaper (which was certainly forbidden) and we were able to read how Hitler had liquidated his friends Röhm, Strasser, and the others.

My examining magistrates were against Fascism in all its forms and sympathized with me, if not as a Communist, at least as someone who was having to suffer for the cause of freedom of speech. As far as they were concerned my whole case was a bagatelle maliciously blown up by the police. Naturally Dr Berger had not tried to sell them the Litzi affair, particularly since this had taken a somewhat embarrassing turn: Litzi, in grave danger of arrest after the *Schutzbund* uprising, had married Philby, taken British citizenship, and thus travelled unhindered to England, where her young groom proceeded to enter upon his calling (in Gábor Péter's sense, that is).

It was already high summer when I was sent for again. At first they made me wait without telling me what I was waiting for. Then, all of a sudden, things began to move very fast. Someone read out at top speed something to the effect that the public prosecutor's department had dropped the charges in my case for lack of evidence and I was to be set at liberty immediately. They barely gave me time to grasp properly what had happened, rejoice at it, and say a few words of gratitude, before they bundled me into a tiny office where two warders and two policemen were waiting for me.

The First Warder (as he would be described in a theatre programme) mumbled something through his moustache and laid a document down on the table. Here they did give me time (just) to do up my boot-laces and tie my tie. Then the Second Warder took me through a list and put the individual items of my property therein enumerated, which had been confiscated at my arrest, one by one on the table before me. I was seized with childish delight at the sight of my razor and my old pocket-watch – symbols of freedom. I swiftly signed the list and even more swiftly started putting my things away in my pockets.

At this point the two figures who would appear on a theatre bill as First and Second Policemen moved into action. One of them laid both hands over my belongings and the other offered me a further list to sign. At the same time they cursorily informed me that, although the public prosecutor's department had today set me at liberty, the police had already instituted further proceedings against me at a prior date. The long and short of those proceedings was that I might either be sent back to Hungary and handed over to the Hungarian authorities or I might be interned in Austria for an indeterminate period. In either case I must await the decision in the Rossauerlände police prison.

Again they left me time – if very little – to undo my boot-laces and take off my tie. I looked on with a heavy heart as my watch, my razor, and my other effects disappeared into a numbered bag. The policemen – First and Second – stood up and saluted, and the warders – ditto – saluted back. Then, with one policeman on my right and another on my left, I was escorted from the room.

And to think I had wanted to make something of my duel with

Hitler! I wanted to have run the race! Arrogant fancies! This was no favoured campaigner for a free and truthful literature stepping into the waiting Green Minnie* between two policemen but an internationally wanted member of a clandestine organization, an outlaw facing extradition, whom no lawyer and no public prosecutor and no Csokor and no Writers' Union could help any more, who need not first be convicted of some crime by due process of law but who would sooner or later simply be ground to bits between the wheels of the great police machine.

Every evening we were counted and there was never anyone missing, but each time there were a few tense moments before the domestic staff had got the straw mattresses distributed in such a way that there was at least one for every two prisoners. I was in a small cell meant for one person but generally occupied by three. There were three of us in it the day they put the haggard-looking young man in with us – myself, an extremely thin fellow with a knack of dropping off to sleep immediately in any position, and an enormous man of forty or so who was in on a charge of threatening to murder his wife (which he denied, his version of the story being that his wife – 'the whore, the nympho . . !' – had set the whole thing up in order to be rid of him for a while, and free to work her way through a mixed bag of bedfellows young and old).

The young man with the haggard face looked anxiously about him, yet appeared not to see us; it was as if we were transparent and behind us there lurked something sinister and terrifying. Then, selecting a corner, he slunk smartly off into it as if dodging blows, though it was obvious that none of us was planning to hit him. His teeth began to chatter furiously.

For some reason the newcomer had the effect of temporarily transforming our putative wife-murderer into a passionate sleuth. On the basis of four exiguous clues – the fact that he had been brought to the cell by two unusually earnest-looking policemen, one of whom remained on guard outside the locked door, the fact that he was not wearing a jacket, the fact that, when questioned on this latter point, he came out with an obviously

* Austrian Black Maria (Translator).

prepared story couched in considerably more elegant terms than his person would have led one to expect, and the questioner's feeling that 'he looked like someone who'd done someone in' – working from these four clues our 'Sherlock Holmes' (as the sleepy man mockingly dubbed him) reached the conclusion that a band of Nazis, masquerading in some kind of uniform and acting on the orders of army officers, had murdered some big shot in the Ballhausplatz. Our reaction was one of astonished incredulity.

When the young man was brought back from his first interrogation he was sucking a boiled sweet and his story had undergone considerable modifications. He referred to his interrogator as 'a really fine gentleman'. Sherlock's comment when he had been taken away again: 'Look at the Nazi swine – selling his mates for the price of a boiled sweet. I'd be very interested to know who they've done in.'

After the third interrogation he came back with a cigarette stuck dashingly behind his ear. This time he had been interrogated by a major who appeared to have made a great impression on him. An even finer gentleman than his previous interrogator. After a while the young man stepped over to the door and knocked on it – timidly at first, then energetically, looking about him with an almost triumphant air: he had been given explicit permission to knock on the door like this. The door was opened immediately and the warder offered him a light without even having been asked. He smoked his cigarette elaborately, playing for time, and as he did so we heard a slight scrabbling noise at the peep-hole: he was being observed from outside.

When the cigarette was little more than a stump he burst out unexpectedly, 'What's the matter – shouldn't I have told him it was Lieutenant Planetta? When a major asks me? Do you think the lieutenant won't come out with my name? When the major asks him? Don't make me laugh. Anyway, the major said . . .' He paused, his cigarette already finished. 'They've promised they'll take us all in the army. They said we'd all be NCOs if we co-operate . . . Why should I be the stupid one . . ?'

They took him away again and did not bring him back. For two days nothing happened. The sleepy fellow slept. The 'detective' resumed his colourful reflections on married life. Then an elderly man was put in with us. He said he was a Macedonian, and he spoke several languages. He seemed to know a bit about politics, despite his claim that they were trying to deport him for smuggling tobacco. As an experienced lag he informed us in the routine whisper that Nazis wearing soldiers' uniforms had occupied the Ballhausplatz a few days before and murdered Chancellor Dollfuss. High-ups in the government and at the German Embassy had been behind the plot. But the high-ups were not being hanged for it. No, only Lieutenant Planetta and a few other small-fry were being hanged for it. Whether our recent cell-mate was among them is something I never discovered. I never knew his name.

One afternoon a few days later I was fetched from the cell. I was told to take my things and was hurried along to the office the short way through the courtyard. A flustered-looking gentleman with whom I had not had dealings before stood up and came towards me as I entered. His face had that unmistakable expression of polite condolence. After a cursory attempt to spare my feelings he told me that my father was dead. (I did not experience any emotional shock at that moment. It was only later, when I was alone in the room a friend put me up in for the night, that I began to weep quietly.)

Then the gentleman's expression switched to one of great amiability. Briefly he informed me that the deportation proceedings against me had been dropped and that I was to be set at liberty immediately. I must still leave the country, but I was free to do so unescorted and by any frontier I chose. I also had a week in which to wind up my affairs.

He added in a confidential tone that I had the federal chancellor in person to thank for this favourable turn of events. I did not feel it was a suitable moment to ask who in fact was federal chancellor after Dollfuss's murder. When subsequently I heard the name Schuschnigg mentioned I recalled a young Roman Catholic politician who had a certain amount of time for culture and who was on good terms with Csokor.

I pictured the stocky, slightly greying figure of Csokor in his permanently scuffed shoes and his Wagnerian headgear jogging upstairs and downstairs from floor to floor and from room to room in order to turn the new chancellor's 'yes' into a 'yes' of the old civil service.

It was already dusk when I set foot on the street outside, a free man. There were *chevaux de frise* and machine-gun emplacements everywhere, including many that were new since my arrest. The city looked as if it was in a state of civil war, although there was none on at the time and none was to come.

What was to come happened without resistance.

A week was more than I would normally have needed to 'wind up my affairs' in Vienna. I found my things in predictably apple-pie order at Mrs Kranz's, discovering later that the old lady had even darned my socks.

The most important part of my luggage, however, took up no more room than my trouser pocket. This was a number of sheets of lavatory paper written closely in pencil – the beginning of the play I had been working on during my last few weeks in prison. Writing in the cells was of course forbidden, but one could purchase lavatory paper from the warder, and the warder felt that, since we were already on a business footing, he could sell me the stub of a pencil as well for a modest sum. Happiness, sometimes, is the stub of a pencil.

The new play that I had begun was called *Haben*.

All I had to do before leaving Vienna was to collect the money for the journey which my family had deposited with my debt-prone Hungarian journalist friend, Mari Bojtár. Mari was overjoyed at the news that I was out of prison but had no time just at present to bring me the money or receive my visit. During the course of the week I had at my disposal she made nine different rendezvous with me in nine different cafés. On six of those nine occasions she actually turned up; on five of those six occasions she let me pay for her coffee; and on one of those five occasions I was even permitted to stand her the taxi fare. But for an astonishing variety of unlikely reasons she never had my money with her. I began to fear it might have vanished without trace in the maw of her chronic impecuniosity.

143

One hour before my last train was due to leave I was sitting waiting for her in the Café Museum. Eventually she came rushing in, utterly exhausted and bathed in sweat. She had with her, as she mentioned repeatedly and with emphasis, the full amount. In Belgian currency, if you please. Why it should have been in Belgian currency when it must have arrived in either Hungarian or Austrian currency is one of the impenetrable secrets surrounding Mari Bojtár. I could not have cared less what currency it was in. I climbed into the Buchs–Zürich train and left Austria for ever.

'For ever' lasted until October 1945 – just over ten years. Not bad going for an eternity in this twentieth century of ours.

15

*A true description of a double wedding – Mr
Arthur Koestler's white trousers – The invitation*

J.H. 35 – that is to say, at the time of his Swiss intermezzo –
'was a dark, easy-going young man. He was a Communist by
philosophy, but took no interest in politics, paid his party dues as
one pays income-tax, and lived entirely for his plays . . .' The
words are taken from Arthur Koestler's autobiographical *The
Invisible Writing*. After a brief and not quite accurate summary of
my early career, Arthur goes on: '. . . Since then he had been an
exile, wandering through Europe with a suitcase full of unper-
formed plays which represented his capital and future.'

I cannot remember when I first met Arthur Koestler. Probably
it was some time in Berlin. But the friendship that was to remain
intact over more than three decades first began in Zürich.

Picture to yourself two young Hungarians – one rather taller
than the other, one rather stockier – engaged in the process of
killing the lunch break and with it the unwelcome pangs of hunger
by means of a walk along the Limmatquai. They have problems –
the one of a dramaturgical nature, the other of an epic nature. The
taller of the two is deeply involved in murder by poisoning in a
peasant setting; his stockier friend's preoccupation is with the
strategy of a revolutionary army in the first century B.C. Had they
worried their heads about their own banal little problems they
would have succumbed to despair long ago. It is this feeling of
responsibility for centuries past and to come that is keeping them
on their feet. Each believes in himself, and both believe in each
other. This is the foundation of their friendship.

Often the two of us met a third friend – an Italian who, being
convalescent, could not accompany us on our long walks. He

already had one international literary success behind him and his name was still in the literary news: Ignazio Silone. I never exchanged a great many words with Ignazio, and even the usually animated Arthur was capable of long silences, but in those wordless minutes we fought our fight. Not together – each with himself. That we did after all win through to common findings – each for himself and in his own hard-fought way – did not emerge until some decades later.

Arthur and I were married together in Zürich. To be more precise, Arthur and Dörte, and Micky and I were married together in Zürich. Of his half of the ceremony Arthur has written, 'To save our self-respect' – as Communists, as freethinkers, as disciples of freedom in all its forms, including the sexual – 'the marriage had to remain a reluctant passport affair'* so that Dörte could obtain a Hungarian passport. In Arthur's and Dörte's case this was certainly true, but Micky and I found it impossible to take the matter so lightly: Micky was expecting a child.

Nevertheless, to the worthy registrar who received us and our Zürich friends Rudolf and Lilly Humm under the solemn stainedglass windows of his register office we must have presented a curious sight – like a band of gipsies come to catch up at one go on all the formalities of bourgeois existence that they had neglected for years. First Micky and I sat down opposite him and Arthur and Humm signed the register as witnesses. Then I changed places with Arthur and Micky changed places with Dörte, only Humm remaining where he was and his and his wife's wedding rings – on loan – serving for the second ceremony as they had served for the first. Afterwards the Humms, as the only beringed couple of the sextet, stood drinks all round.

The child turned out to be a girl and we called her Andrea. The nurses at the clinic, however, feeling that this sounded more like a boy's name (as it is in Italian, for example), promptly dubbed her Anderli, and Anderli she has remained, through many countries and many languages, to this day, when she is the thirty-five-year-old mother of three children.

* Arthur Koestler, *The Invisible Writing*.

A true description of a double wedding

The birth of a person in turn begets forms and papers. Off I trotted to the Hungarian Consulate to have the validity of my passport extended to cover Andrea H. Then I presented the passport to the Federal Police, Department of Aliens, who duly took cognizance of the existence of the new-born refugee and slapped across the page devoted to her a rubber stamp to the effect that the above-named might not accept employment in Switzerland nor engage in any lucrative activity – conditions by which the new-born scrupulously abode.

Willy-nilly, I abode by them myself as well. In my profession I had no hope of getting a work permit, nor would I have wished to tie myself down. I wanted to be and to remain a freelance writer. We lived as we could, gladly accepting hospitality that for the most part was gladly given. An old couple called Meyer invited us to lunch as often as was feasible. They were furriers, and when the time came for Micky to set out with Anderli for colder climes they had a fur bag sewn for the child that came in extremely handy. I also remember an old gentleman (though I have forgotten his name), a pharmacist by profession, who kept us in medicaments as well as giving us bed and a generous breakfast – which often had to last us all day.

Perhaps we were happiest of all in the Humms' tiny spare room, but when the baby came we had to move. We rented a room in a flat in the Seehofstrasse. From the point of view of the Party the place had one defect: another room in the same flat was rented by a vivacious and interesting blonde who was supposed to have had something to do with Trotskyites. Apparently she had had an affair with an Indian Trotskyite leader and was still at that time in touch with Indian politicians of various shades of the political spectrum. Hardly the ideal environment for Party-line Communists.

Once a young Indian girl, on her way home from school in England, broke her journey in Zürich. The blonde woman was working under pressure at the time and asked Micky if she would show the visitor around town a bit.

The comrades got wind of this in no time at all and we were warned from various quarters not to make ourselves suspect by keeping such company. In such matters, however, there was no reasoning with Micky. Party bigot though she was in many respects, she let no one dictate her friends and acquaintances to her. She found the exotic teenager a delightful companion. The girl, incidentally, was the daughter of a very important Indian politician. Her name was Indira Nehru. She later married a member of the Gandhi family and has for some years now been prime minister of India.

The Zürich publisher Emil Oprecht brought out *God, Emperor, and Peasant* in book form and the great Czech producer E. F. Burian, in Switzerland on tour with his Prague Theatre, read another play of mine, *The Dam on the Tisza*, and gave me a contract for it on the spot, yet none of this bore much resemblance to a tempestuous continuation of the battle for the freedom of literature and the stage that had begun in 1932 under the auspices of Dr Goebbels in person. In fact things were threatening to seize up altogether. Why?

Dr Goebbels' slogan had been that I was good at robbing people of illusions. This alone – as I thought – should have been enough to recommend my plays to Rieser, the director of the Zürich Schauspielhaus and a man who was sincerely opposed to the kind of illusions that Dr Goebbels deployed, yet he showed no interest in them whatever.

It was not until much later that it dawned on me: being a destroyer of illusions was a crime not only in the Nazis' eyes but in the eyes of all who lived in and *by* political illusions. And that was not just Dr Goebbels and his henchmen – not by a long chalk. Political illusions – the most childish kind are the easiest to manipulate – were cherished by the political left just as much as by the right. The truth is too many-layered to fit on any theatre bill. The truth stripped of illusions found no buyers in the political market. Even the left-wing theatres were selling political illusions.

Which left me with my little blue exercise books, and the suitcase they were locked in as soon as they were full.

But I am forgetting Arthur's new trousers!
The seat of Arthur's old trousers being a degree more thread-

bare than was consonant with strict decorum, we sallied forth to find him a new pair. After a long search we hunted down at Woolworth's a pair of white trousers with thick black seams and a wide variety of pockets, including some that were manifestly designed to hold hammers, foot-rules, and the like. They were in fact bricklayer's trousers and as such hardly in line with the latest fashion. But we were proud of our purchase, and it was a lot cheaper than any other pair of trousers in Zürich.

That is how we lived in Europe in 1935.

I had at that time three major points of conflict with myself, three brushes with reality that I could not possibly ignore but that I never discussed with anybody – not even with Arthur, not even with Micky.

Firstly, a Soviet Party official whose name I had not previously been familiar with, Sergei Kirov, was murdered in Leningrad in December 1934. According to all the reports – even those friendly towards the Soviet Union, even the official Soviet reports – Stalin's reply to this one shot was innumerable others. I was sometimes tormented by the feeling that this was no due process of law any more but another St Bartholomew's Day. A massacre that had been going on for months already and that showed no signs of coming to an end. This prompted other gloomy feelings – feelings, however, that never managed to assume the form of thoughts.

Secondly, the Soviet writers had recently held a conference to which they had invited representatives from all over the world. Maxim Gorky had made a speech to inaugurate fresh perspectives. Of Gorky's greatness as a writer I was and still am in no doubt, yet I read through the entire text of his speech twice and it left me completely cold. Was it not rather a feeling of disappointment? I found there no answer to my questions and failed to find in myself the questions that Gorky appeared to be answering. Were my ears already deaf to the new? Ought I not in fact to burn everything I had written to date and only begin again when I could do so without writing anything that was in less than perfect obedience to the commands of the revolution? But the worst thing was that in all the speeches given at that congress,

Maxim Gorky's included, I found not one single sentence that might have inspired me to any kind of personal resolution. Instead of drawing fresh strength I experienced a painful feeling of paralysis.

Thirdly, Lunacharsky was dead. He had died scarcely a year after our meeting. Had my invitation died with him? In his absence would I ever be introduced to the Working People's Republic? Or was it after all best that I should be forced to experience crisis, poverty, unemployment, Fascism, and possibly even war in the West that I might be even more deeply convinced of the necessity for the revolution?

Early one morning a young Swiss comrade called on me. His name was Steheli and he was one of the top men in the Communist Party in Zürich. (Seek him not; he fell in Spain.) The purpose of his call was officially to invite me to visit the Soviet Union for a provisional period of three months, without my family. If the invitation was extended over a longer period – and there was a good chance of this happening – my wife and child could join me.

That was the moment at which all three problems, all three areas of conflict, simply disappeared from my mind.

Joyfully I set about my preparations for the journey.

Part Three

16

A good omen – Presidents, vice-presidents, etc. –
In confidence – Secrets of the Lux Hotel

As my train drew slowly into Moscow's White Russia station a band was playing the *Internationale*. Actually the object of their attentions was some football team that was returning victorious – or not victorious – from the West. But I was delighted at the coincidence and saw it as a good omen.

I was welcomed by a three-man delegation. One face was familiar – that of Heinz Greif, whom I had known in Berlin as a member of Gustav von Wangenheim's 'The Red Mouthpiece' troupe and with whom I had become good friends in Zürich, where he had made an extended guest appearance at the Schauspielhaus. The other two men I was meeting for the first time. Umanskij, a short man with sharply intellectual features, had been the signatory of the telegram asking for the Russian translation rights of *God, Emperor, and Peasant* that I had received shortly after my meeting with Lunacharsky. The third man was Ernst Held, a German from Berlin, slightly younger than myself, a pleasant and for some reason always slightly melancholy man to whom I became very attached from the moment of our first meeting.

Held was representing the organization whose guest I was. He was one of that multitude of minor and not so minor officials employed in the vast network of international organizations operating in the Soviet Union. This apparently higgledy-piggledy but in fact pretty tightly-knit apparatus had the task of making contact with Western artists, scientists, and writers and of winning among them more and more friends for the Soviet

Union. My host organization was the International League of Revolutionary Theatres.

By way of a welcoming bouquet Umanskij brought me the good news that the translation of *God, Emperor, and Peasant* was finished and due to be published shortly by the state publishing house. So it was with something of the feeling of a conqueror that I climbed into the black Lincoln that the theatre organization had rented from the Intourist travel bureau for the sole purpose of driving me to the Savoy Hotel, where an attractive room awaited me. The two Czechs with whom I had travelled, and who were visiting Moscow for the theatre festival which was the occasion of my own visit, drove off in an exactly identical car, the only difference being that they were accompanied by the Czechoslovak cultural attaché – an honour I should have looked for in vain from the cultural attaché of my own country.

On my first afternoon in Moscow Held took me along to the Writers' Union, the foreign department of which had its own offices in the Kusnyetzky Most.

I forget where the sphere of competence of an international organization ended and where that of the international department of a Soviet organization began. Comrade Apletin, who bade me a hearty welcome, belonged at any rate to the Soviet Writers' Union and headed its foreign department. He did so in his capacity as one of the vice-presidents of the union as a whole; the president was the now ailing Gorky and the general secretary Alexander Alexandrovich Fadeyev, a not uninteresting novelist who unfortunately found little opportunity to write.

Apletin, the vice-president, was a short, bald man who, had I not known his profession, I should have been prepared to bet was a schoolmaster. It came as something of a surprise to find that a man whose job was concerned exclusively with foreign literature and authors understood not one single language apart from his native Russian. Over the next ten years, during which I saw a great deal of Apletin, he never appeared to grow a day older, nor did he ever seem to be in either a particularly good or a particularly bad mood.

Nobody in this largest writers' union in the world seemed to take exception to the fact that the vice-president had never written a single book himself nor even produced so much as a pamphlet that he might have presented to his visitors with a suitable dedication. (The German Communist poet Johannes R. Becher once told me in confidence that Apletin was none other than the head – or not even the head – of a tentacular department of the Soviet secret police that kept the discreetest possible eye on foreign writers in the Soviet Union – and outside too. But Becher had a weakness for over-subtlety and as time went on one learned not always to believe everything he told one, especially in confidence.)

At any rate Apletin, sitting under his portraits of Marx, Engels, Lenin, Stalin and Gorky, listened attentively over a period of ten years to every problem and request I brought him. And on each and every occasion, whether he could help or not, he nodded with an expression of deep understanding and concern.

Fadeyev's photograph adorned his office too, but more intimately: it stood in a frame on his desk. Bushy white hair above youthful features, eyes as blue (and as cold) as china, a face that might have belonged to a pagan god, or to a guards officer at the Winter Palace two hundred years before that shot from the battleship *Aurora* – Fadeyev's picture reflected something that struck me as consisting of relentlessness and hopelessness in equal portions and at one and the same time.

Had Apletin's almost clockwork precision ever found itself up against the disintegrating personality of the moody alcoholic whose picture stood on his desk, Apletin would certainly have backed down. The positively harmonious collection of asocial qualities that Fadeyev united in his person together with the virtually unlimited authority he enjoyed was something the likes of Apletin could neither treat with nor compete with. Nor, really, did anyone expect him to. As absolute dictator of the literature of all Soviet peoples, Fadeyev was lord over life and death for all who put pen to paper, lord too over their thoughts and feelings, and that not only in an empire of gigantic proportions but with an influence extending far beyond its frontiers as well. Fadeyev might be neither restrained nor controlled. Fadeyev was a friend of Stalin's. He could do just as he liked.

(Seek him not, by the way. When his master and idol Stalin died, Alexander Alexandrovich found the prospect of living through a period of truths and revelations without his omnipotent protection intolerable. He took his own life.)

While I was drinking tea with Apletin and eating a cake that was much too sweet, a man came in from one of the offices down the corridor. He was about forty and had the soft voice and economical movements typical of a man with heart trouble. Addressing me in Hungarian, he introduced himself as Sándor Barta. The name was familiar to me and I remembered having read one or two short stories by him that had stuck in my mind. Barta welcomed me in his capacity as chairman – or was it general secretary? – of the International Union of Revolutionary Writers, an organization that was anxious not to be confused with the international department of the Soviet Writers' Union. (Seek Sándor Barta not, either. He fell victim to the never-ending St Bartholomew's Day, known in the official language of the Party as a 'purge'.)

Barta's organization had just invited the very fine Danish writer Martin Andersen-Nexö on another of his frequent visits to the Soviet Union – frequent because whereas in his own country the grand old man could barely afford to live, in the Soviet Union royalties were accumulating for him all the time, and whenever he came he was able to spend as much as he liked. I met Andersen-Nexö and his young wife Johanna when they arrived in Moscow. We soon became good friends and we remained so until his death. He used to love to draw me aside and pull other writers, present and absent, to pieces. He was a man of straightforward and intense feelings. Johannes R. Becher, for example, made him feel sick. Making a simple German pun by adding one letter to his name, he called him, simply, 'Johannes the Puke'.

I had met Becher briefly on two earlier occasions so I looked him up immediately after my tea with Apletin. He was spending the day as usual next door in the editorial offices of the monthly magazine *Internationale Literatur*, of which he was editor-in-chief. A fine figure of a Teuton, he took great pride in his appearance and was something of a ladies' man. He saw and represented himself as the poet-king of German revolutionary literature. An expressionist in his younger days – when expressionism and Communism still went very well together – he later switched to classical forms and to the subject-matter laid down by the Party. Later still, when he became a minister in the East German government, a post he occupied until his death, he showed neither discrimination nor inhibitions in the exercise of his ministerial powers, employing them primarily for the purpose of having published and/or performed absolutely everything he ever set down on paper – and what had begun as an over-productive pen gradually became a slave to a condition of chronic graphomania. His wife Lilly – a former editor but during her years in the Soviet Union a professional housewife – devoted herself to procuring the highest possible degree of bourgeois well-being for herself and Johannes. In fact material success gradually became for both of them the aim and object of all political, literary, and cultural endeavour.

In one respect Becher bore an astonishing similarity to my brother-in-law Miklós Halmi: his great passion was making and breaking promises, an activity in which he took an unbounded delight. He was continually trying – always of course in the strictest confidence – to provoke one or other of us into uttering some undesirable criticism or entering upon some insalubrious course of action, with the result that one or other of us would get himself into a dangerous situation. Whereupon Becher would wash his hands of the whole affair, lower his already confidential voice to a reproachful whisper, and explain to his victim in detail just how ineptly he had gone about things.

If the affair unexpectedly turned out to have disagreeable consequences for himself as well he lost his nerve completely; he subsided into a state of blind panic and informed on one and all to the Party leadership. He several times offered the Party proof of his remorse in the form of suicide attempts, one of which – against all expectations – almost succeeded. The leaders of the German Communist Party, of whom few enough could conceive why the Party needed poets anyway, were nevertheless sensible of how embarrassing it would be to lose in such a scandalous manner a member whose name was so widely known. They proved in such cases to be of a forgiving, not to say a compassionate and above all open-handed nature. And Lilly nursed her Johannes back to health.

Like most of the German Communists in the Soviet Union, Becher regarded the Russians as little better than aborigines. In other words he would never have dreamt of learning their language. Maids who could speak German were always to be found in Moscow, if not always so easily. At the magazine he had the services of an excellent interpreter, a young Russian woman by the name of Gerassimova, who sat in the outer office that Becher and Barta shared in common. On the day war was declared between Germany and the Soviet Union, Gerassimova came to work in the uniform of the political police – as a first lieutenant, if I remember rightly. For the time being, however, she continued her editorial work.

Even among the other Germans Becher had no regular friends. His only real friends were two Hungarian couples – Andor and Olga Gábor, and Georg and Gertrud Lukács. The positive moral influence of these four people kept him more or less in line during the Moscow years. Without them, alone with Lilly in the Pankow Reservation after 1945, he went completely and utterly off the rails.

Somewhere in the depths of my tiredness, which for the most part I had brought with me from the West, a vague and barely perceptible sense of unease began to make its presence felt. It may have been absurd of me but I was disappointed to find that I was not kept in a state of constant amazement at the novelty of the world I now lived in. I had come to this capital of every international revolutionary movement in order to find something I had never experienced before, something that in both form and content had only very recently come into being, something that was still in fact in the process of coming into being. Gradually, however, I had to get used to the fact that everything I needed I could obtain only in the form of laboriously preserved but none the less decayed relics of an earlier bourgeois existence.

In Gorky Street (called in old novels the Tverskaya) there was a lavishly designed and painstakingly restored delicatessen shop that rejoiced in the name of Gastronome No. 1. Nobody called it that, though. It was known to all and sundry simply as Yelisseyev's, after its quondam owner, doubtless some long-dead representative of the capitalist commercial system. The Moscow man or woman who wanted to treat himself to the feeling that he had in fact achieved something in the last two decades could derive no proper satisfaction from the thought that he shopped at Gastronome No. 1 in Gorky Street. He must be in a position to say to himself, 'I can afford to buy my breakfast in the Tverskaya, at Yelisseyev's.'

At least, that is how it was when I got to know Moscow, and that is how it was when I left Moscow ten years later, in other words from the thirty-fifth to the forty-fifth year of my journey with this oddest of travelling companions, the twentieth century.

And when something really new and significant did emerge it promptly fell into line with the restored Yelisseyev's. The underground stations – certainly no product of a bourgeois society. Magnificent buildings both below and above ground, designed in a variety of styles, carefully executed in the choicest stone, and maintained in a condition of spotless cleanliness. But – nothing but a lot of overgrown Yelisseyev's. Mingled with one's first inspiring impressions was a feeling of dustiness and age.

The Savoy's menu was dispensed against my tourist coupons three times daily by waiters as old as they were old-fashioned, who gave expression to their zeal in the time-honoured, cumbersome gestures of their profession, and shuffled up and down in worn-out gymshoes, dreaming vainly of some fresh form of support for their fallen arches. But the food was both tastier and richer than I had been able to indulge in in the West in recent years.

The opening performance of the festival was *Swan Lake* at the Bolshoi Theatre. Connoisseurs assured me that the current Russian ballet was quite as good as the old court ballet of the Tsars. Andor Gábor, a Hungarian writer staying in Moscow, informed me with one of his wise, clown-like smiles that no event of any importance could take place in the Soviet Union without being either preceded or succeeded by a performance of *Swan Lake* danced by civil servants in tutus. I felt it again that evening –

that barely perceptible uneasiness I felt every time I saw how inextricably old and new were intertwined.

I was looking for a fresh start under socialism and did not immediately find it.

Hard by the splendid entrance to Yelisseyev's an unobtrusive door gave admittance to the Lux Hotel. The Lux, I should point out, was not in fact a hotel. Depending on which part you were looking at at the time you might have called it either an apartment house or a barracks. Nothing about that rambling, unassuming, even slightly dilapidated building betrayed the fact that within its walls the cauldrons of the world revolution bubbled and seethed non-stop. The atmosphere appears to have been a bit too rarefied, though, as on top of a high mountain: nothing in those cauldrons ever got cooked right through.

J.H. 35, then, steps through the door of this curious building called the Lux. He does not live there, so certain exertions are required of him before he may enter. He must stop at a little office and get himself a pass – known as a *propussk*. If, like J.H. 35, the visitor is a foreigner and if his passport, as almost invariably in the case of foreigners, is in the hands of the immigration authorities for the acquisition or extension of a residence permit, then he must deposit the only valid identity paper remaining to him, namely the receipt for his passport, a pink, printed slip, filled in in ink, and franked with a round rubber stamp.

The pass, when J.H. 35 got it, bore not only his name and the name of the person he intended to visit but also the hour and minute of his entering the building. It was the responsibility of the 'visitee' to make sure that the time between his visitor's entering the building and the time of his reaching his room was no longer than was justified by the distance to be covered. At the end of the visit the 'visitee' had to enter the exact time on the pass and add his signature. Only on presentation of a properly completed *propussk* might the visitor resume possession of his passport or its receipt.

In my day at least visitors to the Lux were not subjected to a search, as they were at the offices of the Party's central committee, for example. Before you got a valid pass to enter that building you had to hold your hands above your head while practised fingers felt you over from top to toe and went carefully through your briefcase as well. I personally endured this procedure on numerous occasions. One Nikolayev in Leningrad once constituted a historic exception, but only once – when he entered the Party headquarters in order to assassinate the local Party secretary, Sergei Kirov. No one knows how it happened, but on that one occasion there was no search; the briefcase in which the weapon was concealed was likewise left unexamined.

It was the lapse that led to the murder which gave Stalin the opening for his apparently never-ending massacre.

Permits, applications, official recommendations . . !

In my ten years in the Soviet Union I saw many people – some were my friends, some I did not know from Adam – who held in their hands or carried in their pockets pieces of paper that were capable of wrecking their entire future. Little scraps of paper – but what prodigious power they had!

Take Elga Schweiger, a more than ordinarily beautiful Budapest girl, elegant, well-educated, sure of herself and of her talent for her craft. She came from an intellectual family that had been loyal to socialism for three generations. When she and her likeminded mother went to live in the Soviet Union it was out of a combination of personal conviction and family tradition. And when I arrived in Moscow and Elga and her mother helped me over the initial difficulties of settling in, they did so not simply because they felt sorry for me as a refugee but because it was virtually a reflex action with that family to do everything in their power to give people the highest possible opinion of life in the Soviet Union.

Yet at the time I met Elga Schweiger she was already carrying round in her handbag a piece of paper that, if she could not manage to get it annulled, threatened to plunge not only her but her mother, her relations, and heaven knows whom besides into practically insoluble difficulties. The piece of paper was an order to leave the Soviet Union, to leave the family's chosen homeland outside which the life and work of its last three generations was deprived *ex post facto* of all meaning and purpose.

After Kirov's murder, when everyone was expected to reveal information about and throw suspicion on everyone else, someone in Leningrad made a discovery that led initially to Elga Schweiger's arrest. It was discovered, and reported in the appropriate quarter, that if four of the ashtrays Elga had recently designed for a Leningrad factory were placed together in a particular way, the resultant shape was not unlike the Fascist swastika.

It was not until Elga had spent several months in prison, vainly appealing to the fact that neither she nor anyone else was in the habit of placing four ashtrays together either in the incriminating arrangement or in any other arrangement, that her mother at last persuaded someone in the department responsible to set her free – with a piece of paper to say that she must leave the country.

As long as Elga continued to assume that what she was up against was the stupidity of individual officials, she bore her fate with composure. She was intelligent enough not to let other people's stupidity upset her. Time began to run short, however, and she appealed to one court after another without ever obtaining more than a brief reprieve in which to make a further appeal that won her a further, even briefer reprieve. In her wide circle of important acquaintances she found not one person with the courage to get her expulsion order annulled, and if she found one with the courage then he lacked the power to do it. The mighty Communist Party, the Soviet state, and the entire Communist International could not avail against the manifestly crack-brained fancy of a demented informer.

To take such a blow as that calmly was beyond even Elga's intelligence. She wanted to understand what it was all about and she got more and more embroiled in a self-justificatory monologue. As a revolutionary and the daughter of revolutionaries she felt deeply hurt and offended; she felt ashamed to face other people; her beauty began to fade; she was afraid at night . . . When she no longer found anyone at the Central Committee, at the Comintern, or at the Lux Hotel who would issue her with a *propussk*, she admitted defeat, let madness win the day, and left the Soviet Union on the first British ship that would take her. What happened to her after that I was never able to discover.

Secrets of the Lux Hotel

Documents, papers, rubber stamps . . .

One day – it was one of my first days in Moscow – I saw in the street a man who often returned afterwards to haunt my dreams. The impression that figure made on me was so deep as to stamp its significance on my unconscious, although I knew too little about this new world at the time to grasp that significance consciously.

The man was a middle-aged peasant. He was leaning against the wall of a house. There was nothing special about the house; it was simply where his last strength had left him. His peasant shoes looked as ancient as the earth, as ancient as serfdom once was in Russia. It was summer but he was wearing a fur cap with the ear-flaps down and a ragged fur coat. He held a small, flat lunch-bag pressed between his knees. One had the impression that everything he owned in the world he had on him. He was staring fixedly at a slip of paper in his hand. The hand, however, was trembling so violently that his eyes cannot possibly have made out what was written on the paper. In fact he was staring beyond the paper into nothingness – perhaps into the nothingness that the paper had made of his future. Its text must have been wobbling illegibly before his bloodshot eyes, but he had surely read it countless times already; over and over again his silent lips repeated the words that were written there. And sweat, the cold sweat of fear, streamed down his face . . .

Notes, chits, slips of paper . . .

Life and death . . .

17

*Mustard in tubes – yes or no? – My hosts
exchange glances – Walter the Nosy Parker –
In praise of Soviet law – Our first flat: a guided
tour*

YOU could get very good mustard in Prague, only not in tubes;
it came in little glass jars. Mother Pieck's instructions, however,
were quite explicit: the mustard must be in tubes. So three comrades had to traipse round every shop in Prague in a vain attempt
to find Mother Pieck at least a few tubes of mustard. To me fell
the painful duty of transporting the little glass jars of excellent
Mostrich from Prague to Moscow and handing them over to the
bitterly disappointed housewife. The combined efforts of a son,
two daughters, and a daughter-in-law proved barely sufficient
to pacify her; Mother Pieck was inconsolable, but she generously
and repeatedly stressed the fact that she did not blame *me* in the
slightest, thereby gradually awakening in me the most absurd
feeling of personal guilt.

Mother Pieck was the wife of Wilhelm Pieck, top man among
the German Communists, and at that time – with Hitler wielding
the big stick in Germany – resident in the Lux Hotel, Moscow.
When J.H. 35, armed with his pass, had completed his mission
with the mustard, she and her daughters withdrew from the room
and left me alone with my old friends from Berlin days, Arthur
Pieck and his wife Grete.

Grete and Arthur began sounding me about my first few days
in Moscow. After each of my answers they exchanged glances,
either unaware of or indifferent to the fact that these did not
escape me. The significance of those glances, however, was for

the most part unclear to me. I understood only that they had already heard something from Ernst Held, that they were deeply concerned about every aspect of my well-being, and that they were my sincere and true friends.

At one point Grete pricked up her ears and set another coffee cup on the table. A moment later the door opened and in came the head of the Pieck family and – since early 1933, when Ernst Thälmann had been arrested by Hitler's police – head of the millions-strong family of German Communists: Wilhelm Pieck. The strong family feeling and striking family resemblance between all the Piecks made them particularly sensitive to and others vividly aware of the fact that they were currently without hearth and home. It was only because history obliged them to that Mother Pieck and the rest of them, long accustomed to the moderate prosperity of solid professional revolutionaries, endured the discomforts of life at the Lux (a life, incidentally, that was comparatively privileged and the subject of universal envy).

If, for example, a Lux housewife wanted to cook or possibly even bake something that exceeded the capacity of the tiny electric stove installed in her room, she had to resort to the communal kitchen that served the entire floor and there share the stove with Mrs Gottwald or Mrs Kopecky, perhaps, or it might be with Mrs Thorez, at any rate it was always with Mrs Gerö and – which was really the limit – with Mrs Ulbricht, the highly unpopular Comrade Lotte. The inconveniences involved not infrequently led to thinly veiled feuds that even extended to the husbands as well, men who held high and in some cases the highest positions in the Third International – guarantor of the long-overdue world revolution. There was one insignificant-looking little man with a blond Hitler moustache who got on everybody's nerves. He was always poking his nose into the cooking-pots with an officiousness not untouched by envy and he was a tireless weaver of intrigues. This was the unpopular Lotte's husband – Walter Ulbricht.

It was a black day for the Pieck family and for humanity when, more than ten years after my first visit to the Lux Hotel and in an entirely new political constellation, this man decided completely to transform the appearance of his face by the addition of a curious

pointed beard and to venture his advancing years upon a series of
ghastly political adventures that culminated in walling his own
country in. No, he was not a nice man, the comrade from central
Germany whom we all called Walter – not even then. (It was the
custom among the German Communists to address one another
in the familiar form and by Christian name alone, which meant
that I too had to call the No. 1 man in the party 'Willem' – something I never managed to do without embarrassment.)

'Willem', then, stepped into the room, uttered a greeting, and
stood motionless with an inquiring and not unfriendly gaze
directed at myself. It was all a bit theatrical, for the man was
used to addressing crowds. His hair was almost white, his clean-
shaven face on the thin side, but almost threateningly compen-
sated for by his belly. Grete mentioned my name and the expression
of amiable curiosity shifted into one of welcome; it was still consciously theatrical, but full of genuine kindness and by no means
unpleasant.

'Ah, it's *you*!' he said, as if my being there had been a source
of great relief to him. He came two steps closer, allowed a further
pause to ensue, and finally with a sweeping gesture offered me his
hand. Grete poured fresh cups of weak coffee and the old man
gave himself over entirely to enjoyment of the steaming
beverage. For the space of several minutes he perhaps managed
to forget even his permanent irritation over Walter.

Over the coffee and cakes he and his son talked together in
lowered tones. I did not understand much of what they were
saying but I understood enough to know that it had to do with a
lot of minor and to my mind petty requirements of individual
comrades. One man needed a new suit – no, trousers alone would
not do; he had to have the jacket as well. A secretary needed a
nursery school place for her child. Someone else deserved a
better dentist than he was actually entitled to because he had
lost his teeth in the struggle against the Nazis. Many of the people
under discussion – no names were mentioned – were due to go
'into the country' soon. It was not difficult to guess that these
nameless comrades were going back to Germany to work underground, in other words to be in constant and immediate peril of

death. Their mission was discussed in the same calm tones as the pot of jam for people suffering from vitamin deficiency and the distribution of the six pairs of rubber galoshes that could not possibly be stretched to seven. 'Of course, we must go through all this again with Comrade Dimitrov.'

I believe it did not once occur to me that before very long my own troubles and requests would be the subject of just such a discussion.

Then Willem wiped his mouth, pushed his cup aside, and turned to me. To begin with his questions were pretty much the same as Grete and Arthur had asked me. This time my answers prompted a threefold exchange of looks, without my being any the wiser as to the outcome of this mute consultation.

The looks met again when I brought out the page-proof of *God, Emperor, and Peasant*, but when I mentioned that the play was soon going to be put on all three of them looked silently down at their plates. I then told them how I wanted to write a new theory of drama that aped neither Aristotle nor Brecht, one that would free the drama from set patterns and not try and force it into straitjackets whether ancient or modern, and this time the three looks perceptibly darkened. I never got a further opportunity of talking about this theory of drama, nor did I ever come to write it.

As if he had simply not heard much of what I had been saying, the old man proceeded to ask whether it would not be possible to find me a job on the editorial staff of *Internationale Literatur* or the *Deutsche Zentralzeitung* – a newspaper published in Moscow for the Germans living in the Soviet Union. I managed to stutter something to the effect that the theatre had always been an important political instrument and that it still was today; the theatre was, as I saw it, my field, and it was there that I wanted to earn my living and fight my share of the battle. As an independent writer. A self-supporting writer. I pointed out that I was already thirty-five and could not afford to waste much more time. 'And the world needs plays, Comrade Willem, the Soviet Union included.'

This time there was a longish pause before the looks were exchanged, and this time they were accompanied by kindly but embarrassed smiles. Willem: 'First of all we'll get your family here.' A further pause, then: 'I'll be talking this over with Comrade Dimitrov, of course . . . Arthur, *you* tell Walter, if you will . . .' Then he pushed another piece of cake towards me and said, 'Don't worry – we'll keep an eye on you . . . Yes . . .'

Accompanied by that movement of the plate of cake, his words had something of the character of a solemn promise. Nor do I want there to be any doubt about the fact that in my own affairs I never had occasion to be disappointed in Wilhelm Pieck. He always endeavoured in his way to stand by me.

When Micky and the child arrived (Anderli in the fur bag that the Meyers had given her) I had to look around for some accommodation for us. In the almost inconceivable housing shortage obtaining in Moscow at that time, however, finding a flat was no easy task.

A giant of a Ukrainian, Khariton Sergeyevich Sagaidak by name, employed by the Ministry of the Interior in the prison service's department of economic affairs, once explained to me the principle of letting accommodation under Soviet conditions. He had a neat little flat in the Taganka district to let – two rooms, kitchen, and toilet (no bathroom) on the ground floor of a long block.

Comrade Sagaidak began his explanation by pointing out to me how important it was not only for the economy of the Soviet Union but also for socialist justice that a man such as himself should be able from time to time to take on the management of some remote establishment – the case in point being certain insalubrious mines in the vicinity of Magadan, a little-known Soviet city accessible only by air over the taiga or by sea through Japanese waters.

On the other hand, Khariton Sergeyevich went on to inform me, any kind of housing speculation must in the Soviet Union be most strictly forbidden. 'You'll pardon my frankness, comrade, but no one in this great Soviet fatherland of ours must be allowed to profit financially from the fact that he has a house or flat while another man has nowhere to call his own.' He closed his eyes for a moment as if in prayer. Then he took a piece of paper and a propelling-pencil of foreign manufacture and began to note down figures as he spoke. 'Consequently *this* amount – the amount you will be so good as to make over to me – breaks down as follows: for the flat itself you pay nothing, or rather you pay the official rent, which, as you see, is very little.' The figure he jotted down was indeed negligible. 'Now, this sum here . . .' – and he scribbled a further figure that hit me very much harder – '. . . you pay me in advance, that's to say now, for the use of the furniture. No receipt necessary. Yes, comrade . . .' – here he slapped a mighty hand down on the table at which we were sitting, and the fact that the massive piece did not immediately split in two was in itself sufficient proof of its quality – '. . . take a look at the furniture if you like. I had this table sent over from Sweden when I was still serving in Leningrad.' Leaving me guessing as to the connection, he wrote down a further sum for cleaning and yet another one for dispatch, though without going into the question of what was to be dispatched whither or what was to be cleaned and why. He then totted up the various items and arrived at a pretty handsome figure. 'I'll let you have a receipt for *this* amount and get the caretaker to witness my signature. That way no one can say afterwards that I charged anything for the flat.'

He signed, I paid, the caretaker drank his vodka. Then Comrade Sagaidak clapped me on the shoulder (the fact that I did not shatter under the blow being proof of my toughness), looked me deep in the eye, and said in tones of moving pride, 'Make no mistake about it, comrade – our Soviet laws take a lot of getting round.'

But that was later. Our first flat in Moscow – in a once thoroughly substantial block in the Baumann district – was a part of an originally five-roomed flat that had subsequently been divided up. The engineer with whom we got in touch through Elga Schweiger and her mother had two rooms of it; the other rooms housed one family each. In the former servant's room lived Aunt Shura, alone with her gramophone and three gramophone records of which she played only one a day – but that one quite a number of times. Sunday afternoons she usually put on her absolute favourite, the *Warsavianka*. But first she would give a few ceremonial taps on the walls so that the neighbours should listen as well.

Ivan Pavlovich lived with his tired and taciturn wife and four little daughters between four and fourteen in what had been the dining room. He was a textile worker but he also knew a bit about electricity and could repair almost anything mechanical. Whenever he did something for me and I asked him afterwards what his fee was, the answer was always the same: 'Three-fifteen.' Three roubles, fifteen copecks. At first I was very impressed with the solid precision of his calculations. Only later did I discover that three roubles fifteen copecks was the price of a quarter-litre of vodka.

Not that this meant Ivan Pavlovich was a drinker. Not at all. It was just that vodka made almost as good a standard of value as gold. The economic constitution of the country had undergone more than one radical alteration since 1917 and was due for various further changes before 1945, the date when I left. Vodka, however, kept its stable value, did not alter its substance, could be stockpiled within the context of the most modest housekeeping budget, and, depending on the current purchasing power of the rouble, was always reconvertible into legal tender. A family with vodka was a family with bread, ready cash, and the goodwill of its neighbours. Hence: 'How much do I owe you, Ivan Pavlovich?' 'Three-fifteen.' Or it might be: 'Six-thirty.' Larger amounts were rare and were dealt with directly in litre bottles.

Of the four young men and the married couple who lived in the remaining rooms I remember nothing worthy of note beyond the fact that none of them spent much time at home, coming and going at the most irregular hours.

Only the engineer – that is to say ourselves, when we had moved in in his stead – had two rooms, of which one was very tiny and had no separate entrance. The communal kitchen broadcast a wide variety of smells. There was no time during the day at which loud snoring could not be heard behind at least one of the doors. The door of the one lavatory had a persistent squeak and the cistern produced sinister gurgling noises when flushed. Tenants were allowed the use of the bathroom once weekly for the purposes of taking a bath, though most preferred the public Turkish bath. Otherwise the bath-tub was used for washing clothes in. The clothes were then hung up on a bewildering system of strings in the corridor to dry. Row upon row of faded, steaming garments threw weird shadows on the walls, and whenever you set foot in the corridor, no matter at what hour of the day or night, you got yourself dripped on.

Our two rooms were far from completely furnished. In fact the smaller of the two contained only an enormous wardrobe and a curious piece of furniture that Micky unearthed in the market one day and bought like a shot. Rustic basket-work – only one of its kind. It was a sort of cradle or cot mounted on skids. The child slept in it in the smaller room, and as soon as the first snow fell we were able to use the thing in place of a pram. At the very beginning I used to take her for walks on my arm just like the majority of Russian mothers. They must have thought me a cruel parent, though, because I merely carried her about; I neither rocked her rhythmically to and fro nor did I hum her the usual monotonous lullaby the while.

In the larger room stood the housewife's pride – a polished sideboard complete with mirror and matching dining table. We had no beds, however. This in itself was not so bad because after all one can sleep very well on mattresses laid on the floor. But it so happened that there were no full-sized mattresses to be had at that time in any shop or market in Moscow. So we bought three children's mattresses and put two side by side and one across the top, thus achieving a very passable double bed. A bookcase was something I was not able to treat myself to until our second flat – that is to say more than two years later. It consisted of three orange-boxes in all their natural beauty. Who had eaten the oranges and on what occasion I never discovered.

A playpen for Anderli was nowhere to be had, so she crawled all over the whole complicated flat visiting all the neighbours in turn, qualifying for an extra-curricular performance of Aunt Shura's *Warsavianka*, and collecting a smile from anyone she happened to meet in the corridor. And whenever she disappeared from circulation completely we had only to knock on Ivan Pavlovich's door to find her playing with his four girls or sitting up at table with the family, sharing their cabbage soup and herring.

When the first winter arrived I noticed how all our neighbours shut their windows tightly and sealed them with putty or by gluing strips of paper round them, having first spread a layer of cotton wool underneath, which they then proceeded to decorate with coloured confetti. This left only the little window at the top, the *fortochka*, that could still be opened. I refused to cut myself off from the healthy fresh air in this barbaric manner. Before the week was out, however, the Moscow winter had taught me a lesson. I had to call in Ivan Pavlovich to rescue us in the time-honoured fashion from the whistling Russian cold (three-fifteen per window). And this although the central heating was highly efficient and the windows fitted pretty snugly.

Among the objects that the engineer and his family had left behind for our use was a fencing foil, the usefulness of which I was at first inclined to doubt. It was not long, however, before my small family saw me with weapon bared, engaged in an evening ritual of clearing our stuccoed ceiling of the bugs that had assembled there in clumps during the course of the day. The clumps – like bunches of grapes – fell on to a sheet of newspaper, which Micky then whisked into the bathroom and burnt in the stove. By dint of this precaution we obtained a relatively sound night's sleep.

18

Meshrabpom Films – The guardian angel theory –
Imprint of a female form – Shopping in Moscow

I⟦T⟧ was precisely in this environment and under these living
conditions that the oppressive feeling I had been unable to rid
myself of at the Savoy began gradually to leave me. My new
lodgings were neither the best nor the worst one might have
wished for, given the time and place. In fact I believe I was more
envied than pitied. I certainly felt that my circumstances were
more enviable than pitiable.

Looked at from the Savoy, it appeared as if the battle between
old and new had yet to be fought to a conclusion; it seemed
questionable whether the way forward was not in fact longer and
harder than the way back.

Here, however, it was manifest that the world to which these
run-down, decrepit, ex-petty-bourgeois flats had belonged was
gone for good and all and would never again be viable. A new
world must emerge – for the simple reason that the reconstruction
of the old would have demanded more effort and promised less
stability than a new creation, no matter what form that new
creation might take. Moreover I felt at home in the Baumann
district, in crumbling, mouldering old Moscow, in our overcrowded five-roomed flat with the neighbours' laundry dripping
overhead, the harsh tones of the *Warsavianka* and its eternal
accompaniment of snores, and the stuccoed ceilings with their
teeming harvest of vermin. I felt like someone who at last finds
himself in a position to take his fate in his own hands, who can
enter resolutely upon the battle for his own future and for the
future of humanity's millions because that is what he wants to
do and because in any case he has no alternative. Ever since my

173

arrival in Moscow I had known a blessed sense of security. Neither Hungarian Fascism nor German Fascism could touch me here. What were a few trite little worries against this constant feeling of physical safety? The dilapidated ceiling above my head, even if it did need delousing nightly, was both symbolically and actually more than I felt I deserved at the time.

I wanted to hurl myself head over heels into my work in order to show myself worthy of the heroes of this world both dead and living, the heroes to whose struggles I owed this blessed security.

In Lychov Street in Moscow there was a newly founded and not particularly large film company. It was called Meshrabpom Films, in other words it bore the name of International Workers' Aid, one of the largest international organizations giving the Communist Party and the Comintern permanent and more or less effective assistance in every country in the world.

The Meshrabpom studios were supposed to turn out the kind of films that would further the Communist education of broad sections of the masses that took no interest in politics. The company, as I say, was relatively new and had not as yet completed a film, though one was under way. It was a film about Dimitrov, the hero of the Reichstag fire trial who had turned his defence into a triumph over Hitler, Göring, Goebbels, the National Socialist state, and the National Socialist Party and who had now been placed at the helm of the Comintern to give the international struggle a new strategy and tactics. Author and director of the Dimitrov film was Gustav von Wangenheim. Work on it had just been interrupted for reasons as yet unknown.

A further mystery to me was why Comrade Samsonov, the Russian head of the studio, kept me waiting day after day after day before he finally signed the contract for the new scenario – on a subject as yet to be determined – that I was to write for Meshrabpom.

Since I was dealing with a socialist institution I accepted the proffered sum without question, barely even looking to see what it was. However, Fritz Kreiči – a tall man with a dark moustache who exercised some lofty function in these international cultural organizations and who recognized my hopeless ineptitude in business matters – was good enough to stand by me on this the threshold of my new life. When he saw my contract he shook his head in annoyance. Next morning I duly received a visit from the studio's German head, Hans Rodenberg, who apologized for there having been some mistake and exchanged my old contract against a new one containing more favourable terms. 'Samsonov didn't mean it badly, you know. He's just economical. He has to be. After all, we're a socialist business in a socialist state!' And it naturally passed my understanding yet again why Comrade Samsonov, on the occasion of our next meeting at the Meshrabpom studios, should have expatiated at length on how his accountant sometimes tried to cut costs at the wrong end and asked me whether I could not mention to Comrade Pieck when I got the chance how difficult things were at Meshrabpom and how they kept paring his budget down to a minimum. 'Yes,' Rodenberg added, 'Willem could put in a good word for us.'

My reaction was rather one of disappointment. I would much have preferred to be given work and wages on the basis of my capabilities alone and to visit the Piecks for coffee for no other reason than that we enjoyed one another's company. Maril, Fischer, Reinhardt, Hilpert, and others had given me money and offered me their stages because they believed in my talent; Lunacharsky had invited me because he liked my play; Ossietzky, Csokor and many others had lent me their protection because I was in the right . . .

'Anyone who wants to get anywhere in our soviet socialist republics must have a guardian angel,' Rudolf Haus once explained to me. Haus was a successful young journalist. Asked whether *he* had a guardian angel, he gave a contented chuckle and murmured the name of Karl Radek, who was generally regarded as the most gifted of the Soviet politicians and who in 1918 and 1919 had been one of the accoucheurs at what was supposed to have been the birth of the German Revolution. I had no liking for such cynical talk and it was a long time before I was able to make friends with Haus and his wife.

And yet I had no idea how I could have begun to make a living in Moscow myself if Willem had not taken me under his wing and made himself my guardian angel.

Between signature of the contract and payment of the first advance a period of several days elapsed – days, as it happened, during which there were more things than usual available for purchase. Friends and acquaintances who knew that I now had a flat and was trying to get settled in rang me daily – even hourly – with tips. One of them had seen some really fabulous bed linen for sale – not new, no, you couldn't get new, but it was still in good condition. Another knew of a fur-lined coat – never been worn – that could easily be adjusted to fit Micky. The person selling it could put it on one side for me for twenty-four hours, no longer. Olga Gábor had heard of a place where you could get hold of pillows. A secretary at the State Publishing House said the lady she lived with had some tumblers for sale. A little shop near Kursk station had men's galoshes and if I was quick I could still get my size.

I had had a deep loathing of galoshes since childhood and was not inclined to buy any now. My informant went to considerable pains to explain to me that in the Russian winter a man was doomed without galoshes. Once the shoes became damp from the caked and slowly melting snow, pneumonia was almost bound to set in.

I should have bought felt boots for the winter in the summer, but I was blind to the vital importance of this ungainly item of footwear as well. I missed my opportunity and was not able to make good the omission for the whole ten years. Only in the second or third year of the war when the heating was going off everywhere, virtually nothing was being done about the snow any more, and I was having to cover vast distances about Moscow on foot, did Micky at last manage to get hold of a pair of ancient black felt boots for me, the legs of which had probably at some stage got the moth and had for this reason been truncated by a former owner. Until then I got by with galoshes pulled on over my town shoes. My feet never got frozen, only my hands, but that was another story.

Luckily Micky had bought herself a pair of lined rubber boots in Switzerland; they lasted the ten years.

'Why don't you touch Alex Granach for a small loan?' someone

(I forget who) suggested. 'He's rolling in money, he loves helping people out, and it doesn't really matter if you forget to pay him back.'

Alexander Granach, a highly regarded and extremely talented actor at the Berlin Staatstheater in the Gendarmenmarkt, had had to flee the country in 1933 for two reasons – he sympathized with the Communists and he was a Jew. Speaking both Russian and Yiddish perfectly, he got one part after another with the major Soviet film companies and with the Jewish Theatre in Kiev. He was not dependent on Meshrabpom Films with its precarious programme and all too modest fees.

Granach was staying at the Metropol Hotel and I found him in the foyer in intimate conversation with a pretty woman – a woman, incidentally, whose elegance and, despite her obviously limited means, tasteful dress sense suggested that she was from Leningrad rather than Moscow. One never saw Granach otherwise than in intimate conversation with women – when one saw him at all. When he was nowhere to be seen, that meant he was with a woman too. A stocky, broad-shouldered, peasant-looking man with thick black hair and bushy eyebrows, he consumed perfectly monstrous quantities of women of all sorts and descriptions. From the virtually untouched seventeen-year-old drama student to the fat Ukrainian cook, all were welcome in his voracious and indiscriminate arms. And women flocked to him. Their hearts went out to him in gratitude, they worshipped him, and they even brought him other women too.

Yet through it all Alex's heart remained true to a Swiss blonde who visited him – wherever he might be – at far from frequent intervals and spent a week or a fortnight at his side. Granach was most concerned that everyone should recognize the Swiss girl as his lawfully wedded wife. He introduced her as such when he was sober and he bellowed the fact to the four winds when drunk. For the duration of her visits the concubinary hordes had orders to keep away. What is more, they did. In Alex's life there was never a breath of scandal. Also for the duration of these visits from Switzerland he wore a wedding ring, and his visitor did likewise.

Granach cut me short in the middle of an explanation that was only wasting my, his, and his Leningrad friend's time.

'Here's the key to my room. There's an old suitcase full of roubles on top of the wardrobe. Take as many as you need and put them back when you've finished with them.'

As I was heading for the stairs he called me back.

'Do me a favour while you're up there – pull the bed a bit straight, would you? The lady's new and we don't want her finding the hollow the last one left.'

I happened to be in the big department store called Univermag one day just as some magnificent quilted eiderdowns were brought in. Securing a good place in the queue, I promptly bought two of them. They were bright yellow and they became the glory of our little room, shining like the sun out of the corner where the three children's mattresses lay on the floor.

In due course it was borne in upon me that certain things one did not even attempt to buy in the shops. Blockhead that I was, I spent two whole days going from one stationer's to another, building up a motley collection of sheets of paper – squared, ruled, double-ruled, and so on. At first I made a complete fool of myself by asking for a hundred sheets at a time. I soon learnt to ask for ten, in order, if I was lucky, to be given five. It subsequently transpired that all my efforts had been superfluous anyway. I need only have had a word with Apletin's secretary, who would then have written out an application for me to sign, whereupon I should in a day or two have received from Apletin a voucher against which, after a further few days, the so-called 'Lit-Fund', the economic organization of the Writers' Union, would have issued me with the paper for which my request had been approved.

Unquestionably a more complicated process than just going into a shop and buying as much as one wanted, but in time one grew accustomed to the fact that one could neither own anything, nor obtain anything, nor do anything without written approval from above.

Another way in which I made a fool of myself was by waiting in shops for the things I had bought to be wrapped up for me.

Not even the bloodiest piece of beef, not even herrings were wrapped up for one. Wrapping was the customer's affair – if he happened to have brought along the requisite supply of newspaper. Proper wrapping paper was not to be had; and for every other conceivable purpose too one invariably employed newspaper – a custom that caused me some embarrassment at first because it was virtually impossible to take a piece of newspaper in one's hand without finding one of the large official portraits of Lenin or Stalin printed on it.

Every organization or institution had its own buying and selling apparatus, often with a vast corps of buyers and agents, its own price-list, and a multitude of special shops that were not always recognizable as such from outside. One had to resign oneself to the fact that shopping was an involved and intricate business. One's whole life came to revolve around it, in fact. The food and consumer goods available in public shops were insufficient for the daily needs or far beyond the means of the average family. Once Micky discovered a particularly well-stocked grocer's and shopped there with such naïve assurance that at first she was served with no questions asked. Only when we had both shopped there on two further occasions did it emerge that we had hit upon one of these special shops that were only open to the employees of a particular institution. The particular institution happened in this case to be the so-called Lubyanka, headquarters of the much-feared secret police that was just beginning to make its presence felt more weightily even than before. The entire distribution network of all goods was inscrutable and for the most part secret. It was distinguished by both an official and an unofficial hierarchy. I still for example have no idea where, how, and at what sort of price Comrade Fadeyev, the general secretary of the Writers' Union, was able to do his shopping. In the eyes of my neighbour Ivan Pavlovich the 'Lit-Fund', where I was occasionally able to buy things, was an inconceivable paradise of legendary proportions; the works shop where Ivan Pavlovich could sometimes buy his smoked fish and the millet for the family's millet gruel was hopelessly beyond someone like Aunt Shura's reach.

The fact that a pair of trousers could make a man happy and the denial of a pair of trousers reduce him to a condition of physical and mental beggary meant that the distribution of such everyday objects could not be left in the hands of low- or even middle-grade officials. Comrade Pieck, Comrade Togliatti (at that time using the name of Ercoli), Comrade Gottwald, or Comrade Béla Kun, hero of the Hungarian Commune of 1919, had to occupy themselves personally and in detail with the day-to-day needs of their fellow militants. And the new helmsman of the Communist International, Comrade Dimitrov, appointed to teach the proletariats of all lands new methods of struggle and thus lead them to victory, was forced to spend a considerable portion of his time and energy in scrutinizing all kinds of petty requests. When every button was capable of becoming a political question, then no amount of scrutiny seemed superfluous.

A further feature of such a system is that in the end no one has the right to own a thing simply because he needs it. Everything comes as a gift, a mark of distinction, an indication of rank. And as a result of right-mindedness and good personal contacts.

An additional source of commodities for us emigrants in Moscow was provided by the few through-travellers who could afford to take the hitherto little-used route from Scandinavia via Moscow and Vladivostok to America. For the most part these were intellectuals of renown, some of whom deliberately brought saleable items with them, others of whom decided en route to turn a few things into ready cash. I purchased a very fine powder-blue cardigan with a zip down the front from a well-dressed voyager in the mood for trade, and I very nearly got hold of Max Ophüls' fountain pen when the famous film director came to Moscow with the idea of making a new start in a new country, but unfortunately he left again at very short notice before I could complete the deal.

The dark-blue winter coat that I wore for the next twelve years I purchased from a Mr Witmann (or something like it), a young businessman from Stockholm on his way to the United States. He hit town with a goodly selection of merchandise and invited a crowd of friends known and unknown round for an evening in his room at the Metropol Hotel, where he delighted us with an assortment of excellent bargains. (It was hardly good business for him because we cost him far more as guests than we

paid him as purchasers, but as far as he was concerned that was
beside the point; we were a rum crowd, and he was enjoying
himself.)

He waited until one or two guests who were less to his liking
had gone, then opened a suitcase, took out a box, and proceeded
to offer its contents to the remaining men as a present. For a
moment we were considerably taken aback. This after all was
1936; one did not talk about birth control as openly as one does
today. 'Please help yourselves, gentlemen. A little something for
my friends. With love from Sweden. I'm told the local product
is not so fine.' And he gave an improvised demonstration of the
product's quality.

The rubber-goods situation was in fact grim, to say the least.
'Our socialist industry has presented us with the cast-iron
condom,' had long been a catchword with my friends the
Gábors. The men accordingly supplied themselves from the
proffered box, modestly at first, then rather more boldly. Yet
even so there were a great many left; I think it must have been a
five-hundred pack.

'Ladies, what about you? After all, you have an interest too.'

Dead silence. The women stared in front of them, transfixed.
One or two of the married ones made a mute appeal to their husbands for help. Witmann (or was his name Watmann?) was about
to put the gift regretfully back in his suitcase when a cooing
noise became audible from one corner of the room. A German
poetess whom I shall call Regina Bell, and who was not only
unmarried but made it hard for one to credit that she was ever a
party to even the most temporary affair (the only known exception
having been a Chinese poet who had left her after a very short
time for another German woman), stood up, groped her way
across the room like a sleep-walker, plunged both hands into the
box of Swedish wares, scooped a formidable quantity into her
handbag, and gave voice to a shrill laugh. Then, her laugh skid-
ding off into a muffled whine, she tripped over the carpet, recovered her balance, and ran from the room. In a matter of
seconds the remaining women and girls had cleaned up
Witmann's five-hundred pack completely.

Our attitude to these commodities from abroad was by no means that of the true Muscovite who had no such sources.

In 1939 Micky and I paid our first and only visit to Yalta to spend four weeks in a writers' convalescent home. Entering the breakfast room, where primarily the women had forgathered, we were greeted by an impressive silence. No, not an unfriendly silence, not a brush-off, as it were – simply a silence of the most thorough and eagle-eyed observation. From a distance of several paces the women examined carefully one by one all the visible items of clothing that Micky had on: the brown check costume from Berlin, 1932, the raincoat from Vienna, 1933, the shoes, many times resoled, also from Berlin, but vintage 1931, the pullover from her home town of Finsterwalde, 1929, and the muffler from Zürich, 1934.

Finally one of the writers' wives broke the silence. 'But the stockings – they're from here.'

It reassured those women to know that there were limits even to our Western opulence.

My friend Andor Gábor once defined real scarcity as follows: 'The mark of a true shortage of commodities is when people will stoop to swiping odd gloves.' Well, at the time I am speaking of here I quite believe that odd gloves were stolen without any hesitation whatever.

19

The art of drinking vodka – Curiously shaped neon tubes – A journey with Erwin Piscator – Volga, Volga . . .

'A HUNDRED grams!'

I had already learnt that in Russian restaurants one ordered one's vodka by the hundred grams. I had also learnt that somewhere between the two-hundred and three-hundred gram mark lay the amount that a recent arrival like myself could cautiously knock back without too great a fear of the consequences.

'What are you all doing here in Moscow, anyway?' I asked my actor friend Heinrich Greif as we were imbibing our first hundred grams – or was it already his second? – in the Metropol one day, sipping the liquid slowly and with a fitting air of absorption and eating little slices of herring with it. (One of the secrets of enjoying vodka – always nibble something with it.) 'You're not acting, you're not making any films, you're just sitting around.'

'We're waiting.'

'What for?'

Greif took a frugal sip of his drink, raised a slice of black bread to his nostrils, and slowly inhaled its odour. (Another secret of vodka-drinking – sniff a slice of black bread after each sip. Bread and vodka being close relations, they delight in one another's company, and this has the effect of heightening your own enjoyment.)

'Why aren't any of you doing anything?' I asked with the persistence of inquisitiveness and liquor. 'I mean you foreign actors,' I added by way of elucidation. 'What actually is it you're waiting for?'

'And all you foreign writers – what are *you* waiting for?'

'I've only just arrived.'

'You'll be saying the same thing five years from now.' Pause, sip, sniff, nibble, and then, with some solemnity, 'We're all of us waiting for the world revolution.'

'Radek's old joke,' I said in an access of irritation. ' "I have a life appointment – to wait for the world revolution." '

Sip, nibble, sniff, then with quick vehemence, 'Who's still waiting for the world revolution? We've mucked that up good and proper. We Germans mucked it up. First we got the whole world watering at the mouth. Socialism. World revolution. Proletarians of all lands . . . We Germans did . . . With our Marx. Our Engels. We . . .' And in a different voice suddenly, 'What do you think of Wangenheim's latest – me as the young Friedrich Engels?'

'Where?'

'Don't be silly. In a film. If they finally scotch our Dimitrov film Gustav wants to get something historical through. Alex Granach as Marx, me as Engels . . . Both as young men . . . Yes . . . First we whetted their appetites for them . . . the proletarians of all lands . . . Then we mucked up the world revolution for them . . . Mucked it up and fucked it up . . . For the workers of the world . . . In Russia too . . . Only no one sees it now because there's only *one* country calling itself socialist. Smart, eh? No possibility of comparison. Over there they don't have socialism, ergo they have capitalism. Here there's no capitalism, ergo we have socialism. Great. The young Engels can be proud of us . . . The pussyfoots of the world revolution . . .'

Greif leant closer and whispered in my ear. 'The revolution's fucked up for the Russians too. Fucked up and mucked up . . . Only we don't tell them and they don't tell us . . . The world's already got used to the fact that in Russia there's socialism, and we can't disappoint the world . . . So mum's the word!'

Looking out of the window, one saw shining down through the thin mist two bright-red neon tubes of curiously irregular configuration. It took the stranger some time to grasp that these were the outlines of two human profiles. Lenin and Stalin. Reproduced thousandfold in paintings, statues, photographs, films, and on the stage, here they were once more in neon. Monstrous lack of taste?

Or the taste of another age? I was put in mind of the First of May decorations in Budapest in 1919 – and was less inclined to judge by taste alone.

A confused babble of conversation reached us from the other tables. Even so Greif spoke in a cautious undertone. 'They were much too clever, those two, to wait long for the world revolution. *He*' – indicating Lenin – 'beat a brilliant retreat. *He*' – Stalin – 'made a brilliant thrust forward. Where to? Into socialism, at all events. Wherever we fetch up they call it socialism. Communism ... Great ...' His gesture was sweeping but his voice was barely audible now. 'We're all actors – we can play the conqueror, we can play the conquered ... if someone writes the parts for us ... Write us the parts, you writers ... Get on and write us the parts!'

There flashed across my mind a picture of the Pieck family and its paterfamilias who had once doubtless quit his country with the intention of fanning the flames of the world revolution and was now bogged down in the day-to-day routine of professional revolutionarism ...

Greif raised his glass to his lips and set it down again without drinking; he poked about in the dish of herring but did not eat.

Then he laughed out loud – a real thunderclap of a stage laugh. Knowing he was an actor, the people at the neighbouring tables laughed along with him, even without having heard his so hilarious words ...

That, then, was Heinrich Greif. Son of a Saxon post office employee, thirty years of age, six foot six inches tall, lanky and thin, with silky, light-blond hair and a nasal voice. Like a dozen SS men rolled into one. For all his youth he had been a convinced Communist for years. And when he had not had more than his two hundred grams he was a disciplined Communist too, with a disciplined tongue and disciplined thoughts.

And there he was, sitting in the Metropol and waiting. Writing a bit of poetry – not very good poetry, it seemed to me. The Zürich Schauspielhaus, where he had so often played the Nazi in Friedrich Wolf's *Professor Mamlock*, would gladly have engaged him on a permanent basis. And he was in love with a very lovely Zürich girl. But a disciplined Communist waits for orders.

Some years later he married a Russian student. Some further years later he died in Berlin after a botched operation – tragically, but not dramatically.

He was my friend. Before his unnecessary death he played the part I had written for him in *Day of Reckoning* – played it on the same stage as *God, Emperor, and Peasant* had once been shouted off. I did not see him; I just have one or two photos.

All plans to put my plays on the stage passed gradually into oblivion, though *God, Emperor, and Peasant* was in fact published; it made a nice, insignificant little volume. At the same time things began to move fast in connection with my film commission. Samsonov and Rodenberg informed me that the subject of the scenario I was to write had already been approved by one Comrade Angarov of the central committee of the Communist Party of the Soviet Union. It was to be a feature film about the German Volga Republic.

This small political unit did not rank as a soviet socialist republic but only as an autonomous part of the Russian Soviet Federated Socialist Republic. This, by far the largest state in the Union, towering above all others in power and importance, consisted of a large number of different language areas, regions, and more or less autonomous republics. One of these was the German Volga Republic. Its capital, once called Pokrovsk, was now known as Engels. It lay on the Volga. The second largest town was Marxstadt. There were also a number of villages and collective farms. The republic had two official languages – Russian and German. The curious, old-fashioned German dialect spoken there gave a clue as to the origin and evolution of this German-speaking pocket in the middle of Russia: the population had been settled there by Catherine the Great. They spoke bad German and even worse Russian, and in the villages there were families that had never learnt Russian at all. The republic had its own government with various people's commissariats that were in every respect subordinate to the government of the Federation – which was in turn subordinate to the government of the Union.

This multi-lingual federation reminded me of the plans of forward-looking Hungarians before the collapse of the Austro-

Hungarian Monarchy – plans that the Western powers had greeted with an '*Assez! Assez!*' and tossed on the rubbish heap without even a glance.

Of course that lovingly drafted but never realized Danube Federation resembled the system put into operation in the Soviet Union only from a distance. On closer examination one saw the latter for what it was – a paper edifice proudly known as the 'Stalin Constitution' that, as soon transpired, could be flattened with a wave of the hand the moment it became inconvenient or superfluous to the central authority.

I was to make a brief study of the subject on the spot and then we would make further plans. Erwin Piscator was to direct the film, and a Meshrabpom dramatic adviser was to accompany us on our study trip.

I had to do with two dramatic advisers at Meshrabpom Films, both of them Hungarians – Géza Gold and József Lengyel. Of Gold I remember little. (And seek him not – he too fell victim to the massacre that looked as if it would never end.) But I could tell you a lot about Lengyel. They came knocking on his door too one night and he too had to make the long trip from which few came back.

He did come back, though. That thin, fragile, sick-looking man somehow managed to survive. Eighteen years of uninterrupted dying failed to account for his feeble organism. Round about the middle of our century he went back home and settled in Budapest. The shattering experience had turned a dilettante into an important writer. Yet in one respect this true chronicler of inhuman times let his readers down: he did not draw the consequences. After a social order that he had helped to build had done him almost every evil a man can suffer, after his books had made clear beyond a shadow of doubt that it was no accidental error, no remnant of the past that had caused all the suffering but the essence of that social order itself – he left his readers in the lurch and thanked the murderous powers for not having been crueller than they had. But as J.H. 35 left Moscow with Erwin Piscator and József Lengyel and travelled south-east towards Engels, all this lay unsuspected in the future.

J.H. 35 was hardly delighted at having to break off work on his

new play *Have*, but on the other hand he was proud of the job
that had been assigned to him, for it struck him as being politically
of unprecedented importance, and the prospect of working with
Piscator was very tempting.

I had met this interesting man on only a couple of occasions in
Berlin and we had hardly been able to have a proper conversation.
Now we should be working together on the same level, as it were –
as author and director. Granted, the days when his work had
seemed to herald a new epoch in the theatre were past and gone.
His production of *The Good Soldier Schweik* with Max
Pallenberg in the title role and George Grosz's sets had represented the climax. To the question whether the German theatre
still possessed inner reserves and could have gone on to scale
fresh heights, my answer was and still is 'yes'. One of the guaran-
tors of such an evolution was Piscator himself.

Piscator's art, however, was supported on two pillars: on the
desire for renewal that characterized German art between the
two world wars and on a new socialist art in the Soviet Union.
The brilliant Russian producer Meyerhold and other leading
innovators seemed to draw encouragement and inspiration from
this new German theatre. But suddenly all that was new in art
was denounced as 'degenerate' in Germany and as 'formalistic' in
the Soviet Union and suppressed in both countries in favour of
a crude philistinism. The kind of art that Piscator might have
represented had lost both its intellectual supports at one go.

I found Piscator – born seven years earlier than the century –
a good deal aged. He was also very reluctant to talk about art. I
should have liked to discuss with him the film we were going to
make together but he said hardly a word about it during the
entire trip.

He did, however, observe one phenomenon that, had he not
drawn my attention to it, I should certainly have failed to notice
until a much later stage of our journey. Every time our train
stopped – and it stopped very frequently – numbers of seedy-
looking figures would appear on the platform and there would be
a great deal of coming and going, or rather slinking and prowling,
from carriage to carriage. Lengyel, who did not seem at all surprised at these secretive goings-on, was reluctant to enlighten us

as to their meaning; in fact he did his best to ignore the whole business.

For myself, with experience of one world war and its accompanying manifestations, it was not difficult to grasp that what we were witnessing was a black market in bread. Evidently we were travelling through a starving land. According to the map this was the notoriously fertile Black Earth zone. Yet here were these peasants, offering a wide variety of objects in exchange for bread and clearly acting in defiance of the law, creeping like thieves and beggars from one carriage door to the next. In the half-light of dawn the toing and froing and muttered whispering was especially brisk. There was something preposterous and unnatural about it all. One was used to the *town* having no bread and getting hold of essential provisions by the expedient of illicit trade with the villages. But this was a case of the *country*, of a tract of land celebrated for its fertility, being without bread and buying by barter or begging back from the town the bread it had itself provided. The villages were being plundered, legally and for reasons of state, in order to keep the industrial centres more or less adequately fed. They were compelled to get their own food from the towns as and when they could.

'The alliance of workers and peasants' was the official watchword, but in fact there was a secret, insidious class struggle going on. A class struggle between town and country. A class struggle of starvation and extortion.

Piscator and Lengyel sat in silence, frowning deeply. Little by little the same frown appeared on the face of J.H. 35, though he hardly understood anything as yet. He merely saw a multitude of things that to a greater or lesser degree ran counter to nature – individually or collectively – and felt it to be his immediate duty to investigate how they could be put right. He had already felt that way in Moscow and had got from Held, from the younger Piecks, from Rodenberg, and from Umanskij only an embarrassed silence for answer. Fortunately he was not such a live wire as immediately to set about fulfilling what he saw to be his duty and so did not make an uninterrupted nuisance of himself.

When the three visitors were shown round the pride of Marxstadt, the tobacco works, J.H. 35 was reminded of a visit to a similar installation during the course of a school expedition in 1914 and asked, as his modest contribution to the development of the tobacco industry on the Volga, why the ventilation was not left on for a short while after the machines had been turned off in order to draw off the fine dust that was so harmful to the lungs. The works manager went a sickly yellow and became speechless with fear, convinced that his last hour had come. The comrade from Moscow was dissatisfied!

Comrade Oelberg, who I believe was People's Commissar for Agriculture in the tiny republic, informed us proudly and in some detail of an innovation they had recently introduced on their collective farms: three-year crop rotation. J.H. 35 must needs place the agricultural wisdom drawn from his Abony childhood at the disposal of the Volga Germans, informing the People's Commissar in return that three-year crop rotation was considered old-fashioned even on the better estates and that one should sow a crop of papilionaceous flowers (also usable as fodder) in order to restore the natural nitrogen balance. The result was that Comrade Oelberg gave our Lengyel a wink, as much as to say that someone ought to keep a wary eye on this young man and his dangerous capitalistic-imperialistic ideas.

In the towns and villages we called together men and women of all ages. Anyone could come who wanted to, yet even so there was some selection, the system of which remains a mystery to me to this day. We asked them questions about their life, their past, their hopes, and their wishes. Nothing could have been more natural than that they took us for a commission of inquiry investigating heaven knows what. Many of them, particularly the older ones, embarked upon interminable stories, defending themselves fiercely against heaven knows whom and launching into equally fierce attacks upon persons who remained equally anonymous.

We visited what I can only describe as a boarding school for female tractor-drivers. Plump, well-fed girls in surroundings of impeccable cleanliness. Each girl had her own bed linen, yet it was all absolutely identical. On each bed lay a small embroidered cushion. I was not surprised to hear the girls declare unanimously that great-great-great-grandmother had brought the cushion with her as a girl from the old homeland in the days of the great

Tsarina. They told us – or rather reported to us – how many Young Communists, how many Party members, and how many candidates for Party membership there were in the school and to what extent their plan quotas had been fulfilled or exceeded. It all came out mechanically, as if learnt by rote. For the new concepts they were obliged to use the Russian words, declining or conjugating them in the German manner. Uncertainty, suspicion, and fear lurked behind every syllable. Words, they knew, could kill.

Piscator found it all rather boring and, after hearing that they spent their free time studying the history of the Communist Party of the Soviet Union and the life of Comrade Stalin, insisted they tell him how things stood with love. He expressed himself with such modern informality, however, that we left with the would-be tractor-drivers' delighted and uncomprehending laughter ringing in our ears.

An astonishing sight in the farmyards and in the slushy morass of the streets was the beast of burden employed by these Germans in their curious, floating existence between a real past and an unreal, imposed future – namely the camel. This was an animal we had always associated with sand and heat. And here it came lurching towards us through the snowstorms that howled across the frozen reaches of the Volga. (What happened to those camels, I wonder, when six years later Stalin declared the German Volga Republic non-existent and bundled its population off to Kazakhstan?)

Did I insist, they asked me, on going to the theatre in Saratov today? (J.H. 35 wanted to see Ibsen's *A Doll's House* in the small Russian town across the Volga.) Tomorrow, they suggested, might be more advisable. But I was tired of sights that we never got to see – of the half-built or nearly completed power station or cannery or whatever it might be that turned out at the last moment to be inaccessible. I wanted to see a programme adhered to. 'Yes,' was my sullen response, 'I should like to go today if possible.'

Oh, it is *possible*, they told me – obedient, resigned, always anxious to be of service. And the glowing tip of our driver Julia

191

Metzger's cigarette showed me the way through the fog to the pre-war Ford that was our official transport in Engels. Julia, dressed in quilted trousers and padded jacket, with an enormous green woollen scarf wound round her head beneath the ear-flaps of her soldier's cap and drawn across her mouth so that only a cheeky snub nose appeared to poke defiance at the outside world, looked like nothing so much as a little boy packed off to school in dirty weather.

So began that drive over the frozen Volga through the milk-white fog with a mummified girl beside me who, when I asked her when we should be actually on the ice, at first did not answer and then, perhaps a quarter of an hour later, told me with a catch in her breath that we were already halfway across.

I had noticed some time back that the car's progress had ceased to be as steady – relatively speaking – as it had been before. My driver kept making unexpected turns. The ice beneath our wheels seemed to be getting wetter and wetter and the splashing of water louder.

One could tell this story much more excitingly, conjuring up the instant at which I became aware of the danger and realized that the increasingly taciturn girl beside me held my life in her hands. But I am not concerned in this book with struggles against hostile elements so much as with the hostile tensions existing between human beings – in this case between myself and Julia. For a short while I was her deadly enemy, for it was I who had forced her into this situation. And to cap it all, I liked her; she was an attractive girl.

How did we get into such a pickle anyway – alone in a car in the middle of a frozen wilderness?

The railway from Moscow only went as far as Saratov, a town on the right bank of the Volga, i.e. outside the German Volga Republic. On our arrival the three of us had proceeded to Engels in a little steamer that had threaded its way between enormous, drifting ice-floes. While we had been pursuing studies of doubtful worth in the world's first German socialist state, winter had set in properly and the steamer could no longer run. For some reason that was never explained to us the immensely long railway bridge connecting the two banks a few kilometres south of Saratov and

Engels was for the time being out of service. That left only one
way – over the ice. But *was* the river frozen right across yet?
Would the ice be thick enough to take our weight? This was
something one never knew until the first car had reached the
other side. Or failed to reach it. This year the car in question was
the one in which I was being driven by a young and extremely
uncommunicative peasant girl.

My heart did a somersault in my chest as I suddenly saw what
I had got myself into. Had it been simply lack of imagination
that had made me insist on this journey? My ignorance of what
real danger was? Had it been obstinacy? Had I done it for reasons
of prestige? And why had my hosts agreed? Why had they not
refused me the use of the car? Why had they preferred to risk
the lives of two human beings – and an old Ford into the bargain –
rather than assume responsibility for one little decision? Was it
discipline? Was it drill? Was it fear? Fear – of *me*? Of my *power*?

The Ford kept changing direction. The face of the girl beside
me had gradually become ashen, furrowed, and old. At one point
she brought the car to a halt and sat completely motionless,
staring out into the fog. Was she looking for something? What
was she thinking? Had she fallen asleep with her eyes open?
Was she frozen stiff all of a sudden? None of my questions could
she be induced to answer. Fumbling in one of her cavernous
pockets, she produced two cigarettes. (Not the usual hand-rolled;
she smoked real *papyrossi*. After all, she worked for the government.) One of them she stuck in her mouth and the other she
offered me. She gazed at me with an absent look as I told her
several times in both languages that I did not smoke. Eventually
she put the other cigarette back in her pocket. Then, before I had
had time to phrase a further question, she had slipped out of the
car and was gone. For two or three steps I could trace the glow of
her cigarette, then that too disappeared. There followed an
interval of which I have no recollection whatever, beyond being
aware that I was sitting by myself in an ancient car on the thin
crust of ice covering a prodigiously wide river in the middle of a
foreign country, swathed in impenetrable fog. It was a real fore-
taste of the fear of death, complete with roaring in the ears,
shivers, and chattering teeth. I thought I could already make out

the creaking noise that must be the prelude to my plunging to my doom in icy water. I do remember thinking whether there was anything I could do to save myself – and rejecting the thought for fear of the panic that would inevitably ensue. The thing to do was not to think at all.

A splashing of water. From quite another direction than I had expected it, the glowing tip of my driver's cigarette became visible through the fog.

'Where have you been?'

To which I got the longest answer of the whole day: 'Reconnoitring the load-bearing capacity of the ice.'

'What's the position?'

Julia looked me in the eye – neither mockingly, nor sympathetically, nor would I say reproachfully either. She tore the scarf away from her face. Even her composure was no longer intact.

'We have to go round another way.'

She spun the wheel this way and that for a while, then drove for some distance in a fairly straight line. It was very bumpy and the old car took a terrific jolting. Every now and then Julia would stop and lean right out over the ice. Finally I grasped what she was looking for: she was keeping an eye open for fresh camel droppings. When camels cross the ice they stick to where it is safe. We jolted on from one little heap to the next, the camel dung showing us the way.

After another long stretch Julia stopped the car again. I waited. She waited. The fog was still impenetrable.

'Why don't you go on?'

'Where do you want to go now?'

'You know – to Saratov.'

'This is Saratov.'

'And the theatre?'

'Right here.'

As I shamefacedly got my bag out of the back she laughed at me. This time there was mockery there – and relief. And as I was trying to think of a fitting way to express my thanks she stepped on the gas and after a few yards disappeared out of my life. For ever.

20

Composer in danger – Socialist pedagogics and the Young Pioneer's penis – Death of a film studio – 'Keep quiet'

I FOUND Gustav von Wangenheim and his wife Inge waiting for me in the Moskva Café. Gustav opened the proceedings with a certain solemnity. Possibly I was surprised, he said, that he should ask me to meet him in public like this, but his decision was the outcome of mature reflection. We had, after all, nothing to hide; there was no reason for us to behave as if we did.

Inge, whose eyelids were red as if she had been crying, nodded agreement. Gustav fell silent and stared at the table before him. He might have been going over his lines before an entry.

Puzzled as to the meaning of these introductory remarks, I asked, 'What's it all about, then?'

The two of them leant across the table towards me. Inge whispered and Gustav muttered beneath a nose that a series of bitterly cold Moscow winters had tinged with red, 'Shostakovich.'

'What's the matter with Shostakovich?'

This was January 1936, and J.H. 36 was still an inexperienced newcomer to Moscow. In fact he was indebted to this very couple for a great many enlightening remarks about life in the Soviet Union.

Inge could not believe her ears. 'You don't know what's happened to Shostakovich? You must be the only person in the Soviet Union who doesn't.'

'It was even in the *Deutsche Zentralzeitung*,' Gustav said.

I answered not without pride that I was a *Pravda* subscriber.

The Soviet papers were not available to any Tom, Dick, or Harry who felt like subscribing to them. One's superiors in the firm or organization one worked for were the judges of what newspaper one might take. The fact that Comrade Apletin thought so highly of me that I was allowed both *Pravda* and the *Deutsche Zentralzeitung* really meant something. Admittedly half the matter in all the papers was word for word the same, but in terms of the evaluation of personal worth it counted for a great deal in which paper one read it. A person who was permitted to subscribe to, say, *Pravda, Isvestia, Literaturnaya Gasetta,* and two or three monthlies besides could reckon, even without anything in writing, with various special privileges, for example with preferential treatment from the caretaker of his block in respect of all kinds of needs and requests. One's newspaper was one of the innumerable indications of status without which one was lost. Moreover, to maintain the status one had required relentless upward striving as well as a helping hand from above. And this quite apart from the fact that newsprint was a material necessity.

In those early days I read Russian only with difficulty, but I believed I had understood what had befallen the young composer from Leningrad.

'So the critics didn't like his new opera. It could happen to any of us.'

'The critics ... didn't like .. ?' spluttered Inge, producing a wad of newspaper cuttings from her briefcase. 'In the first place they *all* liked it – without exception. Then, all of a sudden: cacophony, disharmony, decadence, chaos . . .'

'Shush!' hissed Gustav.

'Are you still so naïve?' Inge asked me, and Gustav almost brought his lips to my ear as he murmured another name, 'Stalin.'

Slowly a light began to dawn. The talented young Leningrad composer Shostakovich had had a tremendous success recently with his new opera *Lady Macbeth of the Mtsensk District.* He had been praised, fêted, and held up as an example. Until the day Stalin decided to make the acquaintance of the work. Stalin did not like it. And next morning the critics were trying to outdo one another in heaping abuse upon the recent idol. Thus far I had read and understood. I found the story ridiculous and distasteful. Stalin surely could not know – so I thought – that the critics of

Pravda and the other papers were so lacking in independent judgement.

I was completely innocent, however, of the danger in which such a situation placed a writer or composer in the Soviet Union. All his works were immediately struck from the programme and no one henceforth mentioned his name; his earnings dropped to nil; the authorities through whom he might have improved his position would no longer issue him with a *propussk*; he had no means of protesting when his piano was taken away from him to be given to someone more worthy; and finally he might even lose his flat. While he was explaining all this to me Gustav picked out one of the numerous sentences that appeared word for word in every critic's article: the composer was advised to move out into the country and study folk songs.

'Do you know what that means, reading between the lines?'

'Must one read between the lines, then?'

'Oh yes, indeed!' put in Inge.

'Is that a word of advice?' Gustav went on. 'No, it's a tip to the authorities that they should see the formalistic artist for what he is, namely the obdurate enemy of the Soviet people, grasp him with a firm hand, and pack him off somewhere where folk songs are about all that will grow.'

'But what has this got to do with me? With you and me?'

'A fortnight ago I suggested him as composer for the Dimitrov film.'

'In writing!' wailed Inge. 'Can you imagine – in writing!'

But J.H. 36 was too fresh a Muscovite to seize all the implications at once.

'Do you mean Samsonov doesn't want him any more?'

'Samsonov? Do you think *I'd* have Shostakovich now? The thing is, they'll all use my suggestion against me. Samsonov, Rodenberg – all of them who said yes will now have to clear themselves. At my expense, of course . . . An old Communist like me making a mistake like that! An old Communist like me . . !' He hung his head in silence, then said quietly, 'I shall do public self-criticism . . .'

After an uncomfortable pause J.H. 36 asked whether this was not going a bit far.

'In a thing like this one can't go too far.' It was hard to tell which Gustav reproached himself with most – the mistake or the fact that he had made it. 'We're building socialism in one country. We're surrounded . . . hemmed in by enemies on all sides . . . Capitalists . . . Imperialists . . . And I go and . . . *I* go and make a mistake like that!' He leant across the table towards me again and went on in an urgent whisper, 'And you – you must keep clear of me . . . Yes, yes – none of this playing the hero! It's common knowledge that I backed your invitation to the Soviet Union . . . That we're friends . . . Friends . . .'

He relapsed into silence though his lips continued to move, as if savouring the last word he had spoken. Inge's eyelids, I noticed, were even redder than before.

For Shostakovich – whom incidentally I never met – the affair ended badly but not catastrophically. Time went on and the Dimitrov film, which might have helped establish a new style in cinematographic art, never got off the ground. Gustav became increasingly convinced that the blame lay with an unplayed, unwritten, never even thought-of score and a composer who knew nothing of the whole endeavour. But he dropped the subject. If anyone brought it up in his presence he would adopt a melancholy, absent air. His public self-criticism never took place. No one gave him the opportunity, and he was left to rack his brains for the reason why. Nor did it even occur to me to steer clear of his company, but nobody's suspicions were aroused. There were already bigger things afoot.

After our return from the German Volga Republic my own film work took an unexpected turn. Our preliminary work received high praise and our treatment was analysed appreciately. The next thing we were told was that Comrade Angarov, the member of the central committee of the party who was responsible for this field, had had the idea of combining my plot with a short novel by Adam Scharrer and turning the two into a truly magnificent revolutionary film such as only such gifted masters of the medium as Piscator and myself could make a success. At the same time it was pointed out to us that a collective operation was undoubtedly closer to the spirit of Communism than anything individual.

Adam Scharrer was one of the most talented members of the colony of German writers then resident in Moscow and I liked him very much. An old peasant with a real gift for telling a story, he unfortunately shared a characteristic of Communist writers that regrettably spoils and often ruins their work. The unhealthy relationship between literature and politics so conscientiously cultivated by such writers prevented them from taking as their starting-point a frank observation of life and going on from there, powered by a positive curiosity and steered by a feeling of responsibility towards mankind and the world, to truths not to be found in any canon. They forced themselves to see the end-result as proceeding from the paltry store of currently admissible political material, and expected life to string along.

This alone would not have prevented Scharrer's novel and my treatment being carpentered into some kind of collective product. After all, at the time I felt bound by the same kind of upside-down view of the writer's task as my colleagues. In fact I cannot imagine how I reconciled my conscience to the fact that I still continued to work on plays that did not conform to that view, plays that set out from a good old unbiased stare at the world around me, a marvelling gape at human tensions, clashes, and conflicts, and through the addition of something that might be called poetic invention blossomed into universal truths. Once it had been *God, Emperor, and Peasant*; now it was *Have*, completed in 1936; the next one was to be *The Turkey-boy*. Alone, almost in hiding from myself, haunted by the idea that I was guilty of dereliction of duty, I went on working at them. Feeling myself free of an imposed truth that was prompted by political considerations – that was my 'dereliction of duty'.

Months went by. We received further payments on account – not much, but enough to keep our heads above water. Once I won eight thousand roubles in a competition for a film subject. It was not a great deal of money but it made life easier for a while. The simple, everyday difficulties of living one put up with and even forgot after a bit. But the senseless, purposeless hanging around – that got on one's nerves. No one could explain this enforced idleness. The sheer frittering away of time was so striking and affected everyone and everything to such an extent that one could not avoid the impression that there must be some system behind it.

The Austrian writer Hedda Zinner, now resident in East Berlin, is my witness that even so exiguous an object as the penis of a Young Pioneer could serve to squander aeons. Hedda was commissioned by the state educational publishing house to compile an ABC book for German-speaking children in the Soviet Union. Her text was a great success, the publishers had illustrations drawn for it, and the book was all ready to go to press when a lady comrade at the People's Commissariat noticed that the artist, on the authority of experience and the teaching of the Academy of Art, had indicated by means of a little curved line that a Young Pioneer has a penis too. Various champions of socialist pedagogics protested. They found this irreconcilable with socialist morality. Various other champions of socialist pedagogics and morality were of the opinion that schoolchildren of both sexes knew from other sources than little curved lines in books that Young Pioneers had penises and that they would consequently miss the graphic representation of same, which would stimulate their imaginations in undesirable directions.

As far as I know – despite the fact that the Young Pioneer in question would be between forty and fifty by now – the question remains unsettled to this day, and the much-needed school books have therefore never been published.

One day Comrade Samsonov asked to see me but was not in his office when I arrived. No one apologized for the fact, but this was not in itself remarkable. What was remarkable was a quite unusual tension running through the entire building. Clearly no one had his mind on his work. More and more people came in – directors, actors, writers – but despite the throng it was as quiet as an empty church. I slowly gathered that somewhere in a very important place some very important films were being shown to a very important personage – and that some very important decisions depended on the upshot. It was as if we in Lychov Street must whisper lest we disturb the showing in the Kremlin.

Death of a film studio

We had been waiting for some hours when Samsonov finally appeared. He hopped in on his stumpy legs like an agitated dachshund, but his eyes behind his spectacles gleamed with an unearthly bliss. There was no doubt at all *whose* presence he had recently been in and *whose* words still rang in his ears. His voice, which was trembling with ecstasy, was in marked contrast to the content of his short speech.

'Comrades! Mammoth catastrophe! Wholesale rejection! All the films shown by the entire Soviet film industry – all slung out! Including two by Eisenstein and one by Pudovkin. Prodigious, unprecedented, utter and complete artistic débâcle!'

He paused. Then, more objectively, the tremble of ecstasy replaced by a military severity, 'Government decision: this studio to be disbanded. A studio for children's films is to take its place. All the films on our books to be scrapped.'

Just at that moment I happened to catch sight of Gustav. He was smiling a rapt, damp-eyed smile.

The speaker began applauding before any of us could say a word. A violent if brief storm of applause shook the room. Here and there one heard people repeating the names 'Pudovkin' and 'Eisenstein'. Then the two greatest names in film. A dog would not have accepted a crust from their hands at that moment.

When I went to Willem with my grievance I could tell from his face that it was not the first time he had heard it. There were clearly people with whom the penny had dropped sooner and who had come along earlier than I to complain. He pricked up his ears, however, when I asked for his permission to return to the West and for his help in getting me there. Would I have a better life there than here, he wanted to know.

'Materially I can just about scrape by here,' I replied. 'But what's the point? As a revolutionary writer I should lead a wretched existence in Western Europe or America. Certainly I should. Possibly I should even go under. Maybe the long arm of Hitler or Horthy would reach me. But before that I should do something. Achieve something. Something to justify the fact that I was once admitted to the Party.'

Wilhelm Pieck was silent for a long time, as if thinking over my request. Then he slowly shook his head. 'No,' he said. And added quietly, 'I'm thankful I was able to bring a few of you to safety. Keep quiet. Not everyone is as glad to have you all here as I am. My advice to you is – keep quiet.'

21

*The significance of the double eagle – What is
and is not 'Marxist' – More about Walter*

THIS was the period of the changeover to the Popular Front
policy. A slow and rather uneven process, but a changeover none
the less, and one that ushered in a changed world. Stalin had
charged Dimitrov with the task of putting into practice the new
political strategy for international socialism that he, Dimitrov,
had evolved at the Comintern. That much everyone knew. The
identity of the person or persons whom Stalin had perhaps at the
same time instructed to prevent Dimitrov from carrying out a
policy so foreign to the dictator's nature we did not and still do
not know. Or did he not even need to issue such instructions?
Did the political apparatus that Stalin had spent his life building
up on the shoulders of a countless host of cowed and disillusioned professional politicians of all ranks and degrees – did
it thwart every political innovation automatically?

Did the whole thing form part of that vast and bloody
marionette theatre right from the start? Private performance:
The Rise and Fall of the Popular Front Policy, for political adults
only? Whereby the 'people' of the play's title were cast no higher
than supers, and the strings by which both protagonists and
antagonists hung were operated by one hand alone – that of the
great puppeteer, Stalin, who got through so many puppets. And
for the worn-out ones he had another use: he burnt them; he
tossed them into his very own permanently glowing hell-fire.

The performance had only just begun. We were seeing the
rise of Dimitrov's policy, which a thick, sticky, indefinable,
nameless political substance hampered from the first moment on.
A man might be for the Popular Front policy or he might be

against it. In any case he was *for* Stalin. Sincerely. No, not always entirely without guile, but sincerely all the same. For one or the other of Stalin's faces, that is. Oh, the old Tsars knew what they were doing with a double eagle on their coat of arms!

Those who served Stalin's Popular Front face took the other face, that of the tyrant, wittingly into account. It seemed none too high a price to have to pay for the victory of the peoples of all lands. Those who served Stalin the tyrant, however, tolerated the Popular Front policy only as a collection of tactical dodges, and thus contributed to its gradually grinding to a standstill.

But Stalin needed enemies too. Lots of enemies, that he might have lots to destroy. His whole life was founded on hatred and revenge. So was his system of government, the machinery of which he kept warm with the discarded marionettes. Hence the high rate of puppet consumption. Who was his enemy when was something he alone decided. A new puppet took over the part, and the old one was used for fuel.

At that time it was necessary to win the sympathy of various peoples and classes – for the great Popular Front policy against Fascism on the eve of the Spanish Civil War. At the same time, however, old puppets of good, pre-war wood, if already a bit worm-eaten, had to be made to play the villain in a series of corny spectacles and duly qualify for destruction.

In 1936, as part of the Popular Front policy, a new German-language literary magazine called *Das Wort* ('The Word') was founded in Moscow. Its three editors were Bertolt Brecht, Lion Feuchtwanger, and Willi Bredel. The first two lived in the West and their names and work were internationally known. Bredel, a German writer of nondescript talent then resident in Moscow, was virtually the official prosaist of the German Communist Party. In high favour with the Party leadership, he was occasionally in a position to threaten the otherwise unassailable supremacy of Johannes R. Becher, a circumstance that would temporarily throw our Johannes into a state of hysterical panic. It being an integral part of Soviet literary policy to set up new magazines all of a sudden and just as suddenly ban them or others, Becher was inevitably afraid that *Das Wort* might overnight take over the role of his *Internationale Literatur* and he, Becher, be left without a job, without a reputation, and without a scrap of influence in the Party.

My play *Have* was finished at last and an extremely beautiful German girl called Lilo – with whom for some reason I did not fall head over heels in love but became very good friends instead – took a copy of it with her on a trip to France. She had plans for it, she said. Soon after her return – she was lovelier than ever; I remember that pale-grey hat to this day – I received an unusually fat letter postmarked, I think, St Tropez. It was from Lion Feuchtwanger, with whom I was not at that time personally acquainted though he was due to visit Moscow shortly (visits by Western writers being a feature of the Popular Front policy). Enclosed with the letter was the manuscript of a fifteen-page article about my play, which Feuchtwanger had written for *Das Wort* and which he authorized me to reprint as a foreword to the play in the event of its being published in book form.

One of the things the article said was this: '*Have* is Marxist through and through. Of the German plays I know it is the first that does not talk about Marxism or sing about it but is impregnated with Marxism from within . . .'

I had been waiting for some four months already to see Fadeyev. All I wanted to see him about was to offer him one of my plays – any one – for publication in one of the fat Russian literary monthlies. It seemed too trifling a matter to bother the general secretary of the Writers' Union with but I was told that no matter was too trifling once Alexander Alexandrovich made it his concern. What I was not told – and would not have believed – was that Fadeyev would summon me five times to five different offices and not only fail to appear but neglect to send me an apology. I tried to tell myself that he was a very busy man, that he meant no offence, that the men who had realized the workers' and peasants' state had a different sense of time than we, that perhaps he wanted to surprise me with a fait accompli . . . It was no good. I felt I was being badly treated – and condemned myself as decadent and over-sensitive for feeling so.

Finally Fadeyev summoned me to Apletin's office in the Kusnyetzky Most and I arrived to find him sitting behind a pile of my books and manuscripts, which he spent the entire interview arranging and rearranging without interruption. The tall, handsome man with the snow-white hair and the tired but still youthful face came wreathed in vodka fumes across the room towards me and took me in his arms. For a moment he appeared to consider whether he should vouchsafe me the traditional three kisses. Then, evidently deciding that this would after all be more than the occasion called for, he returned to his seat and astonished me by asking whether I would not offer one of my works – of which he claimed to think very highly – for publication in one of the fat literary monthlies. When I tried to tell him that actually that was what I had wanted to see him about he abruptly cut me short, insisting that I should not worry, there was plenty of time, he just wanted to get things straight in principle. Whereupon he dropped the subject, never to return to it again. Ever.

He turned to *his* subject, which was Feuchtwanger and his forthcoming visit. He was aware of the esteem in which Feuchtwanger held my work – come, come, no false modesty – and of the praise he had heaped on my play. Rare for one writer to write with such unreserved appreciation of another. In fact it was the reason for his – Fadeyev's – wanting a few quick words with me. The rest of the interview did indeed proceed at a lively pace. Fadeyev lacked the patience to linger over an idea. He spoke with almost military terseness, never pausing for an answer, and struck each point off a list as he dealt with it: (a) Feuchtwanger is a great democrat; (b) we Communists must associate him more closely with the Popular Front movement; (c) the Soviet Union is surrounded by enemies; (d) vermin must be stamped out (a reference to the trials of Zinoviev, Kamenev, Smirnov, and others, who had already been sentenced and executed, as well as of Pjatakov, Radek, and others shortly to be sentenced); (e) the guilty plead guilty; (f) our public prosecutor is in tip-top form; (g) the West nevertheless refuses to believe us; (h) the West shall believe us and I must have a talk with Feuchtwanger to this effect.

Such, then, was my task. A task I rightly felt I could be proud of. With Fascism growing in strength every day, it was a matter of life or death for the Soviet Union – and that meant for freedom, for mankind. The West had let the chance of world revolution slip; the East must pay the price, and it was paying generously. The diversion by way of socialism in one country might lead to a fresh chance of world revolution, though it was a road – as one saw already – that was not invariably paved with humanity and justice.

Feuchtwanger came, but our talks failed to take the prescribed form. Accepting gifts and hospitality, making public appearances, going shopping, being received by Stalin in person, paying his respects to Lenin's body in the mausoleum, visiting factories – all this took a great deal of time and energy. He was so completely wrapped up in his political gesture of having come to Moscow and bearing witness to Communism – if on the basis of superficial impressions and with the assistance of party hand-outs – that he was virtually incapable of taking an interest in anything else. He was deeply enthusiastic about the Popular Front policy and in order to strengthen the front against Fascism sacrificed the greatest thing a writer can possess: the truth.

Was the sacrifice conscious? Was it a betrayal of self? Did Feuchtwanger fall victim to the same mysterious influence as made the accused in the great show trials lyingly confess their guilt? Did he come under Stalin's hypnotic power of suggestion?

Whatever happened, his talent for reacting to the slightest untruth with a hundred alarm bells proved of no use to him in Moscow. It was something more suited to the peace and quiet of St Tropez (then still quiet and peaceful), that search for truth in accordance with the principles of the writer's craft, principles that enable a man to find the truth through the medium of intense experience and in the absence of preconceived opinions. In Moscow one felt either too strong or too weak to evolve the code of truth from a stance of sensitive and open honesty, to let the true picture of human society emerge from man himself and from the reality of human relationships.

Possibly Feuchtwanger succumbed to the seductions of simplification when he read Bert Brecht's rejoinder to his article about *Have*.

Why is *Have* not a Marxist play? [wrote Brecht] Because a play that describes the greed for property or the spiritual deformations that lie at the origins of property falls short of being Marxist. In the Marxian description of capitalism, as everyone knows, the root of capitalism is not some mysterious and unbridled lust for possession.

I balked at the phrase, 'as everyone knows'. For a writer, as I believe, nothing is known *a priori*. If Balzac or Gorky had written nothing about man and his society but what 'everyone knew' about them, we should be the poorer for their works.

The Marxist, [Brecht went on] is very much less interested in the fact that somewhere some women get hold of a few farms by marrying and then murdering their owners than in the way in which farms the world over are managed and run ...

In the terribly tight corner in which European humanity had fetched up at that time as a result of the unscrupulous japes of my travelling companion the twentieth century, it was easier to accept cut and dried results as binding than to expose oneself anew each time to the risks of experience and its unforeseeable consequences. This was understandable, but it was far from being right. It was even further from being the *only* right course.

The upshot was that the question whether *Have* was or was not a Marxist play remained unresolved. I was surprised to find how little the whole business bothered me. If I remember rightly, Becher suggested that Brecht and I should discuss it openly in *Das Wort*. I was distinctly averse to the idea. The twentieth century was just beginning to show its ghastly face. In the West the war was already under way. I declined to take part in a discussion of dramatic theory.

In any case a literary discussion in Moscow tended to be a pretty perilous affair. In the jargon of the Lux Hotel one heard, 'X or Y is being "hunted".' There was usually no reason such as one could explain. The people who had initiated or were leading the 'hunt' rarely produced a valid justification. They did not have to.

Around that time one of the state publishing houses brought out a book of short stories in German by the sixty-year-old Hungarian writer Andor Gábor. The title was something like

Supper at Hubertus' and the book was an attempt to portray life and death in Nazi Germany – an unsuccessful attempt, I believe, like many others that were made at the time.

Kurt Funk, alias Herbert Wehner, my friend from the Agitprop days in Berlin, now working in the Comintern and doing extremely dangerous anti-Nazi work in Germany and in the semi-legal centres of the underground movement in Paris, Prague, and other places, was then in Moscow clearing up a difference of opinion – potentially just as dangerous – with Walter Ulbricht. Funk was particularly sensitive regarding things German and had a talk with the editor of the *Deutsche Zentralzeitung* about the misleading description of the German environment contained in Gábor's stories. The editor promptly asked for an article and Funk wrote one. The article appeared, was read, and there the matter might well have rested.

Walter Ulbricht, however, was unwilling to let it rest there. He treated Funk's criticism virtually as a police denunciation and instigated disciplinary proceedings against Andor Gábor. The veteran of 1919, not for the first time the butt of similar charges, recognized the danger and went to see Kurt in his room in the Lux, taking Georg Lukács with him. He asked me along too, and I talked to Kurt. Kurt did not believe that his innocent criticisms could endanger the existence of an old Communist in the Soviet Union; in fact he laughed at what he called our 'idée fixe', convinced that it came from our living in such unhealthy seclusion. He did appreciate, however, that there must be a reason for Gábor's fear of this kind of attack, and he managed to get the hunt called off for the time being.

As soon as Kurt had left for a further journey through the German underground (a journey that ended in a Swedish jail), Ulbricht got the file out again and convened a 'literary discussion'. I have a most lively recollection of that 'discussion'. Ulbricht was – and very likely remained – a dab hand at this kind of witch-hunt. He presided – still a young man at the time, fair-haired, without the pointed beard of later years but with a tiny Hitler moustache above his funny little mouth and shapeless chin – and contrived to steer the dialogue in such a way that every mistake or alleged mistake in Gábor's description appeared as a deliberate falsification of dark and sinister intent and every true or what Ulbricht regarded as a true reflection upon the underground struggle came out as a victory of the Party – i.e. of Ulbricht personally – over wilful and malicious falsifiers.

There was of course no lack of testimony from people who supported the charges and even went one better, seeing clear evidence of ill-will on the part of the accused. Walter could always count on that kind of help. Gábor sat silent and sweating, a picture of wretchedness. Everything he said in his defence sounded like a self-accusation. His wife Olga, one of the most industrious translators of Soviet literature, fought for her husband in vehement terms. Ulbricht and his henchmen smiled sarcastically – what did one expect from a man's wife? Georg Lukács spoke up decisively and at length on Gábor's behalf. We should all have been swept along by the force of his dialectics had not friend and foe alike decided long since that, Lukács' expositions being much too difficult to understand, it was wasted effort to listen.

Had Johannes R. Becher taken a stand it would have made all the difference, but he just sat there with a bright-red face, doing his utmost to convey the impression that he regarded himself as the lowest of the low and not taking any part in the proceedings. Bredel behaved as if he was unaware of the danger threatening Gábor and spent the whole time cracking jokes.

As the 'discussion' wore on Ulbricht ceased to devote his entire attention to Gábor alone and began to direct his criticisms at 'the Hungarian writer comrades', which suddenly put all of us in the dock. Eventually he felt the time had come to pop the question whether the damage inflicted by the Hungarian comrades was in fact reparable – a question following which one could already start reckoning with that nocturnal ring at the door-bell. At this point, however, someone entered the room and handed him a note, whereupon a somewhat embarrassed Walter announced a ten-minute break.

The ten minutes passed in gloomy silence, then Wilhelm Pieck strode into the room, took over the chair with a broad, jovial smile on his face, admonished the writers present to get on with their work instead of squabbling among themselves, struck the whole question from the agenda as being of no importance, shook us all by the hand, and closed the meeting. Walter coerced his features into a beam of satisfaction.

What had happened? Eugen Varga, the only People's Commissar of the Hungarian Commune who had gone on to make a solid career in politics – he was secret economic adviser to Stalin and Molotov – had heard about the awkward position Andor Gábor had got himself into and had let Dimitrov know how Comrade Walter was beguiling his time. A note from Dimitrov was enough to turn all intents and purposes into their opposite. Whether Ulbricht even had a new edition of *Supper at Hubertus'* printed I no longer remember.

Every discussion under Ulbricht's chairmanship was a life and death struggle, and one usually had no idea why. One was suddenly confronted by superhuman forces; if one survived one was a lucky exception. Ulbricht himself saw this man-hunt as a 'stamping out of the fifth column' – at least that was what he called it.

I once asked Kurt Funk what he thought of Ulbricht.

'A great *tactician*,' was his answer. And on another occasion: 'A brilliant *practitioner*.'

By which I understood: a poor *strategist* and a bad *politician*. I still understand it that way.

22

The truth about the dacha – *'Yes, yes, yes!'* –
*Why? Why? Why? – The West on trial – Béla's
comeback – The deserted road*

EVERYONE in the West knows that the Russian spends the
summer months at a *dacha*. I fear, however, that people tend to
have a somewhat inflated impression of this summer residence
with the elegant-sounding name.

The point of the *dacha* is that the Moscow summer is as un-
bearably hot as the Moscow winter is cold. The town provides
refuge from the cold, the village from the heat. The villages
around Moscow, however, provided the summer visitor with little
supplementary comfort. The peasants would move out of their
houses into their sheds and stables (in which there were probably no animals left anyway) and Muscovites would move in,
usually at the rate of one family per room. Families not already
populous by nature would be topped up with guests for the
duration. Provisionally the villagers were allowed by law to
make capital out of their houses in this relatively innocent
manner.

The houses rented as *dachas* were built of wood, mostly on
solid stone foundations. The partition walls generally stopped
short of the ceiling, a circumstance that made it easier to heat the
house in winter but in summer meant that one could hear every
word spoken and every sound produced in the furthermost
corners of the overcrowded interior. Yet so refreshing was the
cool air of those pine and birch forests around Moscow that it
was worth spending an hour or two packed like a sardine in the
suburban train just for the pleasure of breathing it at night.

One disadvantage of *dacha* living was that each family had to get its provisions from the city. In the villages – at least in my time this was so – there was nothing edible to be had for love nor money. I was reminded of the bread-barterers I had seen on my way to Engels. An unnatural process – the village getting its victuals from the town. One member of each family thus had to go into Moscow at least twice or even three times a week, queue for hours outside and inside shops, fill a couple of shopping bags with bread, meat, fish, tomatoes, sauerkraut, onions, melons, etc. – all products of the village but only obtainable in this roundabout way through the state-owned shops in the town – and carry them, the contents oozing odorously through their scanty wrappings, back out into the country. Milk one could get in the village – if one knew a family that had a cow and stinted its children. Very occasionally, and at enormous expense, one could get a few unripe cherries.

Water one fetched in buckets from the village fountain. Bathrooms were unknown, and the privy stood at the greatest possible distance from the house. One took one's own paraffin stove to cook on. In fact the *dachas* were never adequately furnished and one had to hire a lorry to take some of the furniture from one's flat. The hiring of the lorry was always a tremendously shady deal.

The first *dacha* we ever rented was in the village of Bolshevo and we shared it with my journalist friend Rudolf Haus (of the guardian angel theory) and his wife Hilde. That is to say we rented one and a half rooms each, with their little boy and our Anderli sleeping in one room between us.

The day after we returned to Moscow in the autumn Rudolf and Hilde were arrested by the NKVD. And their 'guardian angel', remember – Radek – only just got away with his life in the Moscow trials.

At the beginning we still tried to find reasons and connections, but as the arrests went on we gradually got used to the fact that it could happen to anybody. Even to people who had only just escaped the clutches of the Fascists, for the appalling, scarcely credible fact of the matter was that the NKVD had even been known to hand over German anti-Fascist militants to the Gestapo. Any one of us could disappear at any time, never to be seen again. It was simply beyond one's powers to grasp the full extent of that terrible man-trap and of the weird, unreal danger that hung over everyone's head without the least logical connection with his activities, character, convictions, and views, whatever form they might take. One began to live in a curious kind of fog. There was no moral context any more; there was only this endless, shapeless waiting for nothing – and in such a state of apathy that one could not even tremble.

In the final lines of the book he wrote to bear witness to Communism – Moscow trials included – Feuchtwanger wrote:

It does one good after all the half-heartedness of the West to see an undertaking to which one can say from the bottom of one's heart yes, yes, yes! To keep such a yes to myself seemed improper, and that is my reason for having written this book.

So much for the massive political and psychological arguments I had worked out at Fadeyev's bidding in order to convince Feuchtwanger, despite all contradictions, of the necessity for the Moscow trials. He arrived in Moscow more convinced than I was myself and glided with surprising ease over every absurdity. A slice of lemon that a defendant tossed in his glass of tea during the hearing was for Feuchtwanger proof enough. Judges that had the accused served with hot tea could as far as he was concerned do no wrong, no matter which way their verdicts might fall.

Brecht virtually outlined an entire Brechtian drama in order to justify the sentences passed in the Moscow trials:

It is necessary to bring to light behind the deeds of the accused a political concept that can credibly be attributed to them and that has led them into the swamps of common criminality . . . The wrong political concept has led them deep into isolation and deep into common criminality . . . I am convinced that this is the truth, and I am convinced that it will inevitably be seen to be the truth, even in Western Europe, even by hostile readers . . .

Summing up his ideas, Brecht wrote:

The trials have also . . . proved unambiguously the existence of active conspiracies against the régime and the fact that those nests of conspirators have carried out acts of sabotage within the country as well as entering into dealings with Fascist diplomats . . .

One could reel off a whole list of equally reputable names of men who were no less mistaken than Feuchtwanger and Brecht.

It was in such terms that the West delivered up us anti-Fascist refugees in the Soviet Union physically and morally to the never-ending massacre. The Austrian Communist Ernst Fischer mentions in his *Memories and Reflections* – without pretending to completeness and without sparing himself either – a number of other names: Romain Rolland, Henri Barbusse, Louis Aragon, Ernst Bloch, George Bernard Shaw . . .

Sometimes one rebelled against a state of affairs in which one was deprived of the use of one of the faculties of which one was most proud – the faculty of thought. One's rebellion consisted in playing a desperate jigsaw puzzle with invented logical connections and trying to work out cause and effect even where nothing of the kind was present.

When the German writer Ernst Ottwald was arrested in Moscow in 1936, never to be seen again, I was inclined to think it was an accident. I knew him and liked him better than many of our other colleagues; I found it impossible to see in him the spy and traitor that one sought to see in the countless strangers of whose arrest one heard. He was the first of our circle to be arrested, I wanted to know why, and I began asking around.

Ottwald was the author of a story that described in an extremely true-to-life manner the craft and psychology of the professional informer. Up to now the story had been taken simply as proof of his literary talent. Suddenly, however, someone asked how he came to know so much about it. Surely he could only have learnt it at first hand? Did it not suggest an extraordinary degree of selectivity on the part of the Soviet police that they should want to take a closer look at the very man who had studied the technique of the informer? (That he would die in a labour camp was as little foreseeable at that time as the fact that his wife was shortly going to be handed over to the German Fascist police.)

If I told myself that here a completely innocent person had been carried off and subsequently killed I must also concede that hitherto nothing but the merest chance had saved me from a similarly meaningless death. Would chance be as merciful the next time? Or would I one day simply disappear from the surface of the earth for no apparent reason? No – it was better to live with logic, however threadbare.

One day the Hungarian writer Sándor Barta, president of the International Writers' Union, was hauled off from his flat by the NKVD. From that moment on Comrade Apletin simply forgot that he had ever worked in the next-door office to a man called Barta. When Martin Andersen-Nexö arrived on his next visit to Moscow and inquired after Barta, Apletin ignored his inquiries (or rather persistently assumed he meant Barto, a well-known Russian authoress specializing in children's books) for as long as it took the old man to twig the truth without its being spelt out for him.

The awful thing was that as time went on one began to find such incidents funny. One related them to one's friends as macabre anecdotes. And that too provided a certain protection against panic and despair.

Barta, incidentally, died very soon in prison of his old heart complaint. His daughter, then a delightful child, later a bad actress, was consoled some fifteen years later with the post of manager of a Budapest theatre.

Of Alex Granach's arrest by the NKVD in Kiev I learnt only when he was already at liberty again. He rang me unexpectedly from Moscow's White Russia station. Would I come and see him off – he was leaving the country by the next train. I found him pale, thin, and with his magnificent, taurine head of black hair threaded with silver shorn as bald as an egg. The picture he presented was so eloquent that there remained little to ask.

'Where are you off to?'

'Hollywood.'

'How come they let you out?'

His speech was slightly disorganized, punctuated with brief, stifled expressions of anger against some corporal or other – evidently the person who had interrogated him. One almost had the impression that he had found the lowly rank of the man who had tortured him both physically and mentally more humiliating than the torture itself.

'Your Feuchtwanger got me out. A letter he'd written me . . .

from France . . . Because we hadn't been able to say good-bye
while he was here . . .'

The corporal had found the letter in Alex's pocket.

'First he . . . for corresponding abroad . . .' Alex's lips balked
at the words 'beat me'. Instead he repeated three times, '. . . that
corporal . . .' Suddenly he laughed out loud. 'Finally it occurred
to them that a man who got letters from a man who was that far
in with Stalin might look awkward beaten to death.'

Sadly he passed a hand over his shaven pate.

'It'll grow again,' I said.

'I'm not waiting that long.'

'What are you going to do?' I asked, attempting a smile. 'Hit
back?'

But he was in earnest. 'So I am, God willing!'

And soon he did. In his way. In Hollywood they were casting
the Greta Garbo film that later became so famous, *Ninotchka*.
Alex played a Russian official – played him the way he had
personally got to know him.

That was how Alex hit back. A grimace against armies? Well,
it's a weapon that is often underrated. It is not without its
effectiveness.

About Béla Kun I hardly heard a good word spoken the whole
time I was in Moscow. One might have expected that the Hungarian
emigrants, if only to enhance their own importance, would have
represented the hero and leader of their youth with a halo – a
slightly tarnished one, if you like, but still going back to the good
old days.

Not a bit of it. In an environment in which people tended to be
careful what they said my fellow Hungarians behaved with
almost masochistic recklessness when it came to the reputation of
a man with whom, when all was said and done, their own honour
was to a great extent bound up as well. They told the most
slanderous stories about him without batting an eyelid. He was
supposed to have betrayed, cheated, and materially harmed his
best friends; he was said to have sent comrades back to Horthy's
Hungary to do underground work and to have made such inadequate preparations for them beforehand that many – oddly

217

enough the very ones he did not particularly like – got caught by
the Hungarian police.

I would gladly have turned a deaf ear to such talk. I had had
occasion to call on Béla Kun several times during my first autumn
in Moscow. An elderly little man with a face like a frog's, shrewd
eyes, a mind as quick as lightning, an astonishing breadth of
learning, and a ready wit – if in a rather Budapest coffee-house
style, always with a touch of cynicism or a generous dose of
gallows humour – it was hard to see what he had in common with
the Béla Kun they told the stories about. I asked Andor Gábor
one day how seriously they should be taken. Gábor, whom I
believed and had reason to believe, answered, 'Take it all in and
don't say too much.' That was in fact the day someone whispered
in my ear that Béla Kun maintained a secret alliance with
Horthy's police chief Schweinitzer.

It was a theme on which my countrymen positively harped.
They got themselves all worked up, and no sooner had they
calmed down again than they would begin to work themselves
up anew. Then, suddenly, they switched to stories in which the
subject appeared in the light of an amusing companion without
whom life would not be worth living.

They were old or elderly men, all the life burnt out of them,
living in straitened circumstances, shabbily dressed, tortured with
homesickness. One among many with whom I came into contact
was Dezsö Bokányi, the former president of the Hungarian Soviet
Republic, to whom I was introduced without any ceremony in
the street outside Yelisseyev's. Within minutes he had a firm grip
on the top button of my coat to prevent his new audience from
taking flight. This precaution observed, he launched into a series
of the most compromising stories not only about Kun but also
about a number of other comrades, most of whom I did not even
know. With his drooping moustache and his worn-out leather
overcoat, which reached down to his ankles and was an obvious
source of pride, he looked like an old night-watchman.

One had the impression that the one-time great men of the
political emigration hated one another's guts. They clung to the
Soviet Union with quaking hearts as constituting henceforth their
sole source of contact with life, with humanity. Yet they felt at

the same time that the Soviet Union had shamefully betrayed
them and robbed them of their former greatness. So they hated
their new homeland no less bitterly than they had hated their old.

They had nothing of any consequence to do but they made as
if they had. They practised assiduously something they referred
to as politics, plotted one another's downfall, and generally
pranced and capered and whinnied like superannuated parade
horses at the knacker's gates.

Those of them who were trained soldiers were sent to Spain in
1936, where many fell in the field. Were they among the number
of those who fell in Spain of bullets fired in Moscow? In the
Kremlin? In the Lubyanka? I do not know.

Béla Kun, once a great power in the Comintern, where his
word had been law not only for Hungarian Communists but for
Communists of other countries as well, became all of a sudden
virtually superfluous when Dimitrov decided he could dispense
with his services. Did he perhaps sense then that his part – that
of the undisputed leader of all Hungarian Communists – had
already been earmarked by the great puppeteer for another
marionette and that he, Kun, was due to be dispatched within
a matter of months to make way for that other? The other's name
was Mátyás Rákosi, then sitting in one of Horthy's jails in Hungary. (Rákosi was swopped in 1940 for the historic flags that the
Russians had captured in Hungary in 1849.)

Béla Kun was arrested in 1936 and died shortly afterwards.
Not on account of the misdeeds that his countrymen retailed with
such heat. Nor for having lost the one major battle of the world
revolution in Central Europe – apart from the Bavarian experiment – namely the Hungarian Commune of 1919. No – he died
because an improvisation in the great puppet play just happened
to fall out that way.

His personal importance was underlined on the occasion of his
arrest by the fact that all the members of his family as well as
numbers of friends, enemies, and colleagues were rounded up as
well.

Many years after the Second World War, many years after
Stalin's death, indeed at a time when Mátyás Rákosi's bloody

career was already behind him, Béla Kun was posthumously rehabilitated in Hungary. No one could quite see what had happened to justify this retrospective vindication of the honour of the great man of 1919. At any rate the history of Hungary was hastily rewritten and to a lesser extent certain adjustments were made to world history as well. And unquestionably the corporeal remains of someone or other were handed over by Russia and ceremonially interred.

The historical and moral revaluation involved certainly came in handy for the family. Kun's widow moved to Budapest where she now draws a not excessively high Party pension. His daughter and son-in-law had to make themselves useful in the rehabilitation process – a not uncommon feature of the history of the various 'thaws'. Both now pass as Hungarian writers and belong to that body whose task it is to ensure that literature remains perpetually subject to the currently obtaining Party ideology. I hear they are rigorous in the performance of their duties.

So a new image of Béla Kun is being built up that is very far from identical with the image he once enjoyed. And if work on that image proceeds but haltingly it is because the Hungarian man in the street is sufficiently worried about the present and the future to have little energy left over for the amendment of the past.

In the summer of 1937 Anderli was running around in a cap Micky had sewn for her after the pattern of the uniform kepis worn by the Spanish Republicans and hailing one and all with cries of '*Salud!*'

Again we could not afford a whole *dacha* to ourselves and so shared one with Lena, a young teacher who gave a Russian course for foreign writers at the Writers' Union. She was a plump, healthy, appetizing *comsomolka* with a little boy of Anderli's age. The head of the family, a surly and permanently tipsy mathematics student, visited his wife and child only seldom, and on such occasions the couple rowed loud, long, and most indiscreetly.

Rather late in the day I became aware that the young woman took a more than polite interest in myself.

The deserted road

One afternoon – Micky had gone shopping in Moscow and Lena had put the two children to bed so that we did not have to keep the usual unrelenting eye on them in case they slipped into the owner's vegetable garden and pulled up his half-grown onions for immediate, on-the-spot consumption, complete with such earth as remained attached to them (thereby causing themselves to stink to high heaven but winning in the process a fresh victory in their constant, unconscious battle against vitamin deficiency) – I stuck an exercise book into my pocket and prepared to set out for my daily walk.

'Today I'm coming with you, Julij,' Lena abruptly announced.

She could load even the shortest sentence with undertones that robbed a man (a weak enough man, God knows) of all desire to go walking in the forest with another woman when the mother of his child was struggling with shopping bags that weighed almost more than she did herself.

'Lena, I work on my walks.'

'I'll be very quiet, Julij. Very quiet and very, very good.'

In some irritation I set out, with Lena, very quiet indeed, following behind.

Suddenly she stopped in her tracks. 'I'm not going any farther.'

'That's all right, Lena.'

In a surprisingly anxious tone of voice she inquired how far I usually went in this direction. I told her about the magnificent new road towards Moshaisk that bisected the forest not very much farther on and that was the usual target of my walks.

'I always enjoy the sight of that road. There's something so mysterious about it . . . something almost sinister . . . I've never seen a single car on it . . . not even a pedestrian . . . It's like a road on Mars, never frequented by a living soul . . . Maybe I'll write about it one day.'

She came a step closer, cast a worried look about her, uttered in a hushed whisper the one word, 'Dangerous!', and turned on her heel and ran. Early next morning, before we were up, she and her small son left the house.

Three days later the husband appeared. Without a word of greeting, without so much as a glance in our direction, he started packing her things together and toting them to the station.

Before he left the yard of our shared *dacha* for the last time he suddenly turned to me, took a few steps in my direction, and, still without looking at me, began addressing an imaginary person standing slightly to one side of me in the following passionate and not always comprehensible terms.

'Bloody fool! I suppose you think the new Moshaisk highway was built for you, do you? Don't you get it? Really? Who could it be for, then? Huh?' After a few further sentences that made no sense to me he almost threateningly closed the distance between us. 'Right you are! It's for *him*. For *him* and no one else.' I no longer remember whether he pronounced Stalin's name or whether I understood without his having to. 'Here's the Kremlin,' he went on with vague sweeps of his arms, 'and here's his *dacha*. Between them, backwards and forwards, hither and thither – him, no one but him.'

It was hard to tell whether his words concealed rebellion or a certain pride in the fact that this '*him*' and this '*no one but him*' were when all was said and done *his* and not some foreign immigrant's.

'And one day someone's going to get sick of you and your daily stroll!'

With these words he turned his back on me, swung the suitcase up on to his shoulder, grasped the trunk by the piece of frayed string that held it together, and left the *dacha* with two weeks' rent still to run.

'Dangerous . . .'

I forget whether I thought of Lena's warning in the days that followed but I do remember that I changed my walking habits and began to avoid the forest path that led to the Moshaisk highway.

The magnificent road I had used to visit so often and with such pleasure really had been built for one person and one alone – Stalin. To the European mind the idea was scarcely conceivable. Along it he was driven from the Kremlin to his *dacha* and from his *dacha* to the Kremlin. If in fact he did so travel. That no one knew, for it was forbidden to *see* him drive past. It was forbidden even to know that he was in the habit of driving past – there or anywhere else. It was forbidden to mention the fact. It was virtually forbidden to let it enter one's head. Stalin's fear of an attempt on his life (which never in fact occurred) had grown to be an end in itself, a permanent threat to the populace.

Surrounded by the magic circle of this self-generating secrecy, the highway was guarded by a small army of police both uniformed and otherwise. A foreigner failed to see them. A native knew – felt in his bones – when he was in their vicinity. A person caught inside the restricted area – supposing anyone was fool enough to let his steps lead him thither – immediately found himself outside the law. What was it saved me from just such a fate? No – it was no good. What was the use of trying to find reasons? Logic got one nowhere. Nothing did happen to me, and one gave up wondering why . . .

I have felt myself in danger several times since then. I have sat in a prison cell in danger of the death sentence. But I believe the most dangerous moments in my entire life have been moments spent in idyllic innocence walking through a beautiful forest of birches and pines.

23

Spaniards in Moscow – 22 June 1941 – Of silence, and of saying good-bye

IN the Kusnyetzky Most there was a shop that sold nothing. Such a state of affairs would not in itself have been remarkable, for the supply of goods proceeded in a generally intermittent fashion punctuated by long intervals during which nothing was delivered at all. In this shop, however, which was situated in one of the busiest streets in the capital, no one had ever seen anything being sold.

One day a Red Army lorry pulled up in front of it and unloaded, and two sales-ladies began doing business. There was only a single commodity for sale – a map of Spain.

Whereupon every inhabitant of Moscow understood that the Civil War in Spain was *our* war. Would it perhaps make up to some extent for the world revolution that had failed to materialize?

New perspectives had been opened up. A people had elected in a legal and constitutional manner – per the Popular Front – a government with a revolutionary platform. It had subsequently emerged that for by far the larger part of the civilized world neither the law, nor the constitution, nor the democratic majority was sacred. If the interests of power run counter to the legal government, the constitution becomes rebellion and those who infringe it the guardians of order.

Once a Spanish delegation came to Moscow at the invitation of the Writers' Union – not the first group to have done so. The delegates were received with due ceremony and among other things a meeting was arranged in one of the Union's larger halls.

On the podium – beside the representatives of the host organization – sat the Spaniards. They were welcomed with great displays of affection, but then the Civil War was already in its second or third year. The hall was two-thirds filled with Writers' Union employees, the rest of the audience consisting of Soviet writers, with not more than two or three internationally known names among them. The Russian speeches were roughly translated into Spanish and the Spanish speeches rendered with similar informality into Russian. All the speeches were too long and they all said precisely the same thing. Every time a speaker mentioned Stalin's name we all applauded – at first simply, then rhythmically, then chanting the name in the same rhythm, and finally rising to our feet and, spurred on by the crash of our seats as they slammed back, applauding and shouting with redoubled vigour and volume.

And then the miracle happened. The awful, uncanny miracle. One of the Spaniards, a young officer in the uniform of the Republican army, his chest bristling with decorations, did not stand up. As our tumultuous cries of 'Stalin! Stalin!' rang all about him he just sat there as if none of it concerned him one whit.

The first time everyone tactfully ignored him. But soon the next ovation swept the hall, just like the first except that it was even louder, and still he remained seated. The Russians on the podium stared before them into space with rigid smiles and carried on applauding. One or two of the Spaniards leant over and spoke to their comrade, who merely shook his head and remained as he was. The better known writers slipped unobtrusively from the room. Eventually one of the Lit-Fund secretaries, a middle-aged woman of maternal proportions, lost her nerve. Under her breath, so that only those in her immediate vicinity heard her, she whimpered, 'Don't let him do it! Tell him he can't do such a thing! So young . . . so handsome . . . Oh, save him! Somebody save him!'

Disturbing, indeed tormenting thoughts haunted J.H. 38 – and doubtless others too – that evening. As he made his solitary way homeward through the snow-covered streets of Moscow he tried, in wordless, hesitant reflections that were never pushed to their conclusion, to make sense of the incident of which he had just been a witness.

Had we not heard and answered Spain's cry for help more than two years before? Involved in a revolutionary struggle, the Spanish people had counted on the help of the proletarians of all lands and had not been disappointed. In dozens, in hundreds, but also singly and hand in hand in couples, militants from all countries had poured in to fight for Spain's threatened freedom. The Soviet Union too had heard the call and come to the assistance of the young republic, sending tanks and ships and planes and well-drilled, well-armed soldiers.

So far all seemed clear.

The opposing side in the Spanish Civil War was getting outside support as well. Two powers, Communism and Fascism, were fighting it out over the heads of the suffering populace. At the time I am talking of the fortunes of war were not on our side. Nothing decisive had as yet occurred, however, and the republic and its helpers were battling hopefully on. And whenever they won a victory they shouted, 'Stalin!' And whenever fresh supplies arrived they cheered, 'Stalin!'

Or did they? That was the question that plagued J.H. 38 that evening.

In Hungary, many years later, I saw and understood. Whenever the Soviet Union lent a helping hand it also lent a carefully prepared, thoroughly organized, fully operative control apparatus that promptly filled the space allotted to it. From the ideological adviser to the training officer and from the engineer to the executioner, every member of that apparatus had his job and his routine. Added to which there was the fact that the apparatus was constantly engaged in internal battles of its own. It was a mass of latent tensions, divergent aims, and clandestine struggles for power.

Did the Spanish Republican really fall in *his* war? Did he die at Manzanares in a battle of his own or as the doomed plaything of a machine gone berserk and given to lashing out at anything and everything, including itself?

How fine, how heroic it all was in Spain at first! It might have become a new beginning. But who among the men who governed the Soviet Union was looking for a new beginning? Old accounts remained unsettled. Unsettled and inextricably confused . . . The mockery of settling them dragged on and on and on . . .

And meanwhile the Spanish gold mine fell into enemy hands.

The feeling of complete lack of freedom struck at one's sense of human dignity. The naturalness with which one had once regarded so many things – one's life, for example – as one's own became a thing of the past. Everything one had one came to see in terms of a gracious gift – including the permission to survive that day and possibly the next as well.

Socialism – so we had been told in Party classes – gives us a share of the social product in proportion to our contribution to the process of production. *That is why socialism is so just.* Communism – a higher stage of development – is no longer concerned with a man's contribution to the process of production but gives to each according to his needs. *That is why Communism is so human.*

We were not, however, to take offence at the fact that, in the socialist society that we were assured henceforth existed (at least in rudimentary form) in *one* country, we were furnished with rights – including the right to remain alive – and commodities neither according to our productiveness nor according to our needs but according to the fickle moods of an impersonal force known as 'the Party'.

The current personification of that impersonal force was Josef Stalin. The name was but a detail, if a not unimportant one. Stalin's personal existence did nothing to abolish the impersonality, which remained as much in evidence as before. Who knew anything personal about him, anyway? He was the diagrammatic representation of an abstract concept. Only the fact that he subsequently died proved in retrospect that he had been neither god nor machine. (The impersonality and all that went with it, including total irresponsibility and inconsequentiality of action, were not individual properties. They were of the essence of the social order. When one of Stalin's successors, Nikita S. Khrushchev, tried to be a little more personal he foundered – and others with him – in the attempt. After him there was a return to systematic impersonality.)

With whom should one argue? Whom implore? Whose name abominate and curse? The system of impersonal repression wore one out, exhausted one's moral reserves, ushered in despair, and undermined one's powers of thought. One sank into a stupor. One learnt to be a vegetable. The human values one bore within one went into decline.

It was not easy to live like that. But that is how we lived.

Even in Peredelkino.

Peredelkino! A village not far from Moscow. The summer residence of Soviet literature.

I had managed for the last two years to rent a very nice *dacha* room there each summer. Anderli was able to attend the Lit-Fund's kindergarten in the village. At last we had reached the point where we might have begun to feel at home. But then came 22 June 1941, and once again my barbarous travelling companion the twentieth century was riding roughshod over my life. Just as it had done in 1914, only now I knew a bit more about it. More than I had then, that is – still not enough.

War!

It was early of a Moscow morning and I was already up and about. At the radio building I bumped into Rákosi and Pieck, both still very much at a loss. It later transpired that during those first few days of the war Stalin could not be found – and the system was not so organized that anything of importance could be said or done without him. Someone sent me to the Central Committee, where the old Bolshevik Losovsky sent me on to an annex of the People's Commissariat for Defence. There I met a man who had already begun the work that he was to pursue throughout the war years – Ilya Ehrenburg. Pipe in mouth, motionless, sunk in himself, he sat listening through earphones to the Germans' rabble-rousing broadcasts and answering them on his typewriter without a moment's hesitation. He has been accused of having simply turned the tables and answered racial incitement with racial incitement, and it may be true – but who was there to give him a better suggestion?

The charming and lovely village of Peredelkino was almost a torture to me during that time. Every *dacha* was a reminder of failure – of a conversation that had failed to take place. I had some good friends there, real friends, but the friendships were of a strange, uneasy, silent kind. And I failed ever to break that silence, a failure that can never be made good.

Corney Chukhovsky, author of delightful children's verse, a giant of a man with snow-white hair, was my companion on long walks through the neighbouring forests. We were alone on those walks, yet even so we preferred to spend hours saying nothing, with the forest echoing our silence. We sat round the old-fashioned samovar as Russian families do – and said nothing. The silence was disguised by small-talk, but it was still silence. Lydia, the poet's daughter – no longer young, and looking her age – liked to take charge of Anderli and tell her stories from her father's and other writers' works. Was she a widow? Divorced? Had she never married? I had no idea. Not until three decades later did one learn that Lydia, whom no one took for a writer, had at that time been working in secret on a wonderful novel, the novel of a mother whose twenty-year-old son was among the numberless, nameless deportees – her own novel. For thirty years the manuscript remained hidden, even surviving the siege of Leningrad, before it reached the West by a romantic route and became a successful book.*

What did I know of these people – my friends?

As long as I had a radio I listened diligently, and when I heard something interesting I used to relay it to the neighbours. A charming recipient of briefly digested news items was the poetess Vera Imber. One afternoon in 1940 I arrived to find she had a woman guest with her, the translator Asya Aryan. I almost left without having passed on the news, but when the two ladies asked me about it I remembered.

'Yes – Trotsky has been murdered.'

For me Trotsky was little more than an abstract figure. At the time of his struggle with and defeat by Stalin I had not been taking any great interest in politics; there had been events in my

* Lydia Chukhovskaia, *The Deserted House* (Barrie and Rockliff, London, 1967).

immediate surroundings that were of closer and more concrete concern to me. Vera Imber, however, went very pale, rose to her feet, and left the room. A few minutes later she came back – calm, apparently recovered, but with a smile that was to remain with me for a long time to come. In her absence Mrs Aryan had told me something that everyone in Peredelkino knew but none ever mentioned: Trotsky and Vera Imber had been closely related and in their younger years intimate friends. Such a relationship, such a friendship could at that time have cost one one's life. What for me was a thing of the distant past was for everyone here the painful semi-present.

'Should I say something to her?' I asked Mrs Aryan in my embarrassment while Vera Imber was still out of the room.

'No, say nothing . . . say nothing . . .'

Boris Pasternak, with his silver-grey hair and swarthy complexion, was among the *dacha* dwellers I visited most frequently. It wanted so little – as I thought – of a true friendship between us. Yet that 'little' was a leap over an abyss. Who dared make such a leap?

He was fond of caricaturing himself not only in words but in drawings too. 'I look like an Arab and his horse,' he used to say, sketching in his large, protruding teeth. I was inclined to believe that he was an exception – that he knew nothing of the great silence. But looking back on it now it seems to me that the characters of his *Doctor Zhivago* were already at that time stirring in his brain. Did he gloss over the most important thing in silence? As far as I am concerned he did.

I hoped to find the Slavins still in Peredelkino. Lev Issaevich and his wife were of all the Soviet writers there my best friends. The silence that stood in the way of so many friendships was in our case on the verge of being broken. On the verge.

That morning I bumped into them both by accident. They were standing on the platform with a group of five or six others including a young couple I knew – Ilya Ehrenburg's daughter Irina and her husband Boris Lyapin, a prominent young journalist.

Of silence, and of saying good-bye

They stood in silence. Boris, like countless others on that day, had been mobilized, and they had brought him to the station. The platform was dotted with similar groups gathered about one or more soldiers going to join their units. All were silent. This, though, was a different kind of silence. The silence of the doomed.

Experience had seasoned these people. Wars, revolutions, civil wars and historical disasters had taught them to say their good-byes in silence. In silence – and for good.

A few days after that mute farewell on the platform Boris fell near Kharkov.

24

Will Moscow burn? – A non-existent train –
Evacuation of rolling-stock – Anastas brings
the potty

LIFE in Peredelkino became rapidly meaningless as the Red
Army filled the surrounding forests with anti-aircraft defences
and it became more and more difficult to find a path still open to
stroll along. In any case rehearsals of my play *The Encounter*
were due to begin in Moscow (it was not one of my favourite
plays but at least it was a start and we were very happy about it),
so we packed as many of our things together as we could carry
and moved back to the city. Halfway to the station we heard and
saw a prodigious flight of Soviet bombers fly over our heads in
strict formation, heading west with a hellish thundering.

Our child had long been out of harm's way. The Writers'
Union had set up a children's home at Chistopol on the Kama
(a tributary of the Volga) and the sons and daughters of writers
had been duly evacuated during the first days of the war.

Moscow presented an unusual picture. A quiet, unobtrusive
flight from the capital had begun some days before. Probably the
authorities had instructions not to interfere. Whole streets were
deserted; others teemed with people. Handcarts, prams loaded
with trunks, bundles, mattresses, and terrified children filled the
pavements and spilled into the road. Huge grey barrage balloons
floated in the sky – as if we were scurrying about on the sea-bed
beneath the bellies of so many giant whales. Houses and streets
in bird's eye view were being painted on the large open squares
in the neighbourhood of the Kremlin to confuse enemy pilots.
Many windowpanes already sported strips of glued paper, and
everywhere people could be seen hurrying home with rolls of

dark paper under their arms. And I had no choice but to hear that sound I would so gladly have been deaf to – the deep, muffled boom of heavy artillery that leaves the very air trembling after its passage.

(Overheard on a No. 11 trolley bus outside the Univermag department store: 'Why don't you drive off?' 'To Khimki? You must be mad, man – the Germans are there already.')

A man I did not know stopped me at the door of the theatre.

'I've come to see Comrade Bersenyev,' I told him.

'Not here.'

'The producer . . .'

'Gone away.'

'The secretary . . .'

'Likewise.'

'Look, I'm the author of this play . . .'

'What play?'

The accountant came running up. He brushed the other man impatiently aside, thrust a bundle of bank-notes into my hand, and got me to sign a chit. 'Second advance. I needn't explain, I take it? The company will if possible stay together. We're travelling en bloc to the Armenian Soviet Republic. Pity – it would have been a smashing part for Comrade Bersenyev . . .'

The next chapter of my life began with a telephone call from a secretary at the Lit-Fund. The train that was to take the comrade writers east, she told me, would be leaving Kazan station in Comsomol Square tomorrow morning at eight. She hung up before I had time to ask her what train she was talking about. I tried ringing the Lit-Fund back but could not get through. I thought of ringing a few colleagues.

From six out of seven numbers I got no answer at all. With the seventh I got someone's grandma who, without waiting for my question, proceeded without further ado to inform me that Moscow would be burnt to the ground the way it had been in 1812. This was nothing to worry about, she went on. Hitler would lose this war as surely as Napoleon had lost his. Whereupon the old girl burst into sobbing tears.

The first people I saw in the ticket hall of Kazan station were

Georg and Gertrud Lukács, sitting perched on their luggage along with a number of other writers who for one reason or another had fetched up in the rearguard. One I remember particularly was the Italian writer Germanetto, complete with wife, baby, and the baby's bath-tub. Germanetto turned out to be a useful companion. He was a barber by trade, had his instruments with him, and kept our manes as far as possible in trim.

I was astonished at the way the ticket hall, chock-a-block when we arrived, proved capable of accommodating more and more people all the time. The gaps between individual groups, families, and eventually bodies became steadily narrower. Noon struck – many people drew wisely-prepared sandwiches from their pockets, and the Germanetto baby was suckled for the nth time – and still no one appeared who might have told us where the train was supposed to be taking us, let alone where the train itself might be.

Bredel's boy tried to bore his way through the almost inconceivably dense mass of people and force an entry into the first overcrowded train he found. It took him a long time but he eventually made it to the middle of the corridor. From there, however, he was gradually pushed towards the other end until finally he was hurled out of the carriage door on to the platform again. Luckily for him his bundle was tossed out after him; otherwise he would have had to leave it in the train. Picking himself up, the poor lad discovered that the experience had cost him every one of the buttons of his winter coat – a substantial loss on the eve of winter at a time when there was not a button to be had in the shops.

Towards evening fresh crowds pushed their way in from the square with a fresh crop of false rumours. Those of us who had been waiting since the early morning found ourselves being shoved further in the direction of the platforms.

It was at that moment that Fadeyev made his appearance.

This was my first sight of the secretary of the Writers' Union in the uniform of a general. With his tall, slender, well-proportioned figure, virile beauty, and unshakable calm he moved among us like some kind of higher being as we squatted on our luggage and looked for help. He talked to one or two writers

234

only, his throaty voice clipped and military. He collected the complaints that – as usually happens in the presence of superiors – had become insignificant and negligible even as the complainants uttered them. He took no notes but shook large numbers of hands. Once or twice he even smiled. Then he vanished as mysteriously as he had arrived. The train he had promised us simply did not exist.

It was late afternoon and the darkening ticket hall was filled with a mysterious, pale-blue haze. Suddenly we heard a terrific hubbub from the direction of the entrance. There were cries of pain, and then a distant murmuring that sounded as if it were coming closer. Finally we heard shots, and after that all was still again.

A throng of passers-by with haggard faces surged through the street doors into the hall.

'What's up?'

'Pogrom . . !'

'Who against?'

Three voices replied simultaneously:

'Against the Jews.'

'Against the Communists.'

'Against foreigners.'

The shouting, the rumpus, and the shots were repeated a number of times. Things could have taken a catastrophic turn at any moment. In the hall a woman's voice cried out shrilly. We were a hair's breadth from panic, I reflected, myself barely able to control my anxiety. But no panic broke out. And as far as I know there was never a real pogrom anywhere.

I knew a man, a German; his name was Bernhard, and he was a writer and critic. Once upon a time he was living with a Latvian girl named Anna. Latvians are good interpreters and Anna helped me out several times in 1935. Not long after that she was arrested, and we never saw her again. There was a mass campaign on at the time against the Communist emigrants from Latvia living in Moscow; they were deported virtually to a man, no one knew why. Bernhard was now alone, and began to feel very lonely.

This man suddenly appeared among us foreign writers gathered in the ticket hall of Kazan station. He sat down on his bundle, holding a small and extremely battered vulcanized-fibre suitcase between his knees, and it was clear that he wanted to talk to us.

'Where are you off to?' he inquired, opening the conversation.

'We don't know ourselves yet.'

'Then you're lucky.'

And he showed us his identity card. It bore a rubber-stamped entry to the effect that his one and only authorized place of residence from now on was the town of Karaganda in the Kazakh Soviet Republic. I too could not travel where I would and at my own discretion. When someone finally decided to assign me a destination, there would be no buts about it. Lord over my journey and my destination was the professional body to which I belonged – the Writers' Union. Bernhard's marching orders had been issued by the NKVD. He was being banished, but even I was not free. Yet a greater freedom than mine was more than the average Soviet citizen ever enjoyed.

For hours Micky had been plagued with headaches. Lukács was stretched out across his luggage, fast asleep. Gertrud, almost nodding off herself, watched over his sleep. All around us people were dozing with their eyes open, the Germanettos were changing their baby's nappy, others were drinking tea out of battered thermos flasks.

A loudspeaker that had already asked representatives of a variety of organizations to report somewhere or other suddenly asked for the representative of the Comintern. Did that mean the Comintern, that all-powerful body, was somewhere in this chaos too? Like a flash I saw that here was our one chance of survival. Somehow I must winkle out the fellows from the Comintern.

It took me an hour and a half of rushing upstairs and down, in through doors and out through others, a prey to a growing panic that I should never find my way back again, before I located, at the far end of a train that had clearly been assembled on the principle of random selection, a carriage that some dim figure informed me out of the pitchy dark had been coupled for the benefit of certain Comintern comrades. Vaguely hopeful and completely out of breath, I sank down on the running-board.

I became aware after a while of an unmistakably familiar voice in my immediate vicinity. A bald pate of noble proportions bore its almost phosphorescent gleam through the darkness towards me – Mátyás Rákosi, accompanied by Comintern people of various nationalities, hatless and carrying no further luggage than a briefcase. It was with neither pleasure nor promptitude that he gave permission for a small number of Hungarian writers to travel with him in the Comintern carriage. (I omitted to tell him about the Germans and Italians, with whose presence he reproached me the next morning.)

Seven hours later the train started off. One barely had the strength left to ask where it was going. It appeared – if it fell short of certainty – that the train was bound for Kuybyshev, the town that had that night been proclaimed provisional capital of the Soviet Union.

For the railway authorities it was 'evacuation of rolling-stock'. For us it was: 'Flight from Hitler.' But let them give us a rifle each, I thought, and we'll defend Moscow to the death. Should we fall, should Moscow fall, our fall shall be a worthy one. As long as men live on this planet they shall remember the capital of the revolutionary proletariat of all lands. The many abominations of bureaucracy, the dominion of chits and rubber stamps, the incompetents' lust for power, the preferential treatment afforded to drones, the human fox-hunt, the meaninglessness of life and death, the sanguinary puppet theatre, the self-perpetuating massacre ... all the evil that one had come to accept as an essential component of socialism, of Communism – our generation would forgive and forget it all, leaving only the knowledge that tens of thousands, nay, hundreds of thousands, had died defending Moscow and their beliefs ...

Such heroic thoughts filled the first days of our journey. Later, as the thirtieth, fortieth, and even fiftieth days went by without having brought us to our destination, other considerations gradually invaded and occupied my mind – water for my pot of tea, rusks for my griping stomach. In any case I had no choice

237

in the matter. One step out of line, one single attempt to arrange my journey my way, and I should disappear without trace in the maw of the NKVD. One could be no smarter nor more stupid, neither less nor more of a hero, neither quicker nor slower off the mark than the Ministry of the Interior allowed.

The carriages in which we lived for the six days it took the train to reach Kuybyshev had been designed for suburban traffic – in other words the arm-rests were fixed in such a way as made it impossible to lie down. To give our aching backs at least a measure of relief we took it in turns to stretch out on the floor for a few minutes at a time. Another feature of the suburban carriage was that it possessed no lavatory – a circumstance that confronted male and female alike with problems whose solution my imagination – three decades after the event – is unable to reconstruct.

Rákosi spent much of the six days in conversation with me, though I remember nothing of what he said. All I know is that those conversations did not help the portrait I had of him. He talked to me because he did not like talking to Germans, and with Czechs even less so, because the Romanians bored him, especially Anna Pauker, and above all because it was too exhausting to gossip with politicians all day and not come out with anything that his partner might one day use against him in the ceaseless internal struggle that went on within the leadership. With me he talked commonplaces, and was indifferent to the fact that I had expected more of him.

Mátyás Rákosi! Today without doubt one of the most hated names in Hungary. At that time its owner, fifty-seven years of age, was for me and for many Hungarians the hero of the sixteen years he had sat in Horthy's jails and the great hope of our unhappy nation.

It is hard to recall now all those qualities of his that for a time – a fateful, momentous time – won him my loyalty. There is a tale of E. T. A. Hoffmann's that ought to have warned me: *Little Zaches*, about the devilish gnome to whom the fairy Rosabelverde had granted the magic power of making upon other people an impression of dignity, good sense, courage, indeed even genius. What did he look like, the 'Little Zaches' of Hungarian history? A short, squat body, as if the creator had been unable to finish his work for abhorrence; the head disproportionately large, topped by an enormous bald dome and fronted by a pallid, bloated face with a sweet-and-sour smile frozen on to it. Virtually no neck between the high shoulders, so that it was more or less left to the observer whether he called him a hunchback or not. Clumsy in movement, with a tendency towards flatfootedness; short, stubby fingers . . .

But with it a deep, sonorous voice that I found most engaging, at least then, and – in defiance of popular wisdom and observation alike – the kind of gentle, velvety grey eyes that are generally taken to be sure signs of goodness and humanity. Or was that just another bit of the lovely fairy Rosabelverde's magic? The fairy who promised mankind a wonderful future with no war, no poverty, and no injustice, in other words a life that nowadays – well, why not? – goes by the name of Communism.

And his quite extraordinary shrewdness, which even his opponents had to concede! Did not that too, in the absence of the beautiful Rosabelverde's magic, turn out subsequently to be a game he played, a game of putting remembered scraps of information to uncannily skilful use? In time one became aware of a certain repetition, which then became more and more mechanical.

In Hoffmann's tale the magic ended when Zaches, the gnome who could make himself look big, fell into his own chamber-pot and drowned. In Rákosi's case the receptacle was proffered by Anastas Mikoyan. Mikoyan, a member of the Soviet Politbureau, arrived in Budapest on a special flight in the summer of 1956 to make Rákosi's fall final and complete.

It was October and not yet particularly cold, but in many places there was already a seemingly endless carpet of snow on the ground. We spent a lot of our time – hardly precious, God knows – waiting in little stations whose name I forgot as soon as we left them again. If, as was almost always the case, a goods train pulled up beside us on the other line, also eastward-bound, we saw how it was piled high with a mass of machine parts that had all been tossed on pell-mell like a load of old iron. Many such truck-loads passed and we thought little of them. They consisted of the entire movable plant of factories that had been dismantled and were to be set up again somewhere in the east. It was not until the

Moscow film studios arrived in Alma Ata in a similar state and within a short time were reassembled and ready for use, not until I saw the great Cherkassov as the incarnation of Ivan the Terrible stride before the cameras in the heart of the Kazakh Soviet Republic that I realized what that helter-skelter evacuation meant for history.

The fitters travelling with the machines would leave the train only for a short time, spreading out over the snow-covered ground. When they were all back in the train again and the train had moved off, a changed landscape met our wondering gaze. The endless wilderness of white was bedecked with innumerable little brown heaps.

And my wise friend Andor Gábor remarked in tones of the deepest conviction, 'No one's going to beat a nation that shits that briskly.'

At one of the larger stations we saw a group of girls queueing patiently, soap in hand and clean towels slung round their necks, for their turn to wash under an enormous water tank. They looked tired, as if they had already been travelling for many days, and we noticed that they were speaking German among themselves.

'Where are you from?' we asked.

'From the former German Volga Republic.'

Yes, they were from the German soviet republic we had once been going to make a film about, the little state that had embodied so many people's hopes and been the promise of their brightest dreams. The ranks of its intellectuals already decimated by the purges, the German Volga Republic had now been abolished by the central government with a stroke of the pen, wiped out of existence, and its inhabitants dispatched to Central Asia.

And here they were en route, with their clean towels and their freshly-washed feet, en route for an unknown destiny. They all looked somehow alike, and each face reminded me of the driver, Julia Metzger, who had once driven me across the creaking ice of the Volga.

None of them would ever see the Volga again.

On the sixth day I said good-bye to Rákosi. He and the other

Comintern people were going on to the Bashkir Soviet Republic, while our little group of writers and their families was to make its way up to Kazan by Volga steamer. And after that? No one knew where we were to go after that. The *Turgenev* was on its way, we were told. We must just wait – we should find room on it somewhere.

Details . . . The greatest living philosopher of the Marxist school, Georg Lukács, squatting on his bundle of possessions on the quay of the provisional capital of Marxism for a whole night, two whole nights, as sleepless as the Germanettos' bawling baby that spent half those nights in Gertrud Lukács' arms . . .

Kuybyshev – every inch a capital, or rather the caricature of a capital. One token scene: a provincial barber's shop with queues of foreign diplomats (an imposing figure was the Polish military attaché with a huge coloured plume on his shako) waiting patiently outside for it to open, their chins darkening visibly . . .

Or the trip on the *Turgenev*, crammed in the hold with an almost permanent retch caused by the unimaginable stink and our increasing hunger, against which all we had was cups of awful tea . . .

In Kazan we were reunited with the main body of the writer colony. As soon as we could Micky and I made a sortie to Chistopol to fetch Anderli – travelling there black on a little river steamer, sharing our illegal quarters with a positive giant of a flea-ridden butcher's hound (also illegal?), and returning legally and in luxury in a first-class cabin, with little Anderli delighted at the prospect of living with mummy and daddy again. Our 'house' in Kazan was the local Writers' Union, a more or less fully-furnished residence lacking only – of course – any beds or sofas. Lukács and his wife, both on the thin side, shared a desk-top between them. I with my more expansive figure required an entire desk to myself. Micky slept on the floor beside it with all our spare clothing as her mattress and pillow. Anderli made a kennel underneath it, crawled in, and dreamt sweet dreams of Dolly, the dwarf rhinoceros she visited daily in the Kazan zoo. It was a pleasant interlude in friendly surroundings, and as long as we remained in Kazan we got a normal lunch each day. We celebrated 7 November there, the twenty-fourth anniversary of the

1917 Revolution, heard Stalin's speech from Red Square on the wireless (actually he gave it in Kirov underground station, which had been converted into a bunker), and all felt a little less lost than we had up till then.

But Kazan was only a transit station for us. Soon we were to move on – to Tashkent, they told us.

One thing I came to appreciate on that journey was the simple, primitive black-bread rusk. Another was the simple, primitive organization that was just capable of ensuring that each of us got his army bread and his black-bread rusk on time.

At many stations a darkly surging mass filled the platform, looking like the chorus of beggars in some gloomy opera. They approached with outstretched arms and trembling hands, they opened dry mouths to speak, and they implored you in languages you had never heard before for a piece of bread. Refugees, driven from their homes by the Germans, now being driven on across Soviet soil. 'Bread . . . bread . . .' But you had only what you and your family had been issued with for that day.

Had the simple organization broken down in this case? Or had these people just been left to their fate? What, if so, did fate have in store for them? And might not we too stand one day before the same dark, unforeseeable future as they?

25

Camel in the snow – Moscow to Alma Ata in
fifty-eight days – Ever met Tulibayev?

I WANT you to picture J.H. 41 sitting in the non-upholstered
corner seat of an nth class railway carriage, looking out into the
greyish glare of a day in early November. His eye travels out
over the frozen wilderness and he sees, a long way off, a camel.
This camel, the only living creature in sight, is plodding slowly
across the otherwise completely deserted expanse of snow.

And it is pulling an aeroplane behind it.

J.H. – so it seems to him – has seen many absurdities in his
and his century's forty-one years of existence. But an endless,
uninterrupted desert of snow with, in the middle, a black speck
that is a camel tottering along with incredible slowness, and
something else too, something that the mind boggles at identifying as an aeroplane, an aeroplane that is not flying but being
towed along by the camel – that strikes him as the absolute
pinnacle of absurdity.

The carriage is inconceivably old and shabby – unusable in
fact, but nevertheless being used in this train as it rolls onward
with a laborious and unhealthily arhythmic clattering. This after
all is the season of the utilization of all unusable things, including
this camel and this aeroplane. Perhaps even this journey beyond
the Urals represents a last utilization of a couple of dozen otherwise unusable human beings. Including the forty-one-year-old
J.H.

The train itself is doing little more than a crawl, with the result
that the tableau framed by the window moves past only slowly.
The undifferentiated, shadowless light burns out everything that
seems inessential – whether it be a rope linking beast and

machine or possibly the human being who must after all be playing a crucial role in the matter. All that remains is the silhouette –
the camel, and the aeroplane, picked out in sharp definition. A
stenograph, a Chinese character, a heraldic composition, an
epigram . . .

A barely audible rustling sound above my head told me that
my family – its members occupying the upper berth and the
luggage-rack respectively – was awake. First Anderli slipped
through her safety net – actually a tennis net that the ever-
practical Micky had purchased in an almost deserted sports shop
before we left Kazan – and down into her mother's bed. She
snuggled up against Micky for a while, but before long it got the
better of both of them. Hand in hand they slipped down past my
nose in their brand-new yellow-and-brown check slippers, pulled
their overcoats off their beds and on to their bodies, careful not
to make a superfluous movement lest they lose anything of that
lovely bed-warmth, flashed me a quick little smile, and hurried
off for a pee.

The yellow-and-brown check slippers deserve more than a
mere mention. All down the carriage precisely identical pairs of
slippers awaited their owners beneath every seat. Of Latvian
origin, they pointed even before the outbreak of war to the Soviet
Union's new relationship to eastern Europe, a relationship that,
after 1945, became definitive and permanent. Shortly after the
Soviet armies had marched into Poland, into parts of Romania,
and into the little Baltic republics, astonishing quantities of such
slippers, fine, warm slippers with hard-wearing imitation-leather
soles, began to flood the Moscow shops. The country had never
seen their like before. J.H. duly got his family issue of three pairs
from the Writers' Union. They came to symbolize for us the
height of civilized luxury. We went on wearing them until the
end of the war and only then, back in a Western environment,
did we notice that they were no longer – and perhaps never had
been – quite as elegant as we had once thought.

How often after the war, the wiser for various experiences both
great and small, was I reminded of those yellow-and-brown check
slippers from Riga! So many things made me think of them – the

pretty Hungarian leather sandals that Russian women became
so attached to, Hungarian wheat, Hungarian meat, Hungarian
aluminium, and, last but not least, Hungarian uranium . . .

The stove had stayed alight half the night this time, with coal
supplied by one of the most useful members of our party,
Theodor Plivier, ex-sailor and author of internationally known
novels of the First World War, at that time all unsuspecting that
in a few years a new novel, this one entitled *Stalingrad*, would
put his name in the news again. During one of our lengthy waits
in a siding somewhere, Plivier's keen, piratical eye had spied a
couple of coal trucks in the vicinity and the dramatist Friedrich
Wolf's two sons had lent a hand in a spot of innocent plundering.

Plivier was the great provider. Throwing his nose up like a
pointer, he would hurl himself into the crowds thronging strange
railway stations and, where any of the rest of us would have been
lost in the twinkling of an eye, reappear in little less with armfuls
of bought or bartered bacon, tobacco, pickled herring, honey,
garlic, spirit, what you will. (Coal, however, one took without
payment.) Hilde, his wife, a delicate, indefatigable little woman,
waited like a true pirate's bride for him to bring home the booty.

This morning Wolf's two boys were in the queue outside the
little door at the end of the carriage with strict orders from their
mother to wash out of the bottle they clutched for this purpose.
(The lavatory having unfortunately frozen up yet again, everything now added to it could be expected to freeze up as well until
perhaps at one of the larger stations we might be lucky enough to
find the hot water tap working and have enough left over after
making the tea to thaw the pan out.) Meanwhile their father, the
former ship's doctor Friedrich Wolf, waited for the train to make
one of its frequent stops in open country. As soon as this occurred
our Friedrich – a good fifty but with the figure of a thirty-year-old
– ran stripped to his underpants to the carriage door, stripped off
this one remaining garment in a trice, and leapt naked down the
embankment to roll in the virgin snow of the Urals. After a few
seconds of this he hopped back in the carriage cleansed and
refreshed, his frozen body aglow and his face shining with
exhilaration.

Born 1900

Friedrich Wolf was one of those rare people who are always ready to give one a shot of genuine, unadulterated optimism, a property he no doubt owed to his enormous ingenuousness. He combined a beamingly uncritical attitude towards his own work with an almost blind loyalty to the Party. He believed in himself because he walked with the Party, and he walked with the Party because it believed in him. The play he wrote towards the end of the Weimar period, *Paragraph 218*, a passionate protest against the prohibition of abortion in Germany, appeared to cause him no headaches whatever even when, some six years before this journey, abortion was made liable to the severest legal penalties in the Soviet Union as well. As far as Wolf was concerned, whatever the Party said was right and true. To all inconsistencies and absurdities, be they ever so glaring, he was as blind as a bat.

Yet I believe that even his loyalty to the Party had its limits. I am convinced that no vagary of Party policy would ever have made an anti-Semite of the author of *Professor Mamlock*, that play that in the simplicity of its convictions and the straightforwardness of its protest against the Fascists' persecution of the Jews was such a roaring success in the non-Fascist countries of western Europe.

Visiting East Berlin in 1953 for a production of one of my plays, I was shattered to hear that I had arrived just in time to lay a wreath on Friedrich Wolf's grave. None of his nature remedies and toughening-up techniques had availed against the heart attack that killed him. So he was probably spared that insoluble and for him certainly intolerable conflict that the Party's anti-Semitism inflicted on so many honest Communists. Or did he before he died have to witness how one of his sons chose the persecution of dissidents as his profession and his passion? For Mischa Wolf, I hear, heads with the rank of general Walter Ulbricht's secret police. Guardian of the very tyranny his father so deeply hated – in so far, that is, as he recognized it.

The principle is clear. The fathers voluntarily renounce freedom of thought because they hope a system of dictated thought will bring peace among men. The sons must choose; they must opt between persecuting and being persecuted. Many make the choice cold-bloodedly, many with passion, and many are never even aware that they have chosen.

Threatening snow-clouds gathered above us as the camel went its unhurried way, each step accompanied by convulsive movements of its sinuous neck.

I forget which day of our journey that was. All in all it took us fifty-eight days to get from Moscow to Alma Ata, the capital of the Kazakh Soviet Republic. To give you an idea of our speed, the return journey from Alma Ata to Moscow in the summer of the following year took six days – though that was without the digression to Kazan, of course. Now the railway does it in three days, and even that may not be the fastest train connection imaginable.

My family was not yet back from its perfunctory ablutions when my opposite number and fellow-inhabitant of my compartment woke with a mighty snore as if trying with a single trumpet-blast to challenge the whole world to a duel. Lodging securely in his mouth the dentures of which he was quite incomprehensibly proud, he clambered up, placed his lips to his wife's ear where she lay in the upper berth, and whispered a secret.

The name of the secret was – coffee.

Johannes R. Becher and his wife Lilly spent the entire journey in constant dread of a blow that never fell, convinced that it was only their extraordinary precautions that staved it off. They belonged to the few who still had a little coffee left, and they were terrified lest someone, some day, should ask to borrow a spoonful. Not that there was any likelihood of their parting with any, but it would have been a painful moment and might have put Johannes's poetic musings temporarily to rout. The eventuality must thus be daily guarded against – and daily with the identical ceremony.

Following this (invariable) initial whisper Lilly began without further prompting, and with that fearsome lisp of hers, to recite her piece – which also never varied and which led up to the punch-line that they only had just enough coffee left for this morning. Now came the great search, with Lilly rummaging in trucks and cases, in bundles and boxes for the store of beans that she had almost certainly hidden herself – or was that Johannes's job? Meanwhile the other coffee-drinking families would produce their own supplies.

And then came something that we passionate coffee-drinkers could never accomplish without a blush of shame. We ground our coffee, waited for the next station, ran like fury to queue at the hot-water tap, and, if our turn came before the train pulled out again, proceeded to brew our coffee with the hot water from the tap. Having brewed it, we further proceeded to drink the results.

A daily routine had developed, with habits, reactions, and reflexes, with sympathies and aversions, with delights and irritations, with yearning and with disgust.

One day a telegram reached us: writers who had already done film work, which included the foreigners Friedrich Wolf, Béla Balázs, and J.H., were not to accompany the others to Tashkent; our destination was Alma Ata.

Arys was the name of the large but little-used station where we said good-bye to our colleagues. Our carriages for Alma Ata were uncoupled, shunted off into a siding, and promptly forgotten. We might easily have stayed there for months – undisturbed, it is true, but also without anyone lifting a finger to help us, like so many Robinson Crusoes.

We found ourselves therefore faced with three tasks. Firstly to get on the telephone to the railway authorities in Tashkent and, by playing on their nerves with optimum eloquence, persuade them to forward us to Alma Ata. This job was assigned to the Russian writer Shklovsky. Secondly a life-support system had to be organized, based on the nearby market. That was the women's job. Since, however, the market sold no bread – and this was the third task – I was sent off to get a bread voucher from the local authorities.

'Where can I get a bread voucher?' I asked the sympathetic crowd that had gathered round me in the marketplace.

'Comrade Tulibayev issues them,' I was told.

'And who is Comrade Tulibayev?'

'He'll be coming here.'

'And how shall I recognize Comrade Tulibayev when he comes?'

'You'll recognize him.'

And I did. I recognized him by his fine leather coat, his well-fed figure, his greasy face, his bulging briefcase, the sycophantic smiles of his hangers-on, and the snooty bearing of his secretary.

They all look alike, the men who apportion the state's bread.

Speaking of markets, I cannot possibly omit to mention one particular corner of the market at Kazan.

My wise master and unforgettable friend Andor Gábor had once told me that goods were really scarce when people started stealing odd gloves. In Kazan, however, he was struck dumb and reduced to gaping when he saw how not only odd gloves but also odd galoshes were being sold openly and for good money. Left-footed galoshes were slightly more expensive; there was a greater demand for them because they were the ones people tended to lose more often when storming crowded trams. Knitted gloves were a great rarity, for they were usually unravelled and the wool reused.

More important than any of these, however, appeared to be the numerous assortments of bent nails, the enormous variety of buttons (it would have been a paradise for young Bredel), the cog-wheels, and finally – most curious sight of all – the fragmented gramophone records.

26

With Eisenstein and Pudovkin – To Stalin's daughter Svetlana – The three sailor-suits

SHKLOVSKY'S command of language got us a locomotive from Tashkent in three days, and after a further three or four days' journey across the deserted steppe we pulled into the main station of Alma Ata, capital of the Kazakh Soviet Republic and the town that was to be our new home. Something of a homecoming feeling gave us a warm sensation inside. While the women made a bee-line for the market with empty rucksacks and the rest of the party stayed behind to watch our luggage, Béla Balázs and I struck off across the station square in search of someone who might be able to tell us where we were to be housed. The only other person to be seen in the station square apart from ourselves was a police-man, directing the imaginary traffic. He approached us in a most courteous fashion, bade us welcome in this Asian capital, and enjoined us to observe the highway code. He further expressed the wish 'that the comrades will spend the time until the victory of our Red Army peacefully and happily in our socialist soviet republic'.

We were so moved and found him so lovable with his slanting eyes and Kazakh intonation that, had his bearing permitted such a liberty, we should gladly have thrown our arms round him and hugged him.

We were put up in the Red Army Hotel near the town centre. Each family was given a room of its own, and apart from the relative paucity of toilet facilities we had every reason to be content with our lot. We also had work, and were in constant contact with the élite of the Soviet film industry.

With Eisenstein and Pudovkin

My old longing to collaborate with those giants of film, Pudovkin and Eisenstein, at last met with some measure of fulfilment. Admittedly nothing we did together was ever finished, but I found that even from half-finished works I could learn more than I had dared to hope. Eisenstein was working with his students on a production of my *Have* and involved me as author, local expert, and dedicated pupil. The project was interrupted when Eisenstein was unexpectedly commissioned to make a film about Ivan the Terrible. The job caused him the most fearful torments because he knew that Stalin secretly identified with this historical figure, and the knowledge undermined not only the free play of his imagination but also any sense of physical security.

Pudovkin had already approached me in Moscow the previous year with a view to collaborating. We outlined five or six treatments together, none of them completely, but I remember it as a period of wholly absorbing and satisfying work. Perhaps for Pudovkin it was no more than a five-finger exercise, but for me it was higher education. And after my experience at Meshrabpom Films (Comrade Samsonov: 'Mammoth catastrophe! Utter and complete artistic débâcle!') I could not blame Pudovkin for preferring to put off finishing anything for as long as possible. (When he visited me in Budapest some ten years later there was virtually nothing left of his once boundless energy – nothing but a deep sadness and disappointment. And a waiting for the end of a life that had begun so richly.)

One of the Russian film-writers, possibly the most talented of all, I missed very particularly. We had become friends and would have become even better friends had he not been brutally removed from our midst. I refer to Alexei Kapler, of whom Stalin's daughter Svetlana wrote in 1967, 'After ten years' banishment and concentration camp his life resumed its normal course.'

Why had Stalin banished him? Why had he put him in a concentration camp?

In Moscow and then later in Alma Ata I picked up whispered scraps of the story of Kapler and Stalin's daughter, which at that time was hot and dangerous news. A quarter of a century later

Svetlana herself told it to the world. The dictator's daughter loved the writer, and it cost him ten years of his life. Then, however, his life 'resumed its normal course'. Are you sure, Svetlana Jossifovna? Can anyone, after ten years' banishment and forced labour, get back on to a normal course? Can a life so cruelly and senselessly torn in two ever grow back together again? Does the social order in which a man must die for ten years for loving a teenage girl even offer the possibility of a normal existence? We were all to some extent looking for a way to a normal life or at least away from an abnormal one. You, Svetlana Jossifovna, found one. So did I. But who will show millions the way, and how, and where?

The Kazakh writers gave us Hungarians – Balázs and his wife, Micky, who though far from being a Hungarian still counted as one, and myself – a particularly friendly reception, their sympathetic attitude towards Hungarians being based on their conviction that the Kazakhs and the Hungarians were related peoples. (The Alma Ata public library has a copy of every book representing this school of thought.) The king of the Kazakh poets – or perhaps one should rather call him a bard – the aged Dzhambul Dzhabayev, even invited us to his snow-white *yurta* or nomad's tent where, accompanying himself on the *dombra*, he gave us a performance of his latest songs, of which unfortunately we understood only the words 'tractor', 'kolkhoz', and 'Stalin'. But we had a festive and splendid evening. The old man's *yurta* stood right beside the stone-built house with which the state had presented him on the occasion of his umpteenth birthday. 'The house is falling down,' he told us. 'The tent will stand for ever.'

What old Dzhambul said made more sense than one might have supposed, for the Kazakh capital stood in the middle of an earthquake zone. Situated almost 3000 feet above sea level on the edge of an immense plateau at the foot of the magnificent Ala-Tau, the town was both designed and constructed to withstand the constant danger. Large notice-boards in all the main streets gave instructions as to what to do in the event of the mountains' beginning to move. But that had not happened for decades.

To Stalin's daughter, Svetlana

Here on the Chinese frontier, as everywhere in the Soviet Union, there were taboos one was not allowed to mention. For example it was bad form to inquire what lay beyond the Ala-Tau mountains. Military secret. But a Kazakh bee-keeper who was trying to explain to me why the price of honey had suddenly gone shooting up, did whisper in my ear with his Kazakh intonation, 'When China beyond mountains, bee-keeper take much, much bee over in lorry. Much flower, much honey. Now Red Army beyond mountains, lorry not allowed over, bees not allowed over, much good honey not coming.' According to my atlas, however, the other side of the Ala-Tau is still China. So I think there must have been more to it than the honey.

Anyone who really wants to understand the Russians – at least the present-day Russians – must recognize their bent for impracticality and discomfort. Take queueing, for example. We had plenty of opportunity to queue at the Red Army Hotel; we queued for our meal tickets each day and then we queued twice a day for a seat in the dining room. The queue formed up on the stairs, so that anyone wishing to use the stairs for their proper purpose was obliged to elbow his way up against the stream, since it did not occur to anyone to leave a space free. The Russians know perfectly well that there are more practical ways of solving the queueing problem, and even ways of avoiding it altogether. Yet they do nothing about it. It is as if they are holding the possibility of greater practicality and comfort as a sort of reserve to fall back on. I nearly had a row with my friend Shklovsky on the stairs once when I suggested some minor modification of the system. 'German disciplinarianism!' he fumed, entirely without justification.

Entering the crowded dining room one day I found a small table free right by the door. I sat down.

'I beg your pardon,' an elderly waiter whispered to me with unwonted politeness. 'This table is reserved for His Excellency the count.'

'For whom?'

'For His Excellency the Polish consul,' he expanded, accompanying each word with that curious sibilant with which the old-fashioned Russian servant expressed his humble submission before his superior. Many waiters preserved the custom.

The count was a small, portly man whose baggy black suit betrayed the fact that he had once been portlier still. At his heels came the countess in a dress of violet tulle trimmed with lace. At the beginning of their journey – and who knew whether Alma Ata was the end? – she must have looked younger and fresher. The couple spent the meal supervising the table manners and general conduct of their three daughters, who all wore blue sailor-suits – school uniform – and put away at great speed all that the waiter and their parents placed on their plates.

Their room had a terrace, and whenever the weather allowed – in Alma Ata the sun shone for several hours at least almost every day – the countess and her daughters sat out on the terrace with needle and thread and mended their clothes. Their only clothes. The clothes in which they had fled from the German invasion. The violet tulle dress that suited no season of the day or year required constant attention, and above all the skirts of the sailor-suits were always having to be lengthened – a task that made great demands on the family's ingenuity. And as they sewed, rather than sit in their underwear, they sat in their overcoats.

Where there is a consul there is also a consulate. A room of the Red Army Hotel, Alma Ata, was duly registered as the Polish Consulate, and there an extremely military-looking gentleman received a stream of the ragged, half-starved refugees who, God knows how, had managed to fetch up in this central-Asian town. Whenever I saw one of them I invariably had the feeling that, somewhere along my path from Moscow to Alma Ata, I had come across him before. He had begged bread of me and I had been unable to give him any. The faces may have differed but the eyes – they were the same. The eyes were always the same.

Then one day no one appeared on the sunny terrace. The door of their room was sealed, the door of the consulate likewise. When I asked the elderly waiter what had happened he appeared not to have heard my question. The official local newspaper published an announcement of the arrest according to which the Polish consul, an aristocrat, had played a leading part in a conspiracy against the Soviet Union and was furthermore guilty of illegal business dealings. What happened to his ladyfolk I never discovered.

In Alma Ata I saw a man – they said he was a great scholar, a physicist or a mathematician – who had been flown out of the besieged and starving city of Leningrad a few hours before. I watched him eat his first bowl of gruel.

The fellow ate with his eyes. His devouring gaze remained unassuaged as his mouth moved slowly, lazily, yet with never a pause. Occasionally he spoke. What little one could understand had to do with food.

Months later I met him again. He turned out to be an excellent conversationalist and a witty raconteur. But always, obsessively, he harked back like an addict to the one subject – food. With a keen sense of strategy he contrived to steer the talk round until suddenly we were in the middle of a discussion about marvellous, mountainous, grease-dripping, sauerkraut-smelling stacks of food . . . He paused then and closed his eyes – as if savouring the pleasure of eating himself to death.

His family, in Leningrad, had starved to death.

27

*Of domestic trade – Stalingrad – A tragedy
begins – Remember Comrade Sagaidak? – A
question of wave-length*

THE return to Moscow came sooner than we had dared to hope.
In June 1942 we were allowed to board an antiquated sleeping-car
that still breathed something of the elegance of a bygone age.
There was even a conductor, a spry old fellow who, as our
journey proceeded, evinced a striking talent for commerce.
Whenever we were approaching a town he told us precisely what
commodities were most in demand there and duly produced –
I have no idea from where – what he reckoned to be the required
quantities. Arrived at the station, he then did his business with
positively diabolical speed, swopping salt for honey, honey for
sewing-needles, carburettor parts for soap, dried fish for exercise
books, and so on and so forth. His infallible knowledge of the
market and his exact calculation of exchange rates were
awe-inspiring.

Many people wonder how the vast Soviet empire with its
crippled or possibly still-born system of internal trade could
continue to exist. Here was one expedient: everyone who travelled
about from place to place, particularly when it was part of his
job to do so, began to take commodities with him for sale or
exchange, thus improvising a network of illegal commercial
links that were individually insignificant but added up to an
impressive whole, a second blood-stream, as it were, replacing
the first that had virtually ceased to flow. It was speculation, of
course, and as such was punishable by law, but in this case the
police took a responsible enough attitude and turned a blind eye.
Without the black market the whole country would literally have

starved. Even the government, once it saw that the black market not only flourished but was beginning to play the role of saviour of a threatened and increasingly discontented populace, decided to get in on the act, opening what were known as 'Trade Shops' and selling at prices geared to the black market all kinds of high-quality imported – mostly American – and domestic goods to anyone with the money to buy them. And where did the money come from? From a variety of illegal activities ranging from the free sale of agricultural products to the black fees that doctors were forced to accept if they were to keep their families fed. The result was an economy made up of two irreconcilable elements – the so-called 'socialist' element that the minority dictatorship imposed upon the people and the private element that the people quietly, gently, but with irresistible tenacity dictated to the state. And as the state under pressure of war allowed the private sector to flourish and grow fat, Party and police armed themselves for fresh acts of violence for when the time should have come to take it all away again. Thus the tug-of-war escalated into a new (or was it so new?), officially non-existent form of the class struggle and its concomitant exploitation. It was not long before *Pravda* was publishing jubilant and laudatory articles about gifts of almost legendary proportions which collective farms and even individual members of them had bestowed upon the Red Army. What the articles omitted to mention was how the collectivized peasants, allegedly innocent of exploitation, had managed to amass such gigantic sums and who had had the touching idea of donating them thus voluntarily. The donor? Or the local Party secretary, chairman of the soviet, NKVD chief, or some other representative of the bureaucratic or repressive machine? Yet the leaders of the so-called 'socialist' world believed and still believe – contrary to Marx – that by peaceful or violent intervention in the processes of production and distribution they will one day succeed in doing away with the class struggle for ever.

For the time being, however, there were the Trade Shops. And the churches, quietly reopened with the tacit approval of the state. Every self-respecting Muscovite woman ate chocolate in the tram and prayed for Stalin's victory. And for Russia. The

term 'Soviet Union' passed gradually out of use and the fatherland was once more called by its old familiar name. Even by
Stalin.

In the spring every food market had a stall set aside for Easter
eggs, purchasers of which would then queue for hours at the
church door to have them blessed.

We arrived back in Moscow to find that the house in the
Taganka district still stood, the flat was still ours (the neighbour
who had overflowed into it moved out without demur) and the
only thing not in order was the central heating. The central
heating in tens of thousands of Moscow houses had frozen and
burst during the previous winter. But even that we took calmly.
The same frost as had burst our heating had paralysed Hitler's
offensive north of Moscow in that first winter of the war. The
caretaker knew a man, a prison warder by calling, who for a by
no means unreasonable quantity of vodka would lay an impeccable brick oven. We had one built in the kitchen and, as autumn
drew into winter, made up Anderli's bed beside it. We slept in the
icy living room.

One cold winter afternoon Georg and Gertrud Lukács called
to see us. I was busy treating my chilblained hands, plunging
them alternately into ice-cold and almost boiling-hot water with
a little carpenter's glue dissolved in it. (In this way – so the
doctor hoped – I should be rid of the chilblains in four to five
years' time. The estimate was an optimistic one. Fourteen years
later, in a Budapest prison, my old chilblains came back to
plague me.) Anderli, already a schoolgirl, came in from her
playing after a while, drank her tea, ate her thinly-spread sand-
wich, crept into bed, and promptly fell asleep. Gertrud, exhausted
and undernourished, looked ready to do the same at any moment.
Micky poured tea and produced some cakes she had bought in
the market instead of sugar (we had another source for sugar).
Georg, having no cigars, sat stolidly smoking cigarettes. The
electricity was off – as happened without warning several times
a day – and his short, slender figure was almost lost in the semi-
darkness. Only his sharp profile stood out, and the permanent

drop at the end of his long nose caught and reflected the feeble candlelight.

In those days one hardly ever switched one's telephone-radio off. Our radio sets had all been confiscated when the war broke out (at the end of the war we got them back, and I can truthfully say that my own set was returned in perfect condition). Apart from the papers this dispenser of music at a constant, invariable volume was our only source of news. Our conversation with the Lukács was thus accompanied by the usual incredibly boring music programme made up of too few records too frequently repeated. But no one minded. We were listening with half an ear for the moment when the music would cut out in mid-bar and a thrilling silence ensue . . .

The news! And if this silence fell outside the usual times, and if in addition it was filled with the beautiful, deep, manly voice of the chief announcer, Levitan, one knew that the news would be good. For by then we were already beginning to get good news.

Stalin was pretty sparing with his promises. Very much less generous, at any rate, than his counterpart in the German camp. So that when Stalin ordered the armies that had defended Stalingrad 'not to give an inch', there was a general feeling that he knew something we did not. Until now – the music stopped suddenly . . . long silence . . . Levitan's voice . . .

And so we learnt of the Red Army's victory at Stalingrad.

Around the brick oven and the sleeping child there began an excited discussion as to what would happen now. Might we after all get something to replace the abortive world revolution? Such a victory as was in fact won in 1945 we did not of course dare to dream of in the winter of 1942–3. Our most optimistic forecast was that the Red Army and the Western Allies would catch Germany in a pincer-movement and weaken Hitler to such an extent that the German people would shake off its tyrant and set up a democracy of its own.

And our country? Hungary must become a democratic republic, as it had wanted to be for more than a hundred years.

The first task of any new government in Hungary must be to distribute the land among the have-nots. The free peasants, we decided, could then form co-operatives if they wished. How wrong and dangerous it was to play false with the peasants and ultimately rob them of their right to own the land had been shown in Hungary in 1919. Even clearer proof was provided by the history of the Soviet Union with its disasters, famines, and the chronic bankruptcy of its agriculture.

Secondly, never again could central Europe be allowed to become the prison of the nationalities. The creation of a hotbed of petty national squabbles was likewise to be avoided. The 'Switzerland of the East' must at last become reality.

Finally, as a neighbour of the mighty Soviet federation Hungary would never again be brushed off with a brutal '*Assez! Assez!*' when it sought to determine its own future . . .

That, at least, is how it looked in my dream tomorrow. From this point of view it mattered little whether Russia was already socialist or only called herself such. What was still wrong in Russia we would put right in our country, and the future lay at our feet.

An astonished and more and more confused Micky listened to this discussion of a far-off, foreign country whose future – as she realized with unconscious misgivings – was henceforth to be her own.

And at this point there occurred something that often happens to us Hungarians. In the heat of the discussion, unaware ourselves of what we were doing, we broke into Hungarian. At any other time Micky might have found it funny; happening at this time, it gave her a jolt. Must she now of all times, when victory lay so near, be left out of her husband's world? She looked questioningly at each of us in turn, trying to read from our faces, from the movements of our lips, and from the changing lights in our eyes what we were talking about, and which of us was saying what.

Then she gave up. With an apologetic smile all round she took off her glasses, lay down beside the sleeping child, and in a few minutes, with the tiredness of countless days in her bones, the blood-deficiency of generations in her arteries, and the malnutrition of two hemispheres in marrow and muscle, she was asleep.

Thus was sealed at the level of the unconscious a tragedy that at the conscious level had only just begun, and that had all its suffering before it.

The battle of Voronezh – the Stalingrad of the Hungarian army, only a matter of days after Hitler's crushing defeat – I learnt of in more or less the same fashion. Music . . . pause . . . Levitan's resonant voice announcing the rout of the Hungarian divisions. This time it was in the office of my boss Manuilsky, a tried and tested Comintern man who headed a special department of the Ministry of Defence where he did some very effective propaganda work directed at the enemy armies. (Seek him not now – he fell victim to Stalinism's post-war ravages.) Manuilsky's second in command was the Hungarian Ernö Gerö, 'No. 2' in the Hungarian Communist Party and a name to be reckoned with in the history of Hungary's recent past.

My job in the department was to comb enormous sacks full of confiscated documents both official and private for material and write it up in a newspaper for Hungarian prisoners-of-war in the Soviet Union and a series of booklets and leaflets designed to stimulate peaceful, anti-Fascist sentiments among the soldiers of the Hungarian army.

And then came Voronezh.

A snowy wilderness of inconceivable extent and the appalling, intolerable cold made pitilessly short work of the lives that were delivered up to it. It was pointless for the Hungarian soldiers to give themselves up because there was no one within reachable distance to take them prisoner. Thousands of Hungarian intellectuals who had been serving in so-called labour battalions and waiting longingly for the day when they should at last stand face to face with the liberator froze or starved to death in that vast depression with nothing but snow before their eyes whichever way they looked. The tiny percentage that could be saved and did not subsequently die of dysentery was interned in one of the many PoW camps.

For me it was the beginning of a new field of activity.

Not far from Moscow, in the village of Krasnogorsk, was the one PoW camp I was allowed to visit – when, that is, either Mátyás Rákosi or Zoltán Vas took me with him. Zoltán Vas was the man who had sat with Rákosi in Horthy's jails for sixteen years; he had been part of the deal with the historic flags. (I had a lot of time for Vas. He later became the first Communist mayor of Budapest. A true Budapester, always bursting with ideas, he might have become the first non-bureaucratic bureaucrat – had such a thing been possible.)

In a jeep, or sometimes in a small and ancient bus, we bounced over impassable paths and nosed our way through bottomless mire to this élite camp to which an 'Antifa' (anti-Fascist) school was attached. A number of the inmates were receiving instruction in this school – principally in a kind of popularized Marxism – and it was hoped that the rest would sooner or later be moved to take an interest in politics too.

We had two Hungarian generals in the camp – Major-General Desseö and Lieutenant-General Count Stomm. The latter was an interesting man. Out of hatred of the Nazis he forgot the German language. Anyone who could not speak Hungarian had to address him in English.

This hatred was not unfounded. He had got both legs frost-bitten at Voronezh and they had had to be amputated. Wandering about in the wilderness of snow like so many thousands of others, he had stumbled on an area occupied by the SS. He asked if he could rest and warm himself in one of their still heated huts, but the SS-men, on the run themselves, refused the general – their ally – admittance. This happened several times. Eventually the general was picked up by some Russian ambulance men.

Participation in our Marxist instruction was not obligatory, but it will come as a surprise to no one when I say that few of the prisoners exercised their right to abstain – a right that was naturally associated with short commons.

One of those few was First Lieutenant Pál Maléter, a tall young officer who at first would have nothing to do with us. Then he asked for some books about Marxism, saying that if he saw in Marxism a ray of hope for our country he would apply for further instruction. The books convinced him, and that cost him his life.

As a major-general and Minister of Defence of the Hungarian Revolution of 1956 he was brought to trial after the overthrow of the uprising and sentenced to death.

Maléter had the advantage over many other former pupils of the 'Antifa' school that he *knew* why he died. Major Pórfi among others probably never twigged right up until the end of the show-trials staged partly for his benefit in 1950 why he should first have been made a general and then have to die on the gallows.

Why? Even Lukács the philosopher could never get out of the habit of asking why.

When Georg himself was arrested I was naturally informed immediately. Micky and I called on Gertrud and were amazed at her stoicism. I went to see Mátyás Rákosi – as did Gábor, Balázs, and others – to ask him to do something. Rákosi promised to do what he could, and there is no doubt that he was as good as his word. After all it would have been more than embarrassing for him to return victorious to Hungary without Lukács. But the chances were slender. When Walter Ulbricht intervened on behalf of German comrades who had been arrested – and I heard many times that he was extremely conscientious in such matters – the NKVD sent him packing, and the rebuff had a threatening undertone in it. Even Kurt Funk – carried off to the Lubyanka from his room in the Lux – would hardly have returned so soon had not Togliatti and Dimitrov intervened in his favour.

Lukács, fortunately, was also released.

When I asked what could have been the reason for his arrest he answered, 'The fifth column.' Without exactly blazoning the matter abroad at the time, I disagreed. The activity of a fifth column presupposes the existence of some methodical and useful activity with which the said fifth column then equally systematically interferes. But I was beginning to think even then what I still think now, namely that in the system as it then was, and as it still is essentially today, the wilful destruction was not something directed against the useful and profitable activity. Useful and detrimental intermingled; they complemented one another, as it were. The system needed great scholars. The system also needed great scholars to languish in prison. The system needed generals of the stamp of Tukhachevsky, and it also needed dead generals of the stamp of Tukhachevsky.

Prisoners-of-war . . .

It was a tactful and humane arrangement that virtually no PoW transports were to be seen in Moscow throughout the entire war. Shortly before the victory, however, someone had the bright idea of making up for all omissions in this field with one tremendous parade. Seventy thousand PoWs – Germans, Hungarians, Italians, Romanians – were assembled at a point near Moscow and then marched through the city in a single, seemingly endless column of emaciated, broken, stumbling, filthy, stinking men. Why? If the idea was to impress the Russian people it was a long way wide of the mark. The average Russian has nothing but aversion for that kind of thing. Although the occasion had been announced over the telephone-radio and publicized with posters, the crowds stayed away. The few people that did turn out stood in silence. Not an insult, not a cry for vengeance, not even a shout was to be heard – only, here and there, a woman sighing, 'Poor things.' A mother, perhaps, whose son was at the front? Or a wife whose husband had fallen there?

Peoples could not but recognize one another, though their rulers knew them not.

One day I too became a Lux resident. It did not, however, happen just like that.

It must have been six in the morning when I heard the knock at my door. Not a ring. The electricity was on but my visitor chose to use the knocker. I opened the door and found a giant of a man standing there. At second glance a familiar giant. The owner of my flat. Quick as a flash he slipped a suitcase into the hall.

'Right. That's that, then.'

'Good morning, Comrade Sagaidak.'

'Good morning. That's the law, you see.'

'What is?'

'It's not sufficient for the rightful owner to return to his dwelling; he must also have deposited a part of his goods and/or

chattels on the premises. Which, as you see, he has just done.'
Which is how I discovered that I and my family were homeless.

Something incomprehensible happened to Micky at around
that time. Or to me too? A curious lassitude, even a kind of apathy
and hopelessness overcame her. When did it begin? With the
news of Stalingrad? The more clearly she saw her future as being
set in Hungary among people who spoke a foreign language and
problems that were not her own, the more she lost her otherwise
keen eye for what was real and what unreal. It was as if she was
trying to rebel against fate: 'All right – you set me tasks that are
alien to me so from now on I shall behave like an alien.'

And I? I went dashing off to the PoW camp as often as I could
or buried myself in the huge sacks of confiscated papers, in the
fates of strangers both living and dead, and forgot my family's
cares. I was already living utterly and completely under the spell
of a yearned-for future, where Micky was unable to follow my
thoughts. To the present with its problems that were as insignificant as our everyday life over the last ten years in the setting
of that vast reality – to this present she gave little thought and I
none whatsoever.

Comrade Apletin, who knew that I was due to be sent back to
Hungary as soon as possible and that I myself was waiting
impatiently for that moment, found us a room on a temporary
basis in the National Hotel, an ancient and aristocratic establishment set aside for foreigners.

There Anderli swiftly found a playmate of her own age, a
charming little Chinese girl named Pin Pin. The children fell for
one another instantly, which would have been ideal had not
Pin Pin's father been stationed in Moscow as a diplomatic representative of General Chiang Kai-shek. In Moscow, however,
the child of a Communist writer might not strike up such
acquaintanceships – not even when the parties concerned were
only nine years old. Micky as she had been would have been alert
to such a situation at once. Now she simply disregarded the
absurd danger and chatted at length with Pin Pin's equally
charming mother in the corridor as if unaware of the inevitable
consequences.

We had both had enough all of a sudden – quite irrationally.

When we were bowed out of the National Hotel no mention was of course made of the real reason. The hotel was full and that was that. But I saw Comrade Apletin talking on the telephone with the hotel manager. His face grew gradually darker and he even at one stage said, 'Ssss!' – a sibilant I knew had been prompted by the name of little Pin Pin, inscribed for ever on my secret 'cadre file'. Did I not, knowing the facts, suspect that something of the sort was to be expected? Yes, I did. But I refused to admit the suspicion. I was ashamed for the Soviet Union.

For a while we had nowhere at all. Micky spent the night with a German comrade called Ella, I with the Lukács. Georg had to give up his bed; they had two rooms of the flat they had been allocated by the Academy of Sciences, the third being occupied by a young physicist and his wife and child – soon to be two children.

Then I managed through some Russian colleagues to rent for a few months a room in the neighbourhood of the old Meshrabpom film studio.

To this day that was the only flat I have ever had to share with rats. I can testify to the fact that rats – at least those I have met – are not ill-behaved flatmates. Down the middle of the kitchen – a large room used by no one except ourselves when we washed at the tap – ran an invisible demarcation line that the rats never overstepped. We were equally scrupulous in our observance of this frontier and never once ventured into the other, rather darker half of the kitchen. Above all we never so much as dreamt of cleaning up in the reservation.

Still, the squeaking was unpleasant; it always sounded like the secret call-sign of a conspiracy against us. Moreover it was disturbing how it was almost always at the high-point of the nightly concert that the electricity went off. Had the creatures decided to attack us all the same, the only light on the battlefield would have been the cold gleam of their eyes.

From this – to say the least – ghostly environment I was rescued by a man to whom I would be reluctant to admit my obligation today – Ernö Gerö, the 'No. 2' of the Hungarian Communist Party. Was it his idea, I wonder, to cede his room in the Lux to someone who really needed it, or did his wife Elisabeth still remember those Marxism classes back in 1919, and the Danube steamer with the clandestine comrade and the boiled sweet with which we had been rewarded? The fact remains that they did offer us their flat when they both left for the front, attached to the section of the Red Army that was by then fighting on Hungarian soil.

At that time I still thought highly of Ernö Gerö. Since 23 October 1956 I have hated and abhorred his very name. But at the time of our homelessness that was many years hence.

Through all these difficulties great and small the little exercise books continued to fill up almost in secret, as it were, and every day, no matter what her mood, Micky would sit down at the typewriter and neatly type it all out.

The new play was called *Day of Reckoning*. It was set in Germany after Stalingrad, and it immediately met with Comrade Walter Ulbricht's unqualified disapproval.

He never told me what he objected to in it and I never even tried to engage him in a discussion about it. The play was at variance with the rules of so-called 'socialist realism' in that it had no 'positive hero'. According to the dogmas of Soviet literature such a thing was not only forbidden but also punishable.

While Ulbricht was reading and passing sentence on one copy, another lay on Willem's bedside table. He leafed through it, put it down, and then picked it up again. The subject and one or two scraps of dialogue that had caught his eye began to prey on his mind.

Day of Reckoning was the first play of mine to be performed in Germany after the Hitler nightmare was over. Gustav von Wangenheim produced it and Greif played the part I had written for him. The first performance was in the Deutcshes Theater in Berlin – on the very stage from which *God, Emperor, and Peasant* had been driven thirteen years before.

I did not see the performance and in fact did not hear about it until after the play had been put on in seventy-five different theatres. And after Greif's death. But in the wake of *Day of Reckoning*, the Deutsches Theater put on *Have*, a play that is still today, in a variety of languages from Flemish to Japanese, on the repertoire of many theatres.

My last year in Moscow was different from the previous nine, for I spent it in the one job that interested me above all others. I was made an editor of 'Radio Kossuth', a station doing really important work, for all that its entire staff consisted of three people – Mátyás Rákosi, Imre Nagy, and J.H. 44–5.

I have already mentioned the impression that Mátyás Rákosi's beautiful voice made on me. After all I grew up to the sound of the cello. Now another male voice put me in mind of those Abony evenings – that of Imre Nagy, who was not only an editor but also the other announcer of our Radio Kossuth. We had known one another for almost ten years. He knew a tremendous amount about agriculture, and I had consulted him repeatedly in connection with my plays *Have* and *The Turkey-boy*.

Partition of the great estates among the landless population – that was the key to a happy future for the people of Hungary. So said Rákosi, and so said Imre Nagy. Preparing their texts for transmission, I learned with delight the promise of the Communist Party: the debt of 1919 would – as soon as Hungary was rid of the Germans – at last be redeemed. But for all their similarity, those texts said clean different things. I failed to see the difference at the time, and so probably did many others, but whereas for Imre Nagy every word of that promise was solemn and holy, whereas he spent the rest of his life trying his utmost to fulfil that vow, the identical words in Rákosi's mouth were one unadulterated swindle.

Two paths of Hungarian history – and not only Hungarian history – lay hidden behind those so like-sounding words.

The difference between them tripped and toppled Rákosi.

The difference likewise led to Imre Nagy's martyrdom in a Budapest jail.

And all the unexpected turns in J.H. 45+'s life were to stem from that same identical difference.

With this secret ballast in my invisible luggage I boarded a Soviet aircraft on 12 April 1945 to go home to Hungary. Home to an unsuspected fate.

Part Four

28

My son – A yellow star and a mother's heart –
Introducing an important character

I WAS tired, chilled to the bone, my chilblains hurt, the virus that was soon to give me a temperature was already at work in my blood. But I was happy. For two reasons.

I was on my way to see my mother, my sister, my brothers, perhaps even my son. That was one reason.

The streets were the streets I had walked as a young man. The Suspension Bridge was the same that I had stormed as a student under the salvoes of the police, and there in the river was the island where I had walked with my girl friends. But the stone lions of the bridge lay crooked as if suffering from shock, the chains hung limply down in the water, and the trees on the island had been shot to splinters. One waded through rubble, and one's shoes were red with brick-dust.

The streets were full of people, on foot, each going his own way. Pale, hungry-looking people in search of something or someone . . . Their relatives? The future? A bowl of soup?

And my mother – old and thin and tiny, but alive. Through war and ghetto, still alive, and now living permanently with Juliska. The same mother whom my convictions had forced me to leave so many years before, I now, still following the path of my convictions, found again. And with her my brothers and sister, drawn up in order of seniority, as befitted such an occasion. When I had last been there we were still complete. Now the line began with a gap – Irene had died in the year I called myself J.H. 34. Juliska was there, much aged, but with a hint of indestructibility in her ravaged face. Elek, with an enormous grey moustache, beside her. Their son Laci's place was vacant. He

271

was alive, had been deported, and was even now on his way home – on foot. For Max there were three vacant places. All dead – he in Bergen-Belsen, his wife and daughter in Auschwitz. Bandi and his wife were there, unhurt. And Kari, just back from the death-camp at Bor, alive, though seriously ill.

Six of us including me Mother had brought into the world. With kin, still an impressive tribe. One of the families that had got off fairly lightly.

Back out on the rubble-strewn streets for the long walk across town to Party headquarters. Every now and then an armoured car or a tank would rattle past, or even a whole column. Girls in army uniform – a sight I was familiar with from Russia – directed them with little flags. It was as if two incompatible pictures had been traced over one another – the city and the army of occupation.

At Party headquarters I got my lunch. It felt good to know that a dish of beans and a slice of bread in this city belonged to me. Then another longish walk back to the National Theatre. The second source of my happiness – my play *Have* was in rehearsal. My words, my thoughts, my beliefs at last becoming audible, visible, recognizable. How many years since actors had accomplished their transformation according to a text of mine!

Afterwards, dead-tired, feverish, back to my digs. No heating, no glass in the windows, exposed to the cold of the April night. If I were writing a novel I should give the coincidence the value of a symbol; in this book I must simply state it as a fact: the little pension in which the Communist Party put up its comrades as they returned from abroad was the old Pension Palkovits, where the proprietor's wife had been a blonde.

As soon as I closed my eyes my brothers and sisters, both the living and the dead, stood in a row before me. And somewhere behind them, invisible, my father played his cello to me the whole night through.

Every day was the same. The fever blurred my sense of time. Was it yesterday I met my son Peter? Peter had decided to become a priest, though he was not as yet ordained. He smiled indulgently when, suggesting he enter a secular profession, I

offered to pay for his studies. The Benedictines had saved Peter
and his mother from Auschwitz; they had his loyalty. He did not
say as much at first; his lips smiled it wordlessly.

Father and son – the resemblance in face and figure is striking –
stand for ideologies that are said to be irreconcilable. A certain
reciprocal tolerance, however, helps them over the difficulties.

As was to be expected, one day Peter brought his mother
Margit to Juliska's. In a loud voice Margit asked me, 'When are
you going back to hell with your pickpockets and rapists?'

It was impossible to spend a day or even an hour in Budapest
without hearing of brutalities committed by soldiers. If not
usually couched in Margit's tone and volume but more in
whispered insinuations, the complaint was universal, the accusation cried out to heaven . . .

How should I answer? By saying, 'War is war'? A poor, a
pathetic excuse. All the way from Moscow to Budapest in a
bomber over the Carpathians a solemn feeling had been gathering
in my breast. I had been able for ten years to watch one realization
of the great idea, full of mistakes and loose ends. Now was my
chance to realize the same idea in my *own* country, but better.
And was *this* how it should begin? The inquiring faces of my
family were turned towards me.

In an atmosphere of painfully mounting tension that I felt no
one would be able to check, Mother got slowly to her feet. She
went to the cupboard, took out her sewing-box, and, turning to
Margit, said in a voice of unusual severity, 'The boy came back
to save us. We're saved. So leave him alone!' Then she opened
the sewing-box and took out something yellow.

A yellow star. The yellow star that, only a short time before,
she had still had to wear. She had kept it, using it now as a pin-
cushion.

It was pierced through with a thousand holes like the mother's
heart in the old Jewish song.

'Tell me – what do you actually do all day?' began Comrade
Révai with his usual supercilious insolence. 'Do you hope to win
glory as a playwright?'

'It's my profession, Comrade Révai.'

I ought really to have introduced József Révai long ago, against our common Moscow background. Without a portrait of Révai my life-story would be incomplete.

József Révai was about my own age, perhaps a year or two older. Son of a wealthy Budapest banking family, he had been able in his youth to indulge in all kinds of extravagances, first trying his hand at poetry. Unfortunately only one line of his work survives. It runs, if I remember rightly, 'Die, my father! Die, mother! And you, my first love – croak!' A school that is not without its adherents even today.

When that kind of poetry went out of fashion he switched to full-time politics. The world revolution became his sole profession, waiting for the revolution, whether or not it came, his daily bread – until the Communist victory in Hungary a slender diet, after that a rich one. And at the beginning the world revolution was undoubtedly his great passion, too. But when it failed year after year to arrive and required one continually to readjust one's prophecies, Révai, like so many other members of the Communist leadership, underwent a metamorphosis. The fire of revolutionary passion cooled and the delights of *power* took complete possession of him.

With an education well above the average, a rare example of the Marxist intellectual, extremely good-looking, enjoying the company of women to an extent that in the sanctimonious atmosphere of the dictatorship of the proletariat only few even of the leading Party members could allow themselves, a witty conversationalist and a feared debater, he had carved out for himself in the group of Hungarian emigrants in Moscow that was to exercise power in Hungary from 1945 onwards the role of ruthless dictator of cultural affairs. He had a highly developed taste in literature and art – for his own use. For the masses he had another. In time he had grown accustomed to considering only such things suitable for the people as he found personally repellent. That, for him, was the theory and practice of 'socialist realism'.

Gazing at me through his intellectual-looking spectacles as if from some immense distance away, Comrade Révai sought to explain to me the duties of a Communist writer. He had nothing against *Have*, he said. In fact he liked the play. But there were plenty of plays – some good, some not so good. That wasn't the point. From a Communist with a fairly well-known name one expected something more. I did not know whether he was serious or whether he was making fun of me. 'You're to be general secretary,' he went on, 'of the Hungarian-Soviet Cultural Association. The Party wants you to found it and the Party wants you to make it work.'

'Comrade Révai, I don't know the first thing about that kind of work.'

'A Communist must know everything if it is the Party's command,' he said, closing the discussion with, I felt, a certain malicious enjoyment.

I have always had all the usual nightmares as a first night approaches – fire breaking out in the theatre, the chandelier crashing down into the audience, the leading man collapsing on stage with a heart attack – but since 1932 mine had also featured Dr Goebbels, and now, as 18 May 1945 drew nearer, Comrade Révai was in the habit of appearing to sweep my play from the stage. But none of it happened, and on the night I sat alone in the stage-box as the curtain opened on a new act of my life.

I became aware, almost with a start, of a faint stir in the audience. People were weeping – and it was not just for the fate of the lovers on stage. They were weeping at their own sufferings, their own joys. They were weeping because they remembered yesterday's misery – and even tomorrow's hope made them weep.

They wept to think of the Danube down which not long before the blood-stained corpses had swept after the nightly salvoes. They wept for the beautiful bridges, not one of which had survived the German retreat intact. And now that it seemed the days of destruction were past, they wept for happiness – because happiness hurt.

Then they applauded. And their applause was too great for an author, a play, a cast. It was for life. It was for the change for the better that had just been heralded from the stage out of the tragedy of the recent past. And it occurred to J.H. 45 that perhaps it had not been such a bad choice after all to take the twentieth century for a travelling companion.

Provided, of course, that it permitted itself no further absurdities. J.H. 45 had had his fill of camels in the snow and aeroplanes that did not fly.

The story was going the rounds in the Soviet Writers' Union as early as the first year of the war: Stalin had summoned his favourite playwright Alexander J. Korneichuk and commissioned him to write a play mercilessly pillorying the old Civil War generals who were downright failures when it came to modern warfare. The play came off well – in fact many thought too well. In the towns that they occupied one after another the Germans left it running in Russian and Ukrainian without any changes at all, so exactly did the image of the Soviet general as an ignorant sot and a dangerous incompetent suit their purpose.

Once victory was assured, however, Stalin took his old friends – including Marshal Voroshilov, whom Korneichuk had used as his model – back into favour. He dispatched the marshal to occupied Budapest as head of the inter-allied control commission.

Voroshilov loved throwing huge banquets with masses of people, freely indulging his taste for choice Moscow vodka on such occasions. He would lay on an opulent buffet that had been specially flown in right down to the last paté de foie gras. It did him good to look on as his guests, the élite of this country of which he had been placed in charge, weakened by months of undernourishment, the horrors of the siege still fresh in their memories, hurled themselves on the laden dishes with trembling greed and polished off everything in a matter of minutes.

In my capacity as head of the Hungarian-Soviet Cultural Association I was in almost daily contact with the marshal and his staff. There was even a risk of my getting too involved in the work of the association to the detriment of my writing. It was the first thing that had been able to keep me away from my exercise books for any length of time. It was not the routine work that interested me; I had had enough of Russian courses and lectures in Marxism-Leninism at the Berlin MASch. What so absorbed

276

me was the human side of the job, locating and saving the artists and writers and scholars, great and famous men, who had as it were returned to the wild and had to be gradually won back for human society, reconciled with civilization. Of course at the same time they had to accustom themselves to the Russians and the Communists as well.

The country was alive again, but it was a provisional sort of existence. There were several parties, as in Western countries. There always had been; Hungary's parliamentary traditions went back a long, long way, however ineffective that parliamentarism had proved. The people of Hungary would hardly have understood what a one-party system meant. A party that was not a party?

The Communist Party did, however, make a tremendous impression on the population, and it was not only because it had a victorious army behind it. Numerically the Party was extremely small, much smaller even than people thought. Only a few hundred men had survived the underground years. A similar number returned from abroad, both East and West. There were only a few survivors from labour battalions and camps. Yet these men enjoyed a quite extraordinary prestige. Were they loved? Hardly. Feared? More likely. Did people expect something of them? Everything. Good and bad, without limit. They were thus able to draw hundreds and even thousands with them. And one was not sure whether it was not in fact hundreds of thousands.

Bridges over the Danube? Re-laying the railway lines? The Minister of Transport had given the word and the bridges were begun, the railways in process of being restored to life. The Minister of Transport was the Communist Ernö Gerö. Land for the landless? The Minister of Agriculture had said yes and the partition of the land was already under way. The Minister of Agriculture was a Communist and his name was Imre Nagy.

Have was played at the National Theatre every afternoon – at three o'clock, to give the audience time to get home on foot before curfew. An enormous banner suspended between two ruined buildings announced the production. Ragged, half-starved people poured into Budapest, sometimes after an adventurous

277

journey, in order to see theatre played again. Theatre people from the provinces battled their way through to the capital to hire scripts and costumes for *Have*.

In one mining town the local amateur dramatics group even began rehearsing *God, Emperor, and Peasant*. Their Member of Parliament, a quiet, unassuming young worker who had fought in the underground movement and whom I found extremely likable, invited me to the first performance. His name was János Kádár, and he was later to play a crucial role in the history of Hungary and of Europe as well as in the personal history of J.H.

29

*The girl in blue – My second Peter – Leo's
warning – Rákosi gets the go-ahead*

THE first thing that struck me was the exceptionally beautiful
colour of her shantung costume, and I forthwith dubbed her 'the
girl in blue'. I was deeply involved in a discussion with Helen at
the time – we were at the theatre, and Helen was a kind of artistic
dictator from Party headquarters – and I was not able to do anything further about the lovely girl with her beyond taking note of
her somewhat unusual hair-style and the battered sandals with
which she was incongruously shod.

In the interval I learnt that 'the girl in blue' was called Eva M.,
that she was twenty-nine – sixteen years younger than I – and
that she had joined the illegal Communist Party at the outbreak of
the war. Twice married and twice divorced, she was the mother of
a year-old boy by the name of Peter. (No one could have told me
then that little Peter would become my own dear son and, with
Eva, my wife, the most-loved person of my latter years.)

The next time I met Eva was in Helen's room at Party headquarters. The two of them were engaged in the curious activity of
trying – without benefit of either tools or know-how – to improve
Eva's broken footwear. In seconds I was similarly employed,
though to no better effect, and seriously though we took our work
– these were the only shoes she had – we could not help repeatedly
bursting into laughter.

Soon we could be seen out walking together, with Eva stopping
every ten paces to yank her sandals straight. Our earnest conversation never let up for a second, though. We discussed every aspect
of the production of *Have*, of which she had seen the first performance, and it emerged that she knew a great deal about the

theatre. From the theatre we turned to the work of the Hungarian-Soviet Cultural Association, and before very long it was clear to me that I must have this beautiful woman with the ruinous sandals and the needle-sharp mind, the biting sense of humour and enormous self-confidence, to head one of my departments. I asked her, thinking – though I hardly admitted it to myself – that I should then have her near me all the time. She turned to me with her triangular eyebrows raised inquiringly, gave me a searching look that turned slowly into a teasing smile, and, when I had already given up hope, said, 'Yes.'

Next day the cadre department of the Party, without whose consent no important post could be filled nor any Party member accept such a post, readily gave its amen. And when at last the windows of my pension were glazed, Helen, Eva, and little Peter got a room there too.

I was in Marshal Voroshilov's good books. I mentioned that a play of mine was being produced in Vienna and that I should like to attend the première, and hardly were the words out of my mouth before he was ordering transport for me there and back.

The principle of secrecy did not allow me to be given adequate warning of when and in what manner I should be making the journey, with the result that I arrived in Vienna frozen stiff, having covered the distance in a small training aircraft with little more than a light summer coat between me and the October air. The journey back to Budapest caught me even more unawares. But the production, in Vienna's Volkstheater, was magnificent.

Curiously enough the evening turned out to be a kind of sequel to the *God, Emperor, and Peasant* episode in Berlin. There were demonstrations against both play and author. Exactly why a handful of people gave somewhat halting voice to a few shouts of protest was something I never discovered. A belated Nazi demonstration? Or did they just not like the play? But one does not expose oneself to the risk of physical violence merely because one does not like a play. For on this occasion the demonstrators were actually beaten black and blue by the rest of the audience. And not only by the audience; when the young actor Hans Putz saw what was going on he leapt from the stage – costumed as he was as a Hungarian policeman – and enthusiastically joined in the fray.

Amid the ruins of Budapest I found my former life also in ruins. When Micky had gone to sleep in Anderli's bed that memorable evening of Stalingrad, the future course of our marriage had been predetermined. It led, sooner or later, to a drifting apart, and ultimately to divorce.

Now Eva was there – and it was as if I had known her as long as I had known the sun, as long as I had been speaking our mother tongue. Eva was mine, and for the first time I felt truly at one again with the ruined city.

When my family arrived in Hungary six months after my own arrival (and unannounced, so that neither woman was spared the shock), my life had already assumed a new form and a new content. Both form and content, however, were markedly provisional in character, since at that time Eva would hear nothing of a permanent connection and made me promise never even to mention the subject of marriage.

Now I must tell you about Leo.

Leo was a tall, thin, bald-headed, elderly gentleman whom I found in Eva's room one day. He was the sort of man mature women and teenagers fall for with equal alacrity, and he was wearing a British uniform. At that time one still saw many officers in the uniforms of the Allied armies in the Soviet-occupied zone. Later such a sight became quite inconceivable.

'My father,' said Eva, introducing the stranger. 'The man I was telling you about,' she said, introducing me.

Eva's father offered me his hand in a way which, if not exactly friendly, was not impolite either. After one or two empty remarks he asked me to trust him and to call him by his Christian name. He said he was not a soldier but a war correspondent – that was why he was wearing this uniform. Then he was silent, as if we had exhausted all the relevant subjects. My new friend – or relative? – lit a fresh cigarette from the butt of the old. He was a chain-smoker and remained so until his death in 1960. (He died shortly before my release from prison, having fought tirelessly for my freedom without a thought for our political differences.)

'It appears,' he went on, 'that we are the two men most concerned about what happens to this woman. I am what you call a bourgeois journalist. Though certainly not as far to the left as you, I'm liberal enough to have been on Hitler's "wanted" list. Everyone he could lay his hands on at our paper he wiped out. I got away. To London. This was in 1939. I begged my daughter to come with me. She refused. Why? I did not know. Now I do: political obligations. All right, she's done her duty. And I've come back to get her. Her mother is expecting her and little Peter in London.'

On the table was a photograph that had not been there the day before – a beautiful woman of middle age. Eva's mother. It was not until some years later that I met and grew so fond of her.

'Do I now have to reckon with you as well? Do I have to ask you to let my daughter go?' For a moment he came close to losing his self-control. 'A married man with children of his own?'

Eva, who had been looking out of the window, whirled round to face her father. 'I thought I asked you not to bring that up.'

Leo was silent for a moment. Then he came a step closer to me and said with quiet urgency, 'Don't you realize they look at you askance in Hungary? Even hate you? The man from Moscow. All right, don't tell me – the men from Moscow saved the country from Hitler. But what has been carries little weight in politics. Only the here and now counts. And here and now you're the colonizer. You're the colonizer and the colonized in one person. An oppressor who's himself one of the oppressed.' His voice was little more than a whisper now. 'But one day you're going to have to decide. So is my daughter. Either you unconditionally side with the oppressors if you have the stomach for it or you'll come under the oppressor's knout yourselves. You can appreciate that neither fate is one I should wish my daughter.'

I replied, dry-mouthed at first but with gathering momentum, that he must see his daughter's point of view. Everything she had sacrificed so much for, everything she had risked her life for was now at last on the verge of realization. Freedom, prosperity for all, security, a golden age . . . Should she now turn her back on it? Suffer instead the decline of the capitalist system? The final, cataclysmic economic crisis that was bound to hit the West before long?

Leo gave a loud, provocative laugh. His daughter had to make a visible effort not to lose patience with him.

'Do you want to know what it'll look like here before long? The people are going to revolt against your Rákosis and your Gerös. *A la lanterne!* There'll be barricades ...' Suddenly he was almost beseeching me. 'Don't you see? I want to spare my only child such a fate.'

My answer came out rather over-solemn. 'The Hungarian people will have no further need of barricades. But if it should one day be forced to take up arms once more in defence of its freedom, then I should go with it. With the Hungarian people. And so would your daughter too.'

(More than ten years after this conversation the Hungarian people took up arms. Eva and I were there. With the people. But not with Rákosi and Gerö – against them and all like them.)

That was a proud day, that day in November 1945 when the first free elections were held in Hungary. Or rather it began as a proud day. It ended as a sad one.

The Communists looked forward with confident anticipation to the victory they believed they had earned by their enthusiasm, their determination, their self-sacrifice, their discipline – and the friendly support of the Soviet Union.

The defeat was devastating. In a free and secret ballot the Communists received seventeen per cent of the votes cast. The opposition, the Smallholders' Party, received fifty-two per cent. We were thunderstruck. Never had we reckoned with such ingratitude. Was it possible that people thought so little of us? Did not like us? Did not want us?

Rákosi was disturbingly calm. He had been against democratic elections from the start. The Party, in his view, should vote for all. The Party should elect itself. Now at last the comrades in Moscow would have to give him the green light to seize power as he could by such means as he felt to be necessary.

He got the green light, and he achieved his objective. Beginning with some carefully planned and precisely executed gerrymandering and continuing with an ever more brutal application of naked violence he rose step by step to become absolute dictator. The dictation, however, came from Moscow.

The green light. Whatever the Hungarian Communist Party and its leader Mátyás Rákosi wished to accomplish, they always had the identical means at their disposal – the AVO (Államvédelmi Osztály) or secret state security police. That was Rákosi's green light. The AVO grew steadily in size, strength, unscrupulousness, and cruelty. It stood in the service of foreign interests and of the men who served those foreign interests. Its task was to impose upon a vast majority the commands of a tiny minority – and it fulfilled it.

30

A visit to Berlin (Soviet Zone) – 'Have you brought bed linen?' – Towards the German Democratic Republic

AFTER productions in Budapest, Vienna, Berne, and Prague, *Have* was put on at the Deutsches Theater in East Berlin. J.H. 48 was invited to the first performance by Wilhelm Pieck, a circumstance that lent him such importance all of a sudden that he had no trouble in taking his wife Eva along too.

Altogether we spent a month in Soviet-occupied Germany. Brecht and Helly arrived back at the same time, as did the writer Arnold Zweig and the composer Hanns Eisler. It was a great reunion. For me at any rate – a reunion with Berlin, the city of my youth, the city of momentous decisions, the city of my brightest dreams; a city of ruins, too, facing an uncertain future, which made it also a sad reunion.

But also a reunion brimming with expectations.

The occasion could, however, have been bigger and more important than it was, particularly the meeting between Brecht and myself. We had a great deal to say to one another but got little of it said. Admittedly he did not leave the theatre during the performance this time, as far as I know, nor did he use the occasion to open a fresh discussion of whether *Have* was Marxist or not, but I feel we ought not to have left it at that.

Brecht had come from America, where he had been received with nothing like the respect due to his talent. For him it was more than simply a matter of carving out a new existence for himself and his family in the country of his birth. He clearly regarded the founding of the Berlin Ensemble and the

285

Schiffbauerdamm Theatre as a mission. Many of his circle virtually expected miracles of him.

It was by no means as easy as one tends to think. To create a theatre along pronouncedly avant-garde lines at a time when the dreariest kind of 'socialist realism' constituted the Moscow canon and every deviation from it was tantamount to taking one's life in one's hands – well, it was hardly child's play. Was it the toughness and intellectual superiority of the Brecht-Weigel team and their staff alone that triumphed or were there in the Russian or East German leadership people far-sighted enough to see that a Brecht theatre in the East could become a goose that – politically speaking – laid golden eggs?

Undoubtedly Brecht had to make concessions too. He was obliged to submit to the dictates of a political leadership that laid down the content and direction of literature and subjected everything to a principle of the meanest utilitarianism. The question is whether in fact the writer has any right to forgo independent judgement in matters of politics and philosophy. Can he be allowed to become the harbinger of propositions whose truthfulness he has not weighed up himself but has assumed on someone else's – perhaps a party's – authority? Brecht was a great lover of the pithy formula and the simplifications imposed on him may have suited his purpose for a while. In the long run, however, they must have become a burden to him and begun to conflict with his conscience.

I remember one evening when we tried to talk about this question, but Friedrich Wolf, ever anxious to avoid conflict, swiftly deflected the conversation. Brecht and I lived another eight years together on this planet – and found no time to begin another serious discussion of the sacred duties and rights of the dramatist.

'Oh, are you from Abony?' asked the hotel porter, reading the particulars I had entered in the register. 'I had a marvellous, marvellous time there.'

'When was that?'

'1944.'

I spared us both the embarrassment of any remark, merely

wondering to myself whether that marvellous, marvellous time had coincided with the deportation of my brother Max and his family to Auschwitz. The good man was puzzled when I broke off our conversation. In Germany, three years after the war, I found myself involved in many such exchanges.

The hotel was the famous, the elegant, the superb Adlon – or rather as much of it as was still habitable, namely what had probably once been the servants' wing. One reached it by way of an internal courtyard, having first passed a completely bombed-out section with a bath-tub hanging suspended in mid-air.

The next question was, 'Have you brought bed linen?' If the guest then opened his suitcase and produced sheets and pillow-cases, the staff knew that this was no V.I.P. If, however, the newcomer did not even make a move towards his luggage because – as had happened in our case – a Russian officer and his orderly had already delivered a quantity of high-quality, if still slightly damp, bed linen for his use, the entire hotel knew that it was dealing with a traveller of the highest repute.

Our whole reception was magnificent. Eva and I were quite overwhelmed. Admittedly Becher missed us in the pitch darkness of Anhalt station – at that time one got off in the Western Sector when one arrived by train – but the director of the Deutsches Theater, Wolfgang Langhoff, found us and the little motorcade that escorted us passed slowly through the Western Sector to the Brandenburg Gate, which one could then still drive through when one wished to. Every minute an aeroplane thundered overhead, for this was during the airlift, and suddenly we found ourselves plunged into international politics – something we did not properly understand and in fact only had a vague idea of. And who was there to guard the traveller against getting certain things, possibly the most essential, back to front?

It seemed to J.H. 48 and his wife that they wore the whole portentous Eastern Sector in their buttonholes like a badge of rank. Sometimes, though, we had the feeling that the Eastern Sector was sporting us – Brecht, Helly, Zweig, and Eisler who had returned voluntarily and me, the important visitor from a friendly foreign power – as a status symbol for the world to see.

Born 1900

With the Pieck family I celebrated a happy and heart-felt reunion. Then there was a formal invitation to a simple dinner with Willem at the Politbureau. Walter was there too – my first encounter with the little pointed beard that was to go down in history. Becher, as second host, was everywhere, and Lilly with him, First Lady of East German socialist realism. A happy and heart-felt reunion too with the survivors of the Moscow colony of writers and actors, with the exception of those who had settled in the West and were thus officially anathema.

They were all busy settling in and getting flats and furniture. They ate at The Seagull, the artists' club where we got our meals too, and all in all life was pretty difficult for them. I remember one extremely well-known singer who could not appear because she possessed no evening shoes. With Helly acting as go-between Eva donated hers, perhaps in grateful remembrance of the dilapidated pair of sandals that had first brought us together.

On the Hungarian side we had the pleasantest hosts imaginable in the head of the Hungarian Mission in East Berlin, Imre Horváth, and his wife, with whom we became good friends. (Seek that friendship not, it lasted only until the first real test. A course of action regarded as perfectly 'Communist' by the Horváths – along with hundreds and thousands of others – made me disgusted not only with their friendship but with everything then calling itself loyalty to the Communist Party line.) Horváth, a man of working-class origins but with the manner and bearing of an aristocrat and with an unquenchable yearning for art and culture, took a lively and sincere interest in the promotion of this Hungarian play in Berlin. He and his wife wanted to give a small banquet after the first performance.

During one of the dress rehearsals Horváth came in with some exciting news. He had just been talking to Colonel Tulpanov, he said. Colonel Tulpanov was one of the most important besides being one of the most interesting and authoritative officers of the occupying army, a fine-looking man with a shaven head. The colonel had told him that he had an important job for us. The projected small banquet was to assume enormous proportions and provide the setting for the first unofficial and as it were fortuitous meeting between certain Russian and East German high-ups round a neutral tablecloth.

What is today the German Democratic Republic was – in a context of official-unofficial open secrecy – to be first outlined that evening.

And so began such a piece of mummery as rivalled Potemkin's villages. The Hungarian Mission's pretty but modest villa was too small for the purpose. In a matter of minutes the occupation authorities had assigned us a larger house. For the larger house, however, the furniture, table linen, and silver were hopelessly inadequate. Secret Russian supplies were moved in. Eva and Mrs Horváth spent days combing the antique shops for whatever they could find. Any remaining holes were plugged with pots of laurel and oleander bushes. Meanwhile a vast and sumptuous buffet, more splendid even than Marshal Voroshilov's, was flown in – such culinary splendours as were not to be had in Hungary at that time for any money.

The reception in the Hungarian Mission's new premises went off extraordinarily well. He would be a bold man who maintained that all present on that evening were united in love, but for the founding of a new republic that was not strictly necessary. Colonel Tulpanov, for example, turned to Eva at one point with the unexpected question whether she too found the Germans among the company so repellent. To this day I do not know what the colonel, who incidentally was the supreme guardian of German cultural interests in the Soviet Zone, hoped to achieve with such a question. I was told that Tulpanov never said or did anything without a reason, and I quite believed it. Eva, however, as usual quick on the uptake, answered with a smile unaccompanied by speech.

The multifarious cold dishes and their heavily-spiced contents gave people a thirst for Hungarian wine, and the Tokay and Badacsonyi stimulated appetites afresh. Bemused but victorious, the German guests contemplated their gorgeous if hastily improvised surroundings and wiped paprika-stained grease from their lips and freshly-grown beards. The Russian general with the shaven head said little and kept in the background.

Pieck, Ulbricht, and the former Social Democrat Grotewohl

were the men of the moment. They had dined for the first time at the same table as their powerful protectors and drunk their health in a friendly if somewhat timid fashion. They were all smart enough to see that they were only victors as long as they did not ask where their victory would lead. Or would they, if someone had told them that the trophies that awaited them were barbed wire, a brick wall, and bullets for the fugitives – would they perhaps then have said no?

No – they would have said yes even then.

31

A tragic pettiness – Who'll be villain? – Lukács
tries to explain – The tyrant is dead

WITH us things went both well and badly. We had an organized
state and we called it socialist or at least believed it was on the
way to socialism. It mirrored ever more precisely its archetype
in the East, and everyone was somehow a prey to a deep feeling
of unhappiness.

The peasant was given ever more rudely and violently to understand that he was not in fact lord over the land he farmed, not
even when it had been the new state itself that had dealt it out to
him. He must join with his embittered fellow-sufferers to form
collectives along officially prescribed lines that neither he nor
anyone else was capable of following. The secret police then
made him sign his name to the effect that he did so of his own
accord. On the basis of plans and figures drawn up at random a
new national industry was called into a simulacrum of existence
and workers and peasants forced to live an aimless and illusory
life in this world of illusion.

And throughout it all the twin authors of this senseless suffering – namely Rákosi and Stalin – must be jubilantly extolled.
This extorted, purely superficial worship took on an almost
liturgical character. I once had to deputize for someone and chair
a Party meeting – something I never normally did. I was handed
a printed sheet which not only laid down the exact contents of
my speech but also prescribed the cheers that were to interrupt it
and the respective intensities of the applause that was to greet
each mention of Rákosi's or Stalin's name. A nation was compelled to raise three cheers to its own destruction.

The most shattering tragedies became commonplace. One

lived them, and yet one failed to grasp them – and above all one failed to *write* them, though tragedies ask to be written. The Labdacidae, who provided the great playwrights of the classical stage with their models, were a family of thoroughly unfortunate people. Yet they were people of such stature, and the men who couched their tragedies in literature did so in such depth, in such breadth, and with such grandeur that each step down into the hell of Greek tragedy becomes a step up into heights as yet unscaled by mortal feet. We, on the other hand, learnt by degrees to live in small, even in exiguous spiritual dimensions. I, whose profession it was to write plays, passed the great tragedies by and wrote things of no importance.

Who was there to record the tragedy of Andor Gábor? Who could see that drama of destiny, that character drama, and dared portray it? He died, and the cause of death read 'pneumonia'. But above all he died because no human organism could assimilate such a disappointment and smilingly go on living.

Will someone some day tread the boards to reveal the gap that lies at the heart of the philosophy of Georg Lukács, and set the tragic keystone at last in place? Who will take the pocket tyrants – Rákosi, Gerö, Révai – and show the true historical scale of their tragic pettiness? And who will write the appalling tragedy of our man in the street? The irreparable spiritual and moral breakdown suffered by the worker who for decades had placed his faith in the inspiring watchword 'Unite!' and who must now finally accept the fact that he had been betrayed, that he was inextricably ensnared in artificially created contradictions? We were not the tribe of the Labdacidae, but the tragedy of the world we lived in was no less bleak.

When Eva and I arrived back at Budapest's Eastern station after a month away there was a new and strange quality in the air. Was it thinner than before, or thicker? People breathed with difficulty and spoke with strain in their voices. Moscow had given Rákosi the green light to seize absolute power, never mind how. This meant that any man's life – or it might be his honour, his fortune, or his freedom – could be squandered whenever Rákosi and his secret police with Gábor Péter at their head felt like squandering it. The random pouncing, the total promiscuity of arrest and condemnation were no weakness but in fact the strength of the system. That the life even of the most innocent should be in constant danger was part of the fabric of society.

You cannot have theatre, however, not even the puppet kind, without an adversary. Who was to play the part of Rákosi's adversary in order that a workable piece of theatre might emerge? In reality, you see, he had none. There was no one in all the land who would have risen up against Rákosi. Party discipline was as good as flawless. So one began to look around – as a good pupil of Stalin's – for *potential* antagonists. Who was as it were *eligible* as an opponent, however little he might suspect his own eligibility? Rákosi's short-sighted but – for short focal lengths – sharp enough eyes saw two men he could choose from: Imre Nagy and László Rajk.

Imre Nagy – thick-set, no longer young, unpractical, schoolmasterly, used to Moscow – was for the moment left unharmed. László Rajk had as yet had neither time nor opportunity to show what kind of political line he intended to take. But it was common knowledge that he had never partaken of the bread of the Comintern and never spoken the language of the Lux Hotel. Rajk was not, like the new rulers of Hungary, returned from abroad, and that made him foreign to them. He was also young, tall, good-looking, had taken part in the Spanish Civil War, though not at Moscow's bidding, fought in the anti-Fascist underground, been condemned to death by the Nazis, and escaped as if by a miracle. The young adored him.

The choice fell on Rajk. Rajk must play the villain in the new puppet play and die on the gallows. They did not give him a new script, though. He had to trot out the stale old script of the Moscow trials.

The process of intimidation had to embrace everybody, without exception. If you let anyone off you were not a good pupil of the 'teacher and father of all working people', Stalin. Rákosi called himself his 'best pupil' and wanted to be worthy of the title. So he took the line of greatest inhumanity.

And yet there came a day when Moscow had to get rid of him. On one point even Rákosi had made a fundamental mistake. He cultivated and cherished something he called ideology. He felt both safer and greater for the fact that he nursed this something in his breast. This 'something' was a few garbled scraps of old Marxist texts adapted for everyday use and erected into dogmas. Rákosi believed in those dogmas, and that was his tragi-comic crime. That was why Anastas Mikoyan, acting for the top men in Moscow, made him climb into that aeroplane in the summer of 1956 and leave Hungary, never to be seen there again.

For Stalin there was no such thing as ideology. He created the dogmas himself, unscrupulous and unbelieving. For him every-thing had one purpose and one alone: the growth and prosperity of the great Russian *imperium*.

A Communist ideology is gradually coming to be something only the West believes in. In the West people at least presume that the East still believes in it, whereas the East grew out of the fairy-tale long ago. It is quite conceivable that there will come a day when the East is finally immune against the last vestiges of its own ideology whereas the West for its part completely and utterly loses its immunity against the ideology that is called Communist. It would be a black day for the West – and it could become the great day of the Russian Empire, never mind whether it has a Tsar or a Politbureau at its head.

Georg Lukács once tried to explain to the Party's functionaries what kind of animal a writer in fact is. More precisely, he confined himself to Communist writers, maintaining that they ought neither to be lone wolves nor to be subject to the same strict Party discipline as other Party workers; they should have a firm but at the same time flexible liaison with the Party, the kind of liaison partisans have with the regular army in wartime.

The Party leadership evidently did not like us writers laying claim to such a loosening of the Party tie. One Rudas – he was one of the Rudas brothers I had known back in 1919 – attacked Lukács furiously in the official Party organ for views that he held to be in opposition to Marxism (Stalinist reading). In the atmosphere of the time this kind of criticism, backed up by the full authority of the Party, was tantamount to a denunciation and could have had disastrous consequences for a man who had already seen the inside of the Lubyanka. This would have been the moment for Comrade Révai, powerful guardian of the national culture, to write off something of his debt of gratitude to his master. Not a bit of it: in an article that bore the stamp of Party approval he dealt the already severely maltreated Lukács a few supplementary kicks.

In this kind of hue and cry atmosphere it was impossible that I should remain unscathed. Like so many things that I ought really to have seen coming, the blow took me completely by surprise. Was it an essay I had written or was it a lecture at the Academy of Theatre, where I taught theory of drama? I forget.

Were my views right or wrong? No one bothered to ask. Was what I had said copied from the classics of Marxism or not? That was the question. Cribbed from the classics – all right. Not taken from the works of people whose portraits were carried through the streets on the First of May – suspect and dangerous. Where is the guarantee (asks the guardian of Marxist interests) that nothing has slipped in that is not derived from the authorized quotations? Who was to say that my thoughts had not been directed against socialist realism, against Comrade Rákosi, against the great Stalin himself? The hunt was on.

Luckily for me it was just around this time that I finished *The Bridge of Life*, a play dealing with the truly heroic bridging of the Danube during the winter of 1945–6, and it was awarded the highest distinction for Hungarian literature, the Kossuth Prize. Comrade Révai informed me of the award in the following terms: 'Now you've written something really smarmy – I can finally give you the Kossuth Prize.' At the moment he had more need of a new Kossuth Prize-winner than a reproved heretic. So I was saved – until the next view halloo.

Although an expensive play to produce, *The Bridge of Life* was played in at least twenty theatres at home and abroad – including 'my' theatre in Dresden where I had studied stage design. After attending the first performance in Dresden I went on to Berlin to see Langhoff about a production there. Langhoff took the opportunity of doing the best thing a true friend could have done – he told me straight out that he thought *The Bridge of Life* at best a weak play, that he had no wish to put it on, but that he did want at all events to push through a production of *The Turkey-boy* although he knew that this play could not be performed in Hungary and would not be recommended for export. Langhoff was a man of reputation, however, besides being well-versed in Party wire-pulling. The first performance of *The Turkey-boy* took place at the Deutsches Theater in the autumn of 1954 – again in the presence of Wilhelm Pieck – and it was one of my finest and most successful premières. In Hungary *The Turkey-boy* remained under a tacit ban – for reasons that to this day have never been communicated to me. Rumour had it that the play reminded Rákosi of an argument he had had twenty-five years before, an argument in which he had come off worst. That would have been enough.

Meanwhile Rákosi's absolute power grew year by year, month by month. Countless numbers of people disappeared in the furious storm that Stalin's best pupil raised about him – most of them, as far as one could see, for no reason at all. It was said (though such stories could be neither proved nor disproved) that in a single day Rákosi had eight of his bodyguards executed. I met an acquaintance called Károly Ráth in the street one day. Having each bought an evening paper from a newsboy, we parted and walked off in different directions. When we had gone a few steps we both opened our papers. The first thing I saw was Ráth's name in a list of people who had just been arrested. This time the news had moved faster than Gábor Péter's overworked organization.

Reprisals against the so-called 'kulaks' were characterized by particular inhumanity. Kulaks were actually well-to-do peasant proprietors or such as had once been well-to-do. But there were all kinds of other reasons why one might be put on the 'kulak list' – which meant that one virtually became an outlaw.

One day they started to move former bourgeois, former landowners, aristocrats, and other 'class enemies', for the most part intellectuals, forcibly out of the towns and resettle them in the houses, stables, barns, and sheds of the kulaks in the villages or on isolated farmsteads out in the country. The victims had to leave behind everything but what they could carry with them.

A young actress by the name of Sári Déri, generally agreed to be the most beautiful woman on the Budapest stage, was resettled for being married to a count. The count, incidentally, was completely without any property and had for years been employed as a stable boy at one of the state-owned stables. Not even the intervention of leading theatre personalities could get Sári's banishment revoked. Probably on account of her extraordinary beauty she was treated in a particularly hateful manner. She worked as a day-labourer, washerwoman, kitchen maid, but as soon as it emerged that she was a 'countess', her current employer, fearing possible complications for himself, immediately gave her the sack. In the end she died of appendicitis – for lack of medical attention.

One old man – a retired accountant whom I knew through the Party – when told he was to be resettled showed the official his Party card; the official snatched the card from his hand and never gave it back. This was unheard-of. Were we not continually being told that the Party card was something sacred and must be treated as such? The ill-humour of the authorities grew worse almost daily.

I wrote countless letters to Rákosi in connection with resettlement cases but do not know of one that received the slightest attention. One morning my mother and my sister Juliska with her husband and son – both lawyers – received a resettlement order themselves. Even in the circumstances this took me by surprise. No reason was given, but then government and Party were not in the habit of justifying their activities, and when they did give a reason it was not necessarily the truth of the matter. I found the family in despair; without any hope that it would be successful they were drawing up a petition to which my brother Bandi added his signature, Bandi who as an engineer and one of the country's few shipbuilding experts had recently received an award. I signed too as a Kossuth Prize-winner, and added an accompanying letter, but I doubted whether the petition would reach its destination within the stipulated twenty-four-hour period. Juliska, ready if need be to take Mother on her back again, compared the prospect of resettlement with the ghetto, a comparison in which the ghetto came off best. I telephoned a friend at the Ministry of the Interior and subsequently the Minister himself. Shaken and concerned, they both explained that they had no power to intervene since resettlement questions were decided at top level. My voice by now choked with anxiety at the fate of my mother and Juliska's family, I rang Rákosi's office. A secretary answered the phone. He was a jovial fellow. 'There you are, you see? One shouldn't stick up for strangers so much. It can happen to one's own family too.' The resettlement order was cancelled – my one and only success in this field.

Who was I, I began to wonder, that I could have landed in such a conflicting situation? A creator of the new world or a relic of the old? Was the thing I had fought and suffered for for decades to be reached at all along the road I had once decided to take and was still following? Was what I regarded as the new not in fact the old in sheep's clothing? Was I fighting a hopeless and deadly struggle against myself? The murderous absurdity of it all began to cause me physical pain – a pain that never left me until the day history appeared to promise a turn for the better.

In 1953 Stalin died. A certain relaxation of the terror was inevitable. In Hungary, too. Quick – where was a blameless man who could be dealt part of the responsibility for the country's future?

Imre Nagy was summoned to Moscow and returned as Prime Minister of Hungary.

32

The prisoners talk – Writer at bay – 'Kucsera'

NAGY set about repairing his predecessor's worst offences against human rights and human dignity. Under his government the compulsory co-operatives were allowed to dissolve themselves and agriculture to return to the smallholding principle, becoming in consequence – if to a limited extent – once more productive. The banishments were revoked – though of course the homes of the banished had long since passed into other hands – and the innocent condemned were acquitted in fresh trials. But the lion's share of power was still Rákosi's. He remained at the head of the Party and eventually, after some determined and extensive sabotage – and some changes in the Kremlin – managed to topple Nagy.

Nevertheless it proved impossible to put everything back the way it had been before. The yearning for a society with a human face – be it socialist, Communist, or whatever – that yearning remained. Many people began to see Rákosi – the 'Little Zaches' who had not long since looked so big – in his true light. Communist politicians who had been unjustly arrested during Rákosi's and Gábor Péter's reign of terror began to make known the truth about their trial and imprisonment.

Profound, indeed shattering mental and emotional conflicts came to light day after day. These men had begun their political careers as enthusiastic advocates of a highly simplified form of Marxism. Prison had brought them nearer reality. Their brief activity after their release, their inner struggles, disappointments, and hesitations are among the immediate historical antecedents of the 1956 uprising.

Who was there that afternoon in our flat? Béla Szász? Gyula Kállai? Szilárd Ujhelyi? János Kádár? Géza Losonczy? Just out of prison, they told of their years behind bars. Quiet, calm, objective reports from hell. They made shocking hearing. One was ashamed of having led a normal existence all those years.

What had given us the right to live as we did? What made us think we were building the new world? Was it not all a lie? I had travelled a long and tortuous road in order to help my country, my people, my neighbour to build a new and better life. What had I achieved? As an exile in a foreign land I had almost reached the point where I could look on with cool, objective patience while one attempt after another came to grief. But now I was at home. This was *my* country. These were my people. Were coolness and patience still permissible?

Phoney charges, false witnesses, wrongful sentences, mistaken self-accusations . . . Torture by hunger, by light, by sleeplessness, by electricity – under the supervision of a top expert, the Russian General Byelkin . . . This was no stranger talking but my friend Béla Szász, with whom I had once published a paper aimed at popularizing Soviet culture . . . Szilárd described his treatment in the hideous official terminology of punishment, his eyes behind his glasses seeming calmer than the man within . . . Exact, painstaking, mechanical imitation of the great example . . . This repetition of ghastly crimes, this stubborn continuance along a path that had already once – no, *every time* – led into the abyss, this raving blindness was torment to body and mind. This Massacre of St Bartholomew, the sanguinary puppet theatre, the murderous mockery of justice . . . When I experienced it for the first time, accompanied by Feuchtwanger's 'Yes, yes, yes' and Brecht's 'nests of conspirators', I believe I already felt there was something suspect and disturbing about it, but somehow at the time there was always an explanation. Must one go through the whole thing a second time? For a reprise there was not one jot of credibility left.

During Imre Nagy's brief period in power in 1953–5 I began writing *Fair Play for Gáspár Varró*, the drama of the landless Hungarian peasant who tries honestly and peaceably to follow the Communist path. I found I needed to consult some trial records in the Ministry of Justice. 'Where is there a quiet room for Comrade Hay, who's writing a play?' The Soviet adviser's office was unoccupied. Under Rákosi's government a foreigner had sat here supervising Hungarian justice as others supervised cultural affairs, army, and torture. An experienced man, no doubt. A worthy fellow, without question. One who had the Sinoviev and Kamenev cases already behind him and could restage the whole thing in any country at any time.

In Imre Nagy's time the advisory apparatus withdrew – to resume its old place following Nagy's fall. Before I was able to finish my play Rákosi's censorship had clamped down again, and *Fair Play for Gáspar Varró* was banned.

Meanwhile the tale told by the prisoners Nagy had freed was no longer to be heard only in private homes. Timidly at first, then with increasing assurance it was voiced at the Communist Party meetings of the Writers' Union, then at the Journalists' Association – and so on and on, in ever-widening circles, growing ever louder, more open, and more militant. The Party leadership founded a new institution called the Petöfi Club that was designed to act as a safety-valve. But the pressure of accusation from below was too great; inevitably the safety-valve burst.

This was the point at which I – J.H. 56 by this time – took up my pen. In an article in *Irodalmi Ujsáq* (Literary Journal) I wrote:

Literature must be forbidden nothing that is not in any case against the law. On the contrary the writer, like any other person, must be unconditionally allowed: to tell the truth; to criticize anything and anyone; to be sad; to be in love, to think about death . . . To believe in God's omnipotence; not to believe in God's omnipotence; to doubt the accuracy of certain plan figures; to think un-Marxistically; to think Marxistically, even when this leads to thoughts that are not yet accepted as the officially sanctioned truth; to consider the standard of living of many strata of society as being too low; to expose injustice even in places where the official opinion is that only justice is to be found; not to like individual politicians; . . . to condemn the way in which certain of our leading figures live, speak, and go about their business; to demand humanity even in places where less sensitive souls see no lack of it; to like the new industrial town of Stálinváros; not to like the said Stálinváros; to employ an unusual literary style; to reject the Aristotelian theory of drama; to abide by the Aristotelian theory of drama; to regard works that officialdom deems exemplary

301

as being of poor quality and *vice versa*; to make certain critical ideas heard, and not to give a fig for others ...

If anyone had said to me only a few weeks before that such demands, couched in such terms, would flow from my pen and be printed in an official newspaper in Hungary, I should have thought he was mad. And yet I became one of the most outspoken of all. The Party members in the Writers' Union held more meetings than they had ever held before – and non-members were welcome.

I had the feeling that that window of years ago with its huge dark rectangle still stood open before me. Every word I uttered was listened to. I spoke and wrote, prepared or off the cuff, always pointedly, always provocatively. I shrank from no danger and was a dangerous opponent.

The absolute freedom of literature – that was the ever-recurring theme. Friend and foe came to hear me, ready with a friendly or a hostile answer. There was a landslide in the press as well. Editors sought and found their way through to the truth.

Rákosi was deeply disturbed. He began to be afraid of all writers. They were an unknown quantity to him and he found them difficult to handle. A memorandum demanding certain elementary rights for literature and art was circulated among all kinds of intellectuals and submitted to the Party with many signatures. The Party organization of the Writers' Union, electing a new leadership, declined to exercise the 'dictatorship of the proletariat'. Instead of staging the usual mock election with a single list of candidates the Communist writers did something unheard-of in Communist circles – they held a genuine ballot. An example that others followed.

One date I remember well – 6 December 1955. We writers – that is to say a selected dozen or so of us – were instructed individually by telephone to report to the Metal Workers' Union building for a literary debate.

The first thing that struck us was the extraordinarily large number of cars parked outside the building. In the Hungary of that time you only saw that many cars at one go when a sizable bevy of top Party officials was gathered together. We were directed to the main hall, in which only events of the very greatest importance were wont to take place. Here in this same enormous room the case against 'Rajk and accomplices' had been heard. Had we Hungarian writers risen so high that we were already taking Rajk's place?

I began to wonder whether I had been silly to comply with the invitation. Who could have proved that I was not ill? Or was there still time to make myself scarce?

Still weighing up the possibilities of retreat, I let myself be inched forward until I was in the hall, where I unobtrusively took a seat by myself to one side. A man came up to me. The face was familiar: it belonged to one of Rákosi's bodyguards. He had some printed sheets in his hand. I was against being handed printed sheets by Rákosi's bodyguards. My name sprang out at me in bold type: 'J.H. . . . peddling the idea of the freedom of literature.'

How does one 'peddle' the idea of the freedom of literature? That was unclear. A further five or six names were mentioned in the text in connection with other similar charges, but what would have been most amazing, supposing one had still been capable of amazement, was the fact that the outcome of this evening's proceedings, the resolution to be passed by this assembly that had no competence to pass anything of the kind, was already in print – on this sheet that one had in one's hand. Did not Rákosi, did none of the others see the absurdity of the thing? No, they had grown accustomed to it; they called it – along with many other, much greater impossibilities – 'the dictatorship of the proletariat'. Back in 1919 we had said, 'Congratulations!' We had envisaged such a dictatorship differently then.

A tall, fair-haired, fat-faced man of about thirty, Szalai by name, a man in whom Rákosi showed boundless confidence, employing him successively as head of his secretariat, as a kind of sentinel of the country's cultural life, as Minister of Light Industry, and in a series of other top positions in government and Party, delivered a defamatory speech against writers in general and against the ones in bold type in particular. Beside him sat Rákosi, surrounded by his numerous bodyguard. He had taken his place among the presidium with his usual theatrical simplicity, greeting only *one* of

the writers present – Béla Illés, who was also an officer of the
Soviet army. His face was a flaccid yellow.

A number of Party and union officials and one or two writers
loyal to Rákosi made speeches reiterating the general and
personal accusations – 'peddling freedom' and so on – prescribed
on the printed sheet.

I waited with growing impatience to see who among us accused
would rise to answer. No one. Suddenly a crazy idea flashed
through my mind and I immediately translated it into action: I
wrote my name on a piece of paper and passed it up to the presidium. Before many minutes I was already rueing my impulsive-
ness, but it was too late. I had asked for the floor.

It was my blameless and naïve intention to explain in simple
terms what it was that we writers actually wanted. The need to
open my heart drew me on with the same magnetic force as the
dark rectangle of the window had drawn J.H. 18. But then there
had been a possibility of retreat. Now, as my name was called, I
had no choice but to make my way to the rostrum.

My very first sentence was interrupted: Rákosi himself echoed
my vocative 'Comrades' in a tone of mockery. This was the signal
for Szalai and the others. Rákosi conducted the barracking with
his eyebrows. Thereafter I was interrupted every second. Yells
and cries of derision came at me from all sides.

Suddenly I lost my sense of time and place. I was a small boy
again, back in Abony. Those dogs at the bottom end of the village!
Those ugly, shaggy, stinking, mangy curs in the yards of the
poorest peasants and cottagers! Their hoarse, cracked baying,
their rolling, bloodshot eyes, their hideous, menacing, knife-like
teeth and slavering gums as they hurled themselves in suicidal
fury at the flimsy gates that were all that stood between them and
me . . . My legs felt like running away, but I must not show that I
was afraid.

Sitting opposite me in the front row and standing at all the
exits were numbers of thugs like the one who had thrust the
printed sheet into my hand. I could see the muscles rippling and the
guns gleaming beneath their jackets. They were poised to spring –
a twitch of Rákosi's cheek and I should be torn in pieces. All at
once I knew what it felt like to be delivered up to lynch justice.

A woman came forward from the middle of the hall, moving with a soothing grace, and took up a position before me as if she wished to shelter me with her own body. It was Hilda Gobbi, an outstanding actress with the National Theatre and an old Communist from the underground years. Ten years before she had played the lame girl in *Have*.

Even Hilda's powerful voice was drowned in the general uproar. But her appearance inhibited Rákosi and the signal was withheld. The thugs' muscles slackened and their hands left their pistol butts. And the union official in the chair rang his bell and said, 'Five minutes – your time is up.' This is the moment when the speaker usually counters with, 'Please – just two more minutes.' I said nothing of the kind. I left the rostrum and soon the hall.

Out on the street two writers came up to me – Gábor Devecseri and Miklós Gyárfás, good friends, younger than I, and stronger. 'It's a dark night – we'll stick with you,' they said, and escorted me home. They sat up with me for hours, and neither they, nor Eva, nor I uttered one word.

The Central Control Commission is a kind of Party court. We writers – this time with all the formalities being observed – were summoned for questioning. But the occasion turned out to be quite unlike what the Commission was used to. No one apologized and no one practised self-criticism. The liberally administered 'Party reproofs', 'Party censures', and 'final warnings' frightened none of those present. The chairman of the Control Commission, Comrade Kis, who hated Rákosi with a burning hatred yet served him with untiring fidelity, fearing that at the first brush Rákosi would have his neck, was completely at a loss. One of the younger writers dared to say to the judges, 'It's not censure and reproof we deserve but gratitude.'

At around this time Rákosi is supposed to have decided to draw up the list of the four hundred persons he wanted to have arrested in a single night as the overture to a new long-running St Bartholomew's Day. For reasons unknown to me he kept putting it off – until the summer of 1956, by which time it was too late.

Until that summer's day in Budapest when father said to son, friend to friend, and lover to mistress, looking after a departing luxury airliner, 'Perhaps *he* is on that one.' Meaning Rákosi. For one knew, even if one hardly dared believe it, that Moscow had at last had enough of 'Little Zaches' and had sent Mikoyan to fetch him away. He was packed off for years to Yakutsk in the Far East, where his wife came from. Budapesters delighted in picturing him having to queue up with a string bag whenever he wanted to buy, say, an apple.

Ernö Gerö succeeded him as the new 'No. 1'.

Wherever these secret or open ways led, the first bold steps were taken at the Twentieth Congress of the Communist Party of the Soviet Union early in 1956. However inconsistent and incomplete were Khrushchev's impassioned outbursts at that Congress, they left in their wake something that could not be denied – a yearning that had been gathering strength for decades, a yearning for humanity.

For the despotism governing Russia and its colonial empire a hardly beneficial phenomenon.

'Why don't I like Comrade Kucsera?' ran the title of a longish article that J.H. 56 published in *Irodalmi Ujság* on 6 October 1956 – the day on which the rehabilitated László Rajk (or a collection of bones that had never been his) was interred with much pomp and ceremony.

It must have been four in the morning when I woke Eva with the finished manuscript.

'Shall I publish this? It could have serious consequences.'

After a moment's thought she replied, 'We'll bear them together.'

Which, as things turned out, we had occasion to do.

Who was Comrade Kucsera? Who *is* he?

Kucsera is the bureaucrat as wielder of power, as exploiter of our society.

I really do not like Comrade Kucsera – and I have my reasons. Nor does Comrade Kucsera have any liking for me. There's a reason for that too . . .

Kucsera is the great mistake of our history . . . Kucsera is something soft we have bumped into in the shadowy cul-de-sac of our

306

country's history. Kucsera is the know-nothing by conviction and passion, who looks down on us from the pedestal of his ignorance and clings fanatically to the fallacious principle of the permanent sharpening of the class struggle because it allows him to go on playing the part of political reliability personified with rarity value.

'Kucsera' found such an echo as I should never have dreamt possible. I had to recite it on every conceivable occasion. I recall one of my writer's evenings that was to have been held in a small room but had to be transferred to the big hall of the Academy of Music on account of the crush.

What does Kucsera live off? Undoubtedly off the appropriation of the surplus value. He lives off the fact that we in our society spend a considerable portion of the surplus value not on things of use to the community – schools, hospitals, investment in production, the maintenance of public order, science, culture, recreation, entertainment, and ideological work – but on Kucsera. On Kucsera's upstarthood. On Kucsera's dilettantism. And if the surplus value is insufficient to cover Kucsera needs, then the surplus value must be increased, no matter what the cost to the productive worker.

The name Kucsera became a household word. The Hungarian language adopted it as part of its vocabulary. It was used both as noun and as adjective. In a matter of days I received hundreds of letters, some enthusiastically approving, others threatening.

Many people actually called Kucsera bombarded the Ministry of the Interior with urgent appeals for permission to change their names.

There is no room in history for both Kucsera and us. We have to choose: either Kucsera or humanity. In Kucsera's eyes a lie is not a lie, murder not murder, law not law, and man not human. Kucsera says unity and means himself and the handful of people with whom he is hand in glove and who defy the unity of hundreds of thousands. Kucsera says production and means the sterile cycle that secures his existence. So how can one anyhow like him, this Comrade Kucsera? O Kucsera, do cease to exist! We don't want your life but we do want to call a halt to your Kucserahood!

When the masses filled the streets of Budapest on 23 October 1956, many of their banners read, 'Down with the Kucseras'.

Without a doubt I had touched on the sore point of our society

307

– the emergence of a parasite class, a new kind of exploitation, the rise of the Kucseras.

A few days later the people were up in arms, fighting the like-wise armed defenders of the Kucsera class.

Two fronts had crystallized in our country, and with astonishing clarity. Not the Communists and the non-Communists. The dividing-line went clean through the camp that called itself Communist. The two fronts were the Kucseras and the people who did not like them.

What did the Kucseras want? They wanted a social order that went by the name of 'Communism'. But it was to be a 'Communism' under the dominion of a single, parasitic class – the class of the Kucseras.

What did the anti-Kucseras want? They too wanted a particular social order and they too called it 'Communism'. But in that social order there were to be no bureaucratic rule, no parasites, no exploitation, and no Kucseras. Communism and Communism. The same word with two diametrically opposite meanings. The opposition had never been so unmistakable before. A Communism for humanity and a Communism for Kucseras – that is the great antithesis of the years to come. In what form they will both close in the decisive battle is something no one can say in advance.

33

A première is postponed – The hole in the flag –
A Prime Minister disappears – The time-fuse

THE first performance of *Fair Play for Gáspár Varró* was set for
26 October 1956.

Rákosi's dethronement had put my play in the news once more.
The new head of the Party cultural department was Gyula Kállai,
one of those life-long Communists who had been arrested under
both Horthy and Rákosi and been rehabilitated in the months
of the Nagy régime. He immediately removed the ban. The
production was entrusted to the finest artists of the Budapest
National Theatre. However, when an armed rebellion broke out
in the streets of the Hungarian capital three days before the
projected première I thought it not out of the question that the
occasion might have to be postponed. Little did I suspect that
it would not in fact take place until more than ten years later – in
German, in the German city of Wuppertal.

Early in the morning of 23 October 1956, then, J.H. 56 sat in
the empty auditorium of the National Theatre in Budapest,
watching the rehearsal of his play. As often during rehearsals I
was listening not to my own, endlessly repeated script but to
something as yet unwritten. There were ideas to be clarified, and
I could only really work a thing out by thinking up a play about it.

Brecht was dead. He had died in the summer and it had fallen
to me to go to Berlin and lay the Hungarian writers' wreath on
his grave. I found Helly and the Ensemble in a fever of activity.
The long-awaited and lengthily prepared London tour was
imminent. How sad that Brecht did not live to see that dawn of his
international triumph. What a shame that he left behind him an
unanswered question. Was he not in the very process of breaking

309

free from political dogma? Or was his art to be no more than an effective vehicle for the opinions laid down by the powers that be? Is the writer in our society no more than a retailer of the products of the ideologist?

Brecht's followers were to hold fast to the dogma and undermine and kill the drama. Is that really what his work is about, though?

That was my last visit to East Germany. My last meeting with Langhoff, too. I remember sitting with him, bragging about the marvellous results of the Hungarian thaw. An old lady, a professor's wife who was also present, asked casually, 'What raw materials do you have there?' 'All kinds,' I replied, 'even uranium.' 'Oh dear,' was her comment, 'you poor things!'

The curtain closed at the end of the first-act rehearsal – and at that moment a new drama began of which there was no mention in the programme. A group of young writers entered the theatre and came up to me.

'You must come to the Writers' Union immediately. Big things afoot. A mass demonstration, arranged last night by the polytechnic students. Like nothing the streets of Budapest have ever seen before. The writers have got to do their bit too.'

J.H. 56 was vice-president of the Writers' Union.

Dense, acrid clouds of tobacco smoke. The Writers' Union was full of people coming and going, hurried, preoccupied, yet with a certain solemnity in their bearing.

'We must draw up a list of our demands under twelve points.'

'Please take your seats, friends.'

'Twelve points . . . fourteen . . . ten . . . sixteen points . . . One point is enough: out with the Russians!'

'The Russians out of Hungary . . . Independence . . . Normal trade relations . . . If they want Hungarian uranium they must pay the world market price, and the same goes for aluminium. We're not going to be robbed.'

'National independence . . . Reforms . . . Democratization of political institutions . . . Imre Nagy's return to public life . . .'

And again and again, 'The demonstration . . . the procession . . . the rally . . .'

'Friends, please be seated.'

'Where's Veres? Where's the president?'

'Here's Kállai . . . Gyula Kállai, from Party headquarters.'

Through the thick curtain of smoke came Peter Veres, the president of the Writers' Union, with his white, peasant moustache. Beside him appeared Kállai's round head and thick lips.

'Take your seats . . . '

'We must go to Party headquarters . . . '

'To Ernö Gerö . . . '

'Who knows Gerö well?'

'Gerö's away.'

'No, he's back . . . '

'He's there but engaged till evening.'

'Gerö must see us straight away. That would be the limit . . . The city's full of demonstrators . . . '

'Sit down!'

'I've never seen so many people on the streets in my whole life . . . Students . . . '

'Workers as well . . . '

'More every minute . . . '

'The Party must head the demonstration . . . The twelve points . . . '

'A motion: we appoint two deputations. One draws up the demands – Veres, Kállai . . . The other deputation . . . Who's for? Against? Unanimous . . . '

J.H. 56 finds himself in the second deputation. 'Because you know Gerö . . . '

'Right – we go straight to Gerö . . . '

And off we went. Party secretary Máté came along too but the spokesman was to be J.H. 56 – because he knew Gerö so well.

Party headquarters seethed with excitement, with people darting hither and thither, others hanging about, and all talking in urgent whispers. Corridors normally silent but for the echoing footsteps of the guard now buzzed with non-stop talk. There was tension, but also gaiety, much hope, and here too a certain solemnity.

Hegedüs, the Prime Minister. If only he didn't look so ridiculously like Rákosi, was one's first thought. 'In fifteen minutes there's a break and Comrade Gerö will come out and see you.' Hegedüs was dying to hear from us what was happening out there on the streets and we to hear from him what they thought of it all *here*. (They say Hegedüs was one of the few who drew the consequences and was subsequently able to start leading a useful existence.)

'The demonstration will start moving after the twelve points have been read out . . . Veres and Kállai and some others are drawing them up. Veres will read them out by the Petöfi Monument . . . Thousands of people are waiting for the writers' deputation . . . '

'And the Party leadership . . . '

Gerö emerged from his office – aged, his eyes sick. He was shivering; he always seemed to be shivering then. 'Yes, comrades?'

'We have come to invite the Party leadership to head the demonstration . . . '

'No.'

'It would be impossible to stop the demonstration now even if one wanted to. What do the demonstrators want? Socialism. Communism. It's our own promises we want to honour. The Party *has* to say yes.'

'No.'

'This demonstration has been brewing since Rajk's state funeral, Comrade Gerö.'

'Since your Kucsera article, you mean?' Gerö threw in, as if to confuse me.

The writers' deputation tried to convince 'No. 1' that the enormous crowds on the streets were a force whose effect it was impossible to determine in advance. 'If just *one* of the top comrades came with us . . . '

'No!'

This man, whose career had begun among the masses, was already deaf to any mention of the common people.

I remembered the muzzle flashes and the sharp, stomach-turning rattle of the guns the police had greeted us with on the Suspension Bridge in 1919. Could it, in our state, in our society, happen again?

'Comrade Gerö! Promise us one thing at least: if the crowd starts moving, if it can't be stopped, say there won't be any shooting.'

The deputation formed a solid group around us. From the farthest corners of the room friends and strangers surged forward to hear his answer.

Gerö looked around him. A sallow smile slid over his ascetic face. 'That I promise you.' And in confirmation he offered me his hand. It was a manly, reassuring handshake.

I never saw him again after that meeting.

On the evening of the same day Ernö Gerö, the first man in the land, had the as yet unarmed crowd of demonstrators fired upon. No one knows the death toll of that evening.

The demonstration proceeded from the Petöfi Monument to the Bem Monument. From the revolutionary poet to the revolutionary commander of 1848-9. From Hungary to Poland. A powerful stretch of the Budapest boulevards. J.H. 56 had seen plenty of street demonstrations in his life but this one seemed larger and more populous than any. And gay, radiant. And unstoppable. During that demonstration a silent, mourning people learnt once more to talk and laugh. At the last minute the Minister of the Interior had decided to grant permission, thus legalizing the giant procession.

Arm in arm we strode along – five, six abreast. I walked with the students from the Academy, my pupils. One lost one another in the crowd, not knowing any more where the procession began and where it ended.

People felt an irresistible need to wave flags, to deck the city out, to raise this day somehow above all other days. On every balcony somebody appeared with a flag. In the middle of the red-white-and-green cloth, however, there was that new device, official since 1949, foreign, tricky, a violation of the national tradition. That was not what one wanted to see today repeated thousandfold on all those snapping flags. Someone took a pair of scissors and cut the hated symbol out – a happy thought that found hundreds and thousands of imitators. A hole in the middle of the tricolour became the provisional badge of our revolution. Soon similarly modified flags were flying from every building. The mutilation made them whole.

We strode, we sang, we laughed. Strangers and semi-strangers threw themselves about one's neck. At every point along our route we were greeted with the wildest enthusiasm. A joyous encounter of the people with itself.

Keeping together, the crowd made its way expectantly over the Danube bridges to Kossuth Square and the Parliament Building. This was the place for great events. And the moment was cut out to become a turning-point of history. But it remained a moment of irresolute waiting, and was followed by further uneventful seconds, minutes, hours . . .

Such moments decide the fate of revolutions. By imperceptible degrees the quietly seething mass underwent a transformation. The crowd as it was before it was kept waiting in the square would have been satisfied with a restoration of the state of affairs obtaining in 1953–4 with Imre Nagy as Prime Minister. The crowd that had had to stare for hours at the silent façade of that vast building was ripe for disappointment at anything that should fail to exceed its expectations.

The first speech made by Imre Nagy – that day 'Uncle Imre' to everyone – after his return fell foul of a technical hitch (or was it plain sabotage?): the loudspeaker did not work. The crowd was exasperated, and when Nagy at last addressed it with an audible 'Comrades!' it no longer wanted to hear the word. The same force as might have stabilized the situation produced an unexpected instability.

A deputation was swiftly chosen to fetch Imre Nagy from his home and escort him to Parliament. A car? Nagy did not have one, had never had one . . . Eventually one of the writers turned up with his little four-seater. It was perhaps the first piece of improvisation. From then on everything was improvised; the struggle ran its course with neither plan nor strategy nor tactics, thrust hither and thither by the most diverse of forces. Imre Nagy knew only two guides: his own inherent decency and a strict observance of Party regulations that bordered on a lifeless formalism. Had he been a little less punctilious in one or the other respect he would probably have found a safer place to meet the people than the Parliament Building, only a few steps from Party headquarters.

When I saw Imre Nagy appear on that balcony it was as if I heard the door slam shut behind him. The door with no handle on the inside. I was and still am firmly convinced that Imre Nagy, in going to the Parliament Building unguarded and without any direct contact with the worker and peasant masses, delivered himself up into the hands of his enemies. From that moment on, and for a long time, he was no longer free but spoke and acted under direct coercion. Is it credible that after an event such as that change of government the new Prime Minister should not have felt the need to present himself to the people or at least address them over the radio? Here I am again; my platform is unchanged or changed in such and such respects. To anyone who knew 'Uncle Imre's' habits, his candid conversations on the street with total strangers, such conduct must inevitably seem absurd.

But what was even less likely was that a husband and father, as Nagy was, when called away from home unexpectedly, knowing that his going might be of fateful significance, should allow days and nights to go by without giving either direct or indirect news of his whereabouts. Imre Nagy sent word neither from Parliament nor from Party headquarters, neither in person nor through an intermediary, to reassure his worried family in the house in the Orsó-utca.

Mrs Nagy rang all the people she still knew from the time when her husband had first been Prime Minister. Then she tried to find out something of him from friends and acquaintances, myself included. Her voice sounded courageous but understandably anxious. That was perhaps the third day of the revolution. I in turn tried to locate the Prime Minister and got through on the telephone to Gerö's secretary, who said he could give me no information about Nagy.

What was the force that nevertheless drove the revolution steadily onward during those days?

The future 'No. 1' in Hungary, János Kádár, in his broadcast speech of 1 November 1956, the ninth day of the revolution, answered this question as follows:

We can safely say that the driving impulse behind this uprising came from out of our own ranks. Communist writers, journalists, students, the young people of the Petöfi Club, thousands and thousands of workers and peasants, veterans of the workers' movement who had been imprisoned on trumped-up charges – all fought in the front rank against Rákosi's despotism and political gangsterism.

Thus spake János Kádár on 1 November 1956.

We are proud of the fact that we have stood our ground righteously in armed uprising and in its leadership, permeated with true love of country and loyalty to socialism.

The same struggle he began by calling a 'glorious rebellion' the same János Kádár subsequently learnt to calumniate as 'counter-revolutionary'. But in this first, as yet undoctored pronouncement, which the monitors of many foreign radio stations recorded in identical terms and which was also printed word for word in the official Party newspaper *Népszabadság*, Kádár declared:

Our people has shaken off the Rákosi régime in a glorious rebellion. It has won freedom for the people and independence for the country, without which socialism is inconceivable.

A spontaneous, self-sacrificial struggle with at most the beginnings of a unified leadership but without as yet a revolutionary staff, and without an effective government in the country, began to sketch in the outlines of a new state. And unquestionably that new state wished to be a socialist state. Truly socialist at last, in contrast to what had prevailed hitherto – in Kádár's words, 'despotism and political gangsterism'.

Following Stalin's death there were only *two* attempts to create genuinely socialist states on the basis of Marxist ideas: the Hungarian in 1956, and the Czechoslovak in 1968–9. Both attempts were crushed by the Soviet Union, stamped out in favour of the exploitatory dictatorship of officialdom.

The time-fuse

On the evening of 23 October 1956 Ernö Gerö's power in the land was still unlimited. Even on the radio only he could say what he wanted to say, and suppress what he wanted to suppress.

A crowd of students, the stimulus behind that joyful demonstration, went in a mood of gay optimism to the radio building to make their demands, which they had drawn up in a series of points and read out several times in public during the course of the day, known to the nation as a whole. Gerö forbade it. The students waited, sent deputations, started to parley. AVO soldiers opened fire on the crowd. In the poorly-lighted street outside the radio building many fell dead or wounded.

The radiantly beautiful day of the demonstration was followed by the first bloody night. The fronts, which had existed invisibly for a long time, formed up in the space of a few moments. On the one side the protectors of the higher and top bureaucracy, the political police – on the other the people. According to the terminology of the day: here the police force of the 'Kucseras' (known as the AVO or AVH) – there the mass of the 'anti-Kucseras'.

Where did the people, who an hour before had had no idea they would ever have to do with weapons, all of a sudden find them? I know of two sources, but there were undoubtedly more. One source was certain factories that went by various names but were all in reality arms factories and whose workers promptly distributed the stock among a populace threatened by the AVO. The other was the municipal police, which sided with the people. Before long there were also the Molotov cocktails that the young concocted themselves. All this alone would perhaps still not have tipped the scales in the people's favour. But the crews of the tanks that Gerö ordered into the capital from the provinces that evening as a precautionary measure went over to the people too.

Ernö Gerö – not merely 'No. 1' in Hungary but also an important figure in NKVD circles, a fact which he made a point of keeping dark – was not allowed to rest content with breaking his word in giving the order to fire. Troop movements in and around Budapest, which enabled the Soviet Union to tighten its control over Hungary and increase its pressure on Yugoslavia, were decided at a higher level. Under the influence of the news from Poland Hungary became a powder-barrel during the course of those days. The Kremlin sometimes has nothing against explosions but it likes to decide for itself when they shall occur. It was Gerö's job to take care of the exact timing. There was nothing to inhibit him. Hungary was for him a neutral battlefield – just as Spain had once been. To feel an emotional attachment to any country other than the Soviet Union he would have regarded as an offence against something he and his like called 'Internationalism'. His job was to provoke, so he provoked. He was required to give the order to fire that evening, so he gave it. The rulers of the empire in the East wanted to be sure everything remained under their control. The time-fuse had to tick, and the bomb had to go off.

That was why Gerö's radio speech in the evening of that unforgettable day was full of deliberate insults and inflammatory demands. In an hour when the people expected its rulers to reflect and to make promises of improvement Gerö denounced the people as a mob, as riff-raff, as a counter-revolutionary Fascist rabble.

This scrupulous fulfilment of orders, however, failed to profit Gerö. The fuse ignited all right, but it did not immediately go out again according to plan. The feeling of complete powerlessness that had kept the people under in Stalin's and Rákosi's time evaporated at the sight of those shot-up Soviet tanks and the toppled statue of Stalin.

Gerö's hand, trembling with rage and fear, pressed frantically down on the plunger. His fury had consequences no one had anticipated.

A young assistant lecturer from the Academy of Theatre arrived at the flat, covered in dust and limping from a sprained foot. Eva showed him in, her eyes blazing with a new fire that was to appear in them often from this time on. The young man had only just got away with his life. Where from? Kossuth Square, before the Parliament Building.

25 October – third day of the armed struggle in Budapest. In broad daylight and in proudly self-assured formation hundreds of

young people marched to Parliament to hand Gerö a memorandum. One expected great things of memoranda in those days. Whose idea was it to keep the young people waiting until the square was once more full to bursting? Whose idea was it to post AVO soldiers with quick-firing weapons on the roofs of the surrounding buildings? And whose idea was it suddenly, like a bolt from the blue, to give them the order to fire? They say that more than three hundred dead littered the asphalt of Kossuth Square that day.

And who destroyed the Russian tanks in the square? Hungarian soldiers? Youths? Russian tanks whose crews wanted to go their own way?

That evening Gerö left the palace on the bank of the Danube – the Parliament of a country that had not seen parliamentary government for a long time – no longer as Hungary's 'No. 1'. In order to avoid unpleasant complications the Russian leadership – and this time Mikoyan was accompanied on his hurried trip to Budapest by chief ideologist Suslov – decided to remove a man who had so much blood on his hands.

But for Gerö there was no such disgraceful exit as had so recently been Rákosi's lot. The idea, new for the Soviet Union, that it is possible to remove a person from public life by the simple expedient of pensioning him off – no bullet in the back of of the neck, no show trial, no banishment – was in Hungary first tried out on him. He can still be seen today, old and half blind, taking his constitutional in the streets of Budapest.

The man who succeeded him was Janos Kádár.

34

Portrait of a politician – A party is founded –
Two comrades make themselves scarce

JÁNOS KÁDÁR was the man of the moment. To be more precise –
of the moment just gone by. Every time. No, he was not one of
those who blazed with a sudden brilliance and were then violently
extinguished – like Pál Maléter, for example, the military hero
of those revolutionary days. Kádár one had been expecting. In
fact him in particular. Only – one had already been waiting a bit
too long. His entry on to the historical stage was muffed; the
magic of his personality fell slightly flat. For his personality *had*
a certain fascination. To some extent it still has – or rather again
has. The fascination of weary compromise. All his historical
deeds – for deeds there have been, and misdeeds too – have been
done in moments of the most extreme exhaustion. But done.

I first mentioned Kádár in this book in connection with an
amateur performance of one of my plays. He was the slim, fair-
haired young man who as Member of Parliament for the mining
town of Salgótarján invited me to meet actors and audience at the
first night of a local production of *God, Emperor, and Peasant.*

Soon after that Rákosi had him appointed Minister of the
Interior – without of course any power over the secret political
police. That was before the monster trial mounted against László
Rajk. There is supposed to exist an incriminating tape-recording
on which Kádár can be heard persuading the already imprisoned
Rajk to admit to false charges out of loyalty to the Party. In return
Rajk was to have been executed only in appearance; actually he
was to have been dispatched to Yugoslavia to live there at first
under an assumed name. Is the tape-recording genuine? If so,
was Rajk betrayed by Kádár or Kádár by Rákosi and Gábor

Péter? The question in any case soon became purely academic, because in May 1951 Kádár himself was arrested, not to be released again until the autumn of 1954. He is said to have been given a particularly bad time in the torture-chambers of the AVO.

I met him frequently after his release. He read *Fair Play for Gáspár Varró* in manuscript and gave me some good advice. He let me have a mass of material, both written and in conversation, for my 'Kucsera' researches. He valued and respected literature and we writers were very attached to him. Following Stalin's death we made repeated and more and more vigorous demands for his release and then for his complete rehabilitation until little by little Rákosi was forced to give in.

I particularly remember one meeting with Kádár. It was at the traditional journalists' party at the Hungaria Café, which he attended with his wife. In the atmosphere of the thaw Eva asked him straight out when he was finally going to take over the role of first man in the land. Giving his gentle, embarrassed smile he answered with surprising frankness that it would be a year at least before the time was ripe; until then we should not be able to get by without Comrades Rákosi and Gerö.

Yet a bare four months later Mikoyan arrived to escort Rákosi from the scene. Kádár is supposed to have been offered the inheritance but to have refused on the grounds that it was Gerö's turn first. Only after the blood-bath in Kossuth Square, when Gerö too had to be removed, did Kádár accept the office of First Secretary. This continual hesitation may have had its roots in the fact that Kádár had already passed the high-point of his never exactly stormy popularity.

One could think of no one more suitable, but the appointment was greeted without enthusiasm. We writers supported him in every way we could. On the evening of 25 October I spoke on the radio to the young people: 'Imre Nagy is our man: his platform is our platform too. János Kádár has learnt in Rákosi's jails what dangers the Hungarian nation needs to be defended against.' I can still remember the painstaking care with which I weighed up and balanced the different wordings.

After all that had happened, no one who bore the title 'First

Secretary of the Party' could really be popular. Kádár decided upon a step that would indeed have been the only right one – had he taken it honestly. He dissolved the Party and announced the founding of a new Communist Party for 1 November. Nothing was easier than to dissolve the old Party; it crumbled of its own accord. And nothing was more difficult than to found a genuinely new Communist Party. The new Party that actually emerged was in essence the old one resuscitated. It is said that Kádár wished at that time to create a small, simple, neat, unpretentious Communist Party that should correspond to the actual political situation and compete for the leading position in the country in conjunction with but also in a spirit of political discussion with other democratic parties. He was apparently under no illusion regarding the fact that he could only hope to create a minority party in this way and that it must inevitably remain questionable whether he would ever secure a majority. But Kádár does not appear to be a power-hungry man. As a born second fiddle he perhaps had no fear of beginning honestly and patiently at the bottom.

Truth or legend? I do not know. But in any case it makes absolutely no difference – for neither Kádár nor his Party ever actually took such a course.

I shall never forget how I made the acquaintance of the new Party. I went along to the inaugural meeting with our friend Agnes, a sincere Communist of long standing. On the way we talked about our future, immaculate little minority party that was to make good everything we had bungled up to now. The founders of the new Party had forgathered in an internal courtyard of the block in which a part of the gigantic Party apparatus was accommodated. We both stopped short on the threshold and exchanged disconcerted looks. In the middle stood Kádár, and all around him, right into the furthermost corners of the courtyard, were exactly the same faces as we had always been accustomed to see at Party headquarters – the selfsame comrades as had got the Party into its present hopeless mess.

Agnes was the first to recover the power of speech. She understood my silence. Tears were rolling down her cheeks as she said,

'I'm going to give it a try . . . ' I could not make up my mind. Did I strenuously weigh up pros and cons? Or did I just let my form-less, conflicting emotions run their course? I do not remember. Whichever it was, I then said very firmly, 'I'm not even going to do that. It's hopeless.'

We said good-bye, and she stayed. On my way out I passed a door on the ground floor with a lot of men and women queueing up outside and others emerging with little envelopes. It was the cashier's office, the comrades were Party employees, and the day was the first of the month. The wages being paid out were meagre. But at that very moment wages and salaries were being paid out at countless other cashier's offices, and not a penny of them without the sanction of the Communist Party. Never had it been so clear to me that we were living in a new kind of social order, one that we neither wanted nor had foreseen. That social order, however, could not simply cease to exist just because we regarded it as pernicious. We were living in a society of bureaucratic exploitation.

When I got home I said nothing for a while. For the first time since 1919 I was out of the Party. I was by no means sure that Eva would follow my example. She had not come to the Party through me; the Party formed part of her life and part of her reason for living.

It was days before she was ready to decide. She too stayed out.

Agnes is a Party member to this day. During my years in prison she did everything to help me, Eva, and many other victims of persecution. It cost her her high-up job in the Party administra-tion and afterwards she had to content herself with an extremely humble post. Fortunately her new job has little to do with politics. Her salary is tiny and she lives in poverty, but she will never be completely without means of support. Nowadays even such a state of almost harmonious passivity is matter for rejoicing. Like that one can live. And at least one can look back on some fine, militant years in the Party.

The same evening I had a call from Georg Lukács. He had not been at the inaugural meeting. Kádár sent me his regards, he said, and invited Lukács, myself, Tibor Déry, and one or two other writers to become members of the provisional leadership of the new Party. For a moment I felt an unexpected surge of hope. Perhaps this way it would work? If one were at the helm oneself, with a few like-minded colleagues. Armed with a bit of power . . . I brooded for so long Lukács must have thought we had been cut off. Then I said no. I could no longer muster the belief and hope necessary for the task.

Lukács felt morally obliged to join the new leadership, and so of course did Imre Nagy.

Not many days went by and Lukács was already out of the Party leadership – in fact out of the Party altogether. He and his wife were among the group of Hungarian Communists that the Soviet authorities interned in Romania. His age and reputation saved him from having to stand trial. Not until some ten years later was Lukács readmitted to the Party. Imre Nagy was never really in the Party leadership for a moment. He was arrested, condemned, and executed.

On 2 November 1956 János Kádár disappeared from Budapest. He was last seen in the company of the well-known Ferenc Münnich, a leading Communist politician in Hungary, veteran of 1919, important figure in the Spanish Civil War, and agent of the NKVD.

Part Five

35

'They're back . . .' – Three sad old men – 'Help!
Help! Help!'

'THEY'RE back . . .'

Eva was standing by my bed, fully dressed and ready to go out.
There was a sunken look about her almond-shaped eyes; her face
was pale and her lips compressed and still. She did not even have
to tell me who it was that was back. Nor did we need to waste
any words over the fact that we were now going to leave the flat
together and would very likely never return because we should
not live to see another day.

Where to now? Here too we were agreed. To the Parliament
Building. We felt confusedly that it was at the heart of the capital
that the last battle for our national independence must be fought
and – as already looked inevitable – lost.

Why was the sky a dark purple? We had never seen it that
colour before, not even this early in the morning. Was Budapest
burning? Or did that unnatural hue come from the rising sun
shining through the dust raised by hundreds upon hundreds of
tanks? In the distance we could hear an almost uniform roaring
noise – the din of countless caterpillar tracks coming closer and
closer, growing in volume and menace, interrupted at more and
more frequent intervals by muffled gun-fire. In our immediate
vicinity the only sign of life was the echo of our own footsteps.
We walked through completely deserted streets, apparently the
only people abroad in the entire, silent city on that morning of
Sunday, 4 November 1956.

In silence along the Danube embankment and across the
deserted bridge to the Parliament Building on the other side, Eva
beside me in her green woollen raincoat. When you have been a

Communist your whole life long and have seen life under Horthy and Hitler and Dollfuss and . . . yes, Rákosi and Stalin too, then you have certainly thought more than once about your last steps taken on earth. Yes, but not like this – the only two people on a bridge over the Danube . . !

Was it worth dying today, we wondered, knowing no one would ask us now, knowing that if everything we had lived for died, then we must die with it. If the general death was postponed, then we too would get a reprieve. But might one still hope for such a thing? After a life spent – or wasted? – in the service of a glorious idea that had turned out to be a cover for clean different views with which we had subsequently been duped and betrayed – had we any right to become at the last moment the tools of that betrayal? A mean, mean travelling companion, this twentieth century of ours!

The beneficiaries of the 'Kucsera' order saw it as their duty at this time to appear poor and wretched. Shall I relate how Comrade Katharina, wife of Imre Horváth, the former head of the Hungarian Mission in East Berlin – at that time Foreign Minister – turned up at the flat on the evening of the third or fourth day of the revolution and pleaded for shelter? She feared for her life in her comfortable, well-appointed home. Her husband was on his way to New York, to the United Nations – having, incidentally, taken the slowest boat. He had seen so many fateful moments of decision in his time that he would not at all have minded arriving late this once and being rid of the responsibility.

Katharina Horváth, all a-tremble, begged Eva to recover her bits and pieces – her private car, her silver plate, her furs – from the alleged danger zone. In proportion as her valuables were 'salvaged' from her home she also recovered her self-assurance. A few days later she left for Czechoslovakia, whither many of Rákosi's supporters had fled, there to await a more favourable turn of events. In the wake of the Soviet army she returned to Budapest and came to collect her things, with a word of gratitude for our stewardship. When, however, I later fell into the hands of the secret police, I had to admit that they were extremely well informed regarding every one of the telephone conversations I had had in Mrs Horváth's presence.

Among Communist functionaries and their ilk such conduct was the rule rather than the exception.

The children too fought for freedom in that uprising, as witness the rows of little graves in the Budapest cemeteries. The figure of the Budapest child will take its place in Hungarian history books as soon as Hungary's historians are allowed to write history again. Peter, like all his playmates, spent more of those two weeks in the streets than in the house. My *Banzai* games of 1904–5 had for Peter become earnest reality. The people he was staying with – and could continue to stay with until Leo and Edith fetched him from London in the event of our disappearing from circulation – had to keep a firm hold on his hand all day to stop him joining in the battle. They had a job persuading him that street fighting was forbidden to children under fourteen.

'We want to see Imre Nagy.'

'He's not in the building.'

The officer of the parliamentary guard gave us the information gladly. He seemed to be pleased to have someone to talk to. He was standing in the street outside the entrance nearest the Kossuth Bridge. With him was a soldier. They were waiting. What for? For something to happen. But what could possibly still happen now?

'They're all off negotiating in various foreign missions.' This was said in tones of the deepest hopelessness. What was there left to negotiate?

'Who's still here, then?'

He seemed to consider which of the people present might best suit my purpose, then mentioned the name of Zoltán Tildy.

We set off again, the two of us alone, this time through the labyrinthine corridors of the Parliament Building. Here carpets muffled the echo of our footsteps. We met one of the guards with armfuls of boxes. 'Here – help yourselves, it's good chocolate, let's not be leaving any for *them*.' And he laughed. Hatred and despair sometimes find childish outlets.

The vast, empty building rang with the insistent voice of the radio. 'This is Imre Nagy speaking, President of the Council of Ministers of the Hungarian People's Republic.' And it went on, 'At dawn this morning Soviet troops launched an attack on the capital with the obvious aim of overthrowing the constitutional democratic government of Hungary. Our troops are giving battle. The government is at its post. This I say both to the people of this country and to the peoples of the world.'

The national anthem, then again, *'Attention! Attention! Attention!'* Followed by the same message in various other languages. The translations were poor. This annoyed us both. Suddenly we could think of no more urgent task than to improve those awful translations. One looks for objectives even when one's life is forfeit.

In between the radio gave out another message. 'Imre Nagy, President of the Council of Ministers, requests Defence Minister Pál Maléter and the rest of the members of the military delegation who left to attend negotiations at the invitation of the Soviet commandant at ten o'clock yesterday evening and have not yet returned, to return immediately . . . '

Every Hungarian knows the ballad of the heroic Bálint Török, who was summoned to see the Sultan and never came back.

On the eve of that 4 November, just before he left for the Soviet commandant's headquarters, I spoke with Pál Maléter on the telephone. He had been Minister of Defence only for a matter of hours. He sounded confident, said the negotiations were going well, and added that all that remained to be discussed at that evening's session were certain technical details, mostly concerning the evacuation of Soviet troops from Budapest and subsequently from the whole of Hungary.

That was the day, I believe, on which the composer Zoltán Kodály sent a telegram to the Soviet musicians, asking them to support the withdrawal of Soviet troops from Hungary. One had the illusion that the world had grown sensible.

Several days later, however, by which time I already knew that I should very likely never see my good friend Maléter from the Krasnogorsk PoW camp again, I heard that immediately after our telephone conversation he had met a Polish journalist. To the journalist he spoke in no such optimistic terms. In fact his words sounded like a last will and testament. He appeared to have no illusions and to be well aware of what was in store for him. To me he said nothing of all that. He asked me to ask the writers as a body to watch over the purity of the revolution and to keep it unsullied by any act of personal revenge or instance of lynch justice.

The warning was not superfluous. The tempo of events was too slow for the people, the objective too vague. After the startling victories of the first few days the years of subordination and dependence upon an outmoded form of discipline – the discipline of the Communist Party – began to avenge themselves. The new, democratic social forms, based upon self-determination for the worker, freehold ownership for the peasant, and a higher regard for the leaders of intellectual life, could not possibly become effective within so short a time.

The halting course of events undermined the people's trust. Invisible forces that one had thought incapacitated began to pull themselves together again. There was a danger of an insidious AVO dictatorship emerging. The feeling of insecurity led to outbursts of violent passion. Individual cases of private justice began to compromise the originally crystal-clear morality of the uprising.

In the first days of the revolution there was not a thief in Budapest. The goods in the broken shop-windows were left untouched, just as they had been set out on the morning of 23 October – and they included commodities that the impoverished city badly needed. No one even thought of taking anything. Everything stood under the protection of the revolution.

Some young writers wanted to collect money for the relatives of the fallen. They set up two large chests, completely open at the top, at the busiest points of the city. Humble handwritten notices explained their purpose. The chests were left unguarded till evening, when the writers came to collect them. They were filled to the brim with coin and bank-notes.

On the third day of the revolution some farm wagons drew up in front of the Writers' Union. They brought gifts of food: bread, lard, live geese, whole carcasses of pork – in the midst of the starving city. These peasants had come seeking the writers out; it was for them that the otherwise hardly open-handed villagers had donated all these delicacies.

Peasants and writers! A prospect that only an enthusiastic revolution could open up.

But then came the wasted days, the confusion, the dawning of mistrust . . .

Besides Zoltán Tildy – the leader of the Smallholders' Party who had been elected president in 1945, had subsequently spent eight years as Rákosi's prisoner, and in the last days of the revolution was appointed a minister of state – we also found István Dobi in the Parliament Building that morning, a crafty, hard-drinking old man who had been made president in Rákosi's time and so was also able to appoint the ministers of the revolution, thus ensuring the constitutional continuity. Also present was a former Social-Democrat politician by the name of Sándor Rónai. Three old men looking weary and deeply sad. But perhaps the weariness and sadness were only masks. What they concealed was worse – a bottomless, inconsolable despair.

The big, bloody puppet theatre was preparing a new show. Had the puppeteers already decided how they would allocate the parts? One of them – Dobi – would of course play president again; in the quiet little town of Szolnok on the Tisza he would formally, and with a fluency born of experience, appoint other puppets, including the two comrades who had disappeared, namely Kádár and Münnich, to key positions in a non-existent government. A juicy part awaited puppet Rónai too; perhaps in the very minute in which he offered me his hand he had been made a minister in Szolnok, just did not know it yet. And what was left for the other puppets? For Zoltán Tildy? For J.H.? Convict suits?

The grey, furrowed, sleepless faces of the three old men brightened a bit when they saw two newcomers arrive and heard them ask what they could do. Tildy, overcome with emotion, thanked us in the name of the fatherland. After a moment's reflection he said, 'Go along to the studio – I mean the one here in the building.' It was the only transmitter we still possessed.

332

Three sad old men

As we were going out of the door he called us back. 'I must tell you this: we're not resisting. The youngsters in the parliamentary guard wanted to fight. To the last man. To the last bullet. But I've forbidden it. I've also let the Russian commandant know I've done so.' His voice gave out as he added. 'No help . . . '

By following a thick bundle of cables that had been laid in makeshift fashion along the carpeted corridor we found our way to the studio. It consisted of two or three poorly furnished rooms. There was little staff, and they were at a loss what to do. A few gramophone records rescued at random from the shot-up, burnt-out radio building and placed and replaced on the turntable by two teenaged girls churned out the interminable gipsy music that during those days frayed the nerves of a nation. The good music was kept back for solemn moments.

Just as we entered, a hellish din shook the walls and windows. The first Russian tanks rolled into Kossuth Square, their cannons aimed at the Parliament Building.

'No help . . . '

What is humanity worth if it cannot save a band of doomed fighters who feel themselves responsible for the fight for humanity? Or cannot be bothered to save them? Can man in society live only as a brute? And does he fear his own humanity may hamper his chances of survival?

I reached for a sheet of paper, wrote a few sentences almost without thinking, and showed them to Eva. She nodded vigorously and smiled at me as if I had given her a present.

We ran back along the bundle of cables – back to the little room where we found the three old men just as we had left them. We showed Tildy the sheet of paper, he nodded, we raced back to the studio, and a few minutes later millions of radios and many millions of people the world over received this message:

To all writers of the world, to all scientists, academics and leaders of cultural life: Help us! Time is short! You know the facts. We do not have to explain them. Help the Hungarian people! Help the Hungarian writers, scientists, workers, peasants and intellectuals! Help! Help! Help!

333

While I read out the Hungarian text, Eva wrote the German translation. When I had finished she took my place – soundlessly as befits a radio studio – at the microphone. '... *Helft! Helft! Helft!*' Her place was taken by a slim, dark-haired woman with a hastily completed translation in her hand. I did not know her; she was the English announcer. '... *Help! Help! Help!*' A young man, also unknown to me, took the Englishwoman's place, and then the world heard through the mouth of the Russian announcer how a tiny nation that had just been robbed of the last vestiges of its liberty appealed to its oppressor's surely still-existent residue of humanity for assistance, for protection from inhumanity.

'... *Help! Help! Help!*'

As we left the studio to follow the cables back to Tildy the two girls were discussing which of the records that they had saved for solemn moments they should put on now.

Out in the corridor we saw the first Soviet soldiers coming round the corner.

Back in Tildy's office – a transformation. Everyone had heard our appeal. Their answer: a friendly nod, a grateful smile, a handshake.

Fresh people arrived who had obviously spent the night in the building. The first was a university professor I had known for years, with his wife. Then came a tall, dark-haired, nonchalant-looking man who was new to me. His name, István Bibó, I had first heard very recently; for something under twenty-four hours he had been a minister of state in the reformed Nagy government. Everything I had heard about him had made a powerful impression on me, and taking into account what I heard and read about him subsequently I believe that Bibó could have become the political Maléter of our revolution – a sudden, bright new star.

I learnt some days later that Bibó did not leave the Parliament Building when we did. He went back to his office to represent the sole legal government of the country – as headed by Imre Nagy. There he stayed as Russian soldiers swarmed through the building. He sat at his typewriter and typed non-stop. He did so with such perfect matter-of-factness that it never even occurred to the

Russians to disturb him at his work, any more than they interfered
with the cleaning women when they turned up on the dot to start
cleaning. The man sat at his typewriter and typed and typed. He
typed official announcements, he typed a proposal for the solution of the Hungarian problem, he typed for the nation, for
Europe, for the world. And he signed what he typed in his own
name as minister of state.

'It is the duty of the West not to drop the Hungarian cause
after the first failure . . . Until this question has been satisfactorily
answered, the interrupted East-West dialogue cannot be resumed,'
ran one of the things he typed. Does that not give one food for
thought today?

Bibó is said not to have quit his office for days and nights on
end. And what he typed on his typewriter immediately became
known to the world at large. People later came to believe that it
had not been an ordinary typewriter he typed on but a telex
machine with a line outside the country.

Minister of state Bibó, who placed before the world the only
realistic proposals for unravelling the hopelessly tangled Hungarian question – and with it the whole problem of central and
eastern Europe – was arrested soon afterwards and condemned to
life imprisonment. The power that held the eastern half of the
continent in its grasp was not interested in a long-term solution
of the European question.

'*Assez! Assez!*' one would have heard in the West, had one
sought to explain the true dilemma of Europe and tried to suggest
ways out of it.

Tildy's wife came in with tea and bread-and-butter for us all.
We drank from thick white cups and ate thick slices of bread
spread thickly with butter.

In the midst of the general confusion I pulled Eva to me. 'We
must say good-bye.'

Her flushed face turned towards me and the triangular eyebrows flew up. 'Why?'

'They'll arrest us now . . . line us up separately . . . men this
side, women that side . . . '

Eva's glance was thoughtful for a moment, then she said, 'Wait

335

here.' She went through an open door into an empty office and lifted the telephone. In less than a minute she was back.

'It's O.K.'

'What's O.K.?'

She fondly stroked my hair. 'Well, if after all the worst doesn't come to the worst . . . if they don't line us up in two separate rows . . . then we need somewhere to stay tonight. They surely won't let us over the bridge to our place. I've just spoken to Klára Pán; we can spend the night with her.'

We made our way in small groups towards the exit. Rónai said good-bye to us at a bend of the corridor. He had an office in the building and wanted to fetch something. Or had he discovered meanwhile that in Szolnok he had been appointed a minister?

At the end of the hall we could see the pale rectangle of the open door. Whoever walked out of it was lost to our eyes, his fate a mystery to us. Zoltán and Mrs Tildy . . . the professor and his wife . . .

We reached the doorway ourselves. We passed the Russian soldiers pushing their way in, we left the building, nothing happened.

They let us pass as if they had not even seen us. But from the hatches of the two enormous tanks that flanked the exit two machine guns followed us on our way. We crossed Kossuth Square between the serried rows of tanks as if it had been something we did every day. None of us turned to look back as fugitives do, but our ears were pricked for the slightest sound.

36

Klára Pán's radio – Negotiations with Colonel
Gurkin – A (seven-hour) visit from the police –
The spy who lacked imagination – The journey
to Maria Nostra – Tibor Déry's cow

THE minute we arrived I pounced on Klára Pán's radio. No use.
All the Hungarian wave-lengths were silent, and the set was too
old to receive foreign stations.

'Well, we've survived today . . . ' I heard Eva murmur, as if
to herself. 'Perhaps we'll survive others too . . . ' Suddenly she
buried her face in her hands and remained like that, motionless,
for a long time. When I finally turned her face towards me her
eyes were dry but red-rimmed.

Not until late afternoon did I find a Hungarian-speaking
station talking about Hungary. It was Szolnok calling, a little
town on the River Tisza about sixty miles from Budapest.
Proclamation of a new government. Or anti-government? Kádár,
Münnich, then the names of a number of men who had probably
become ministers in the same way as old Rónai had. They said
nice things about us. They were still proud of us then, still saw
us as 'permeated with true love of country and loyalty to
socialism'.

Münnich signed on as Minister of the Armed Forces. One
wondered what forces might be meant. The routed AVOs that
were now trickling in to some rallying-point? At all events
policeman Münnich was the key figure of those days. With the
air of a genial old gentleman from a slowly vanishing era he was
able to watch day by day, indeed hour by hour, how Kádár, a
sincere admirer of the 'glorious rebellion' and a man who had

337

recently had a dream of a small, fair-fighting Communist Party, turned little by little into a 'No. 1'.

I had always had a lot of time for Kádár. After such dreadful representatives of a foreign power as Rákosi and Gerö the temptation to see Kádár as being completely different was not inconsiderable. Personally he presented a thoroughly human appearance, even if as time went on his face began to set in an expression of numbed weariness. His power, however – and to hope to show a people the way without power was a dream from which he was soon to be rudely awakened – rested on two pillars: the armed might of the Russian colonizers and the backing of the 'Kucseras'. Both demanded a return. To be able to go his own way he had to forgo certain aims – the aims, in fact, of his own way. What power gave with the one hand it took with the other.

And yet the order that was restored was not quite the same as before. Even power had to compromise, or at least accept that, with the logical consequence of natural processes, compromise solutions should emerge. The absolute inhumanity of the Stalin/ Rákosi era had shown itself to be less expedient in many ways than an elastic pseudo-socialism.

On three points, however, the Soviet leadership would brook no argument, and Kádár realized that here he must give in, perhaps even go one better: the kolkhoz system must be reintroduced into Hungary at any price; every attempt at worker management in industry must be quashed; and human lives must be sacrificed, lots and lots of human lives.

Too much inhumanity, however, makes the producers unhappy, and unhappy producers mean a drop in production. Kádár had, willy-nilly, had to pay an appallingly high price in blood and misery for his power. He then attempted to break out of the vicious circle here and there. But would he be able to? Would not Kádár himself inevitably become a tragic victim of that attempt? Or would he prove incapable of living out a human tragedy on his own account, should the need arise? Would he prevaricate with bloody and disastrous compromises? If he had to choose – as he very soon did – would he not choose the latter course?

The Hungarian writers had many opportunities to go along

with such a policy. It often seemed senseless not to. But the belief in a better future for mankind would not allow us to build that future on a betrayal.

The Soviet army overran Budapest, but still the guns were not silent. Day after day the fighting flared up again, in daylight or under cover of darkness, desperate, hopeless. Gun-battles went on sometimes for hours at a time, low-flying aircraft shook the windows, bombs fell in the immediate neighbourhood. Klára's flat was on the top floor – it was almost like being in a tower – and the play in the walls was terrifying.

After queueing for several hours with shrapnel falling all around I managed to get hold of a cauliflower, only to find that Klára had not got a grain of salt in the place. Added to which the central heating was off, and in the cold Eva's old sinus trouble began to plague her again.

The writer Endre Enczi, editor of *Irodalmi Ujság* (now in Paris), rang to say we should move in with him; his wife was a doctor, and Eva needed a doctor badly. We said good-bye to Klára (who soon afterwards fled – though only from her own bitter memories – to Australia; we have never seen her since).

We were accessible to everyone the whole time. People who came looking for us at the flat were given our current telephone number. We walked hand in hand down the middle of the street between torn-down cables and dried-up pools of blood. There were few people about, but we met several who knew us and who gave us a wave or shook us by the hand. Some – even of the strangers – embraced and kissed us. And not one was a Judas kiss.

Enczi's wife came in from her clinic exhausted and upset. Like almost all doctors she had not been out of her clothes for four days, tending the countless wounded and dying. The clinic, flying five large white flags with red crosses on, had been bombarded by the advancing Soviet army. At last the battle toll was slackening off. At last? Was one already beginning to look forward to the final defeat so that the blood-letting might cease? And would it not afterwards be continued? Or begin again in a different way? As another interminable St Bartholomew's Day?

Enczi's wife – with a recommendation from Gerö's ladies –

had once done a spell as doctor at the Party bigwigs' summer colony on Lake Balaton. She had gone there proudly prepared to do her honourable duty; she had come back a broken and embittered woman. She had seen what without the express orders of the Party no mortal might set eyes on: the life of Stalin's demigods on Rákosi's demi-Olympus. A luxury settlement in a luxurious bay, sealed off with barbed wire, guarded by the AVO. Service by nimble waiters – everywhere, even in the water. No food might be set on the table without first having been examined by the doctor. Politbureau members' food she even had to sample. If it was poisoned (as it never was, incidentally), then let a mortal die and not an immortal. If one of the inmates of the Lake Balaton paradise had to have an injection, the doctor was not allowed to open the ampoule herself; only AVO officers were allowed to do that. And the rest of the rules were out of the same mould.

Sudden storms can break out over Lake Balaton. One night a storm drove an excursion boat against the barbed wire. The trippers called out for help. The guards drove them back out into the stormy lake.

Enczi's wife was incapable of keeping such experiences to herself. Her telling of them had been one of the things that prompted my 'Kucsera' article. Now, having seen the blood and the wounds of those who were for changing such a state of affairs, she felt driven to bring it all out again, passionately, painfully, herself almost fainting from weariness.

In a day or two we heard that Kossuth Bridge was open again. *The Bridge of Life* . . . Kossuth Prize . . . When had all that been . . . ? By evening we were back home.

One night Soviet soldiers surrounded the house where the well-known journalist Iván Boldizsár lived and took him away. His wife appealed to the writers for help. The same thing happened to several younger writers. There was a danger of the detainees being carried off to Russia and disappearing for some time, if not for good. There was no time to lose. The committee of the Writers' Union resumed its activities on 12 January 1957. We felt it was right not to make too modest a beginning, and in Boldizsár's case we sent a telegram to Khrushchev. Three days later he was at liberty. Appeals on behalf of other writers we addressed to Kádár. (As it turned out, we need not have aimed so high, particularly not in Boldizsár's case. He had a behind-the-scenes understanding with a number of high-ranking Russians and is a semi-official figure in Hungarian cultural affairs to this day, chiefly in dealings with abroad.)

Major Gurkin, with whom I had had almost daily dealings in 1945 when he had been looking after Hungarian cultural affairs on behalf of the Red Army, was now back and doing the same job, this time with the rank of colonel. I thought it would be a good idea to renew the contact and asked Béla Illés to arrange a meeting.

The meeting came about sooner than I had dared to hope. Present were, besides Gurkin, Illés, and myself, the president of the Writers' Union Veres, the poet Gyula Illyés, whose poem *Some Lines on Tyranny* is probably our revolution's most outstanding literary monument, and a number of Russian officers who came and went without stopping to listen for long. There was also a man with the surname Mátyás, a Hungarian. I had known him for a long time but I could not imagine what he was doing at a meeting such as this.

I apologized to Gurkin for my somewhat halting Russian, saying that I lacked practice and had forgotten a good deal.

'Indeed,' replied the colonel significantly, 'you have forgotten a great deal.'

I had never imagined that a general strike in little Hungary could so upset the mighty Russian empire. Colonel Gurkin was prepared to grant us important concessions if we would only do something to persuade people to go back to work. He promised to look into the cases of arrest as soon as possible and gave us his assurance that no Hungarian prisoners would be taken out of the country in future. In return he wanted the Hungarian writers to resume writing and publishing immediately and thereby set a good example. We agreed on the one condition that we should be allowed to print without censorship what we held to be right and to submit work only to publications with whose political stance we were in agreement. Gurkin procrastinated on this point and would give no clear promise, but he did agree to let us publish a communiqué about our talks, which duly appeared in the official party organ next morning.

In talks with János Kádár we discussed the question of how literary production and publication were to be resumed. How was the absolute freedom of literature that we had demanded in fact to be guaranteed?

We pointed out that the role of the writer is historically determined, citing the case of the 1848–9 revolution. This meant, however, that literature must let itself be guided by moral standards erected not by the Party but by humanity, love of truth, and the writer's own craving for freedom. Kádár, First Secretary of the Communist Party, listened to such arguments with growing impatience.

However, a few days later the agreements with Gurkin and the discussion with Kádár lost any importance they might have had. The Writers' Union was dissolved without warning by a decree that came into effect immediately, Hungarian literary affairs were placed in the hands of a Commissar, and during the night of 19–20 January J.H. 57 and a number of other writers were arrested.

The police raid did not come as a complete surprise. I do not know whether there was some system behind it or whether it was simply a spontaneous working-off of primitive hatred. All I know is that for weeks before the raid we were plagued with anonymous telephone calls. Our telephone was going day and night, often ten or fifteen times in rapid succession. With a series of choice obscenities and dire threats our callers attempted to throw us off balance. It was obvious that things were not going to stop there.

Great emphasis was placed upon the legality of the proceedings – at least as regarded form. The men duly produced a search warrant. A curious fact was that this document bore the signature of that same Comrade Mátyás as had attached himself to the writers' delegation at the meeting with Gurkin.

They had hauled my neighbour, Dr Dubay, out of bed, and since two people must witness a search they also called in the concierge's wife. In pyjamas and a warm dressing-gown the old doctor sat shivering on the bottom step of my bookshelf ladder, reminding me of the prophet Jeremiah in my grandmother's big illustrated Bible.

Under the aegis of the law I was permitted to kiss my wife farewell, even if we were so closely surrounded by seven secret policemen that we had to breathe their very breath. Then two of the men took me between them and led me away. The other five stayed on to search the flat. Throughout the long search Eva treated them with an icy objectivity that, accustomed as they were to passionate scenes, began to cause them increasing embarrassment. What they actually hoped to find were secret documents of the Writers' Union, but no such documents existed either in my flat or anywhere else. The copy of the telegram to Khrushchev shook them a bit. They were policemen, and it made them nervous to have such a delicate document in their hands.

After a seven-hour search they finally left the flat and sent the witnesses home. The old doctor, making his slow, sad way back to bed, can hardly have suspected that he would not live to see my return, nor that his own son, a doctor too, would soon disappear in the same way.

Eva was now left alone in the flat, silent, dry-eyed. She was forty years old, a woman of enchanting beauty and, since the birth of our mongoloid child Michael, fragile health. She stood motionless in the middle of our living room for a long, long time – as if gradually losing all sense of time's passage. She thought about Michael, who she knew was well looked after at his special school. She thought about Peter, whom we had managed to send off to his grandparents in London a few days before. She thought of me and of herself, and of our inseparability – which this brutal separation had for the first time made complete. She looked round the room, selected a corner of the sofa, and sat down in the attitude that was to be for her the attitude of waiting, through unnumbered hours and innumerable days. There she sat, neither weeping nor sleeping, till the next morning.

Next morning some men appeared in our street with a lorry and a saw and killed the old lime tree because it blocked the view into our windows. Then a man began cleaning his shoes at a

343

window of the house opposite – and went on, and on, and on . . .
He was clearly either a shoe-fetishist or a totally unimaginative
spy who could think of nothing else to be seen doing at the
window.

While I was being kept under observation round the clock
through the peep-hole in the door of my cell, Eva too had to
suffer day and night the feeling of being watched.

The true heroes of the time of waiting were our women.
During our imprisonment I lost my ninety-year-old mother,
Tibor Déry his mother, who was even older, and Zoltán Zelk his
wife. I was not able to see Eva until six months after my arrest,
and when we did at last meet it was at the AVO, with my usual
interrogating officer taking part in the conversation. Even later on
our meetings were so few and far between that on one occasion
Eva went through a serious gallstone operation in the interval
without my having noticed that anything was wrong. She had
been forbidden to mention it, and the major had placed her in
the shadow so that I should not be struck by the sudden increase
in the number of her grey hairs.

While I was in the reception prison Eva saw me for the first
time in my striped convict suit. 'How smart you look!' she
exclaimed. The AVO officers must not be allowed to witness how
shaken she was. At that time they had us meet either in the
commandant's office or in the place where the inmates of the
condemned cells received their last visits. In the latter case we
were led past the place of execution. The gallows were not to be
seen, though – only the rectangular holes in the concrete floor
into which they dropped the posts when the need arose.

Visiting day at Maria Nostra was quite different. The women
began their preparations days in advance. Hair-do, manicure, a
new blouse – or if not new at least borrowed from a friend so that
it looked as if one could still afford such things. Then up at four
on the day. The tram still full of yesterday's people – waiters,
musicians – only now going home. The train left at a quarter to
six. Since the mass visits invariably took place on Sundays,
station and train were always full of women going to Maria
Nostra. The railwaymen called the train the 'Widows' Special'.

Arrival at the little town of Szob at half past eight. Five minutes later – off again up the hill in the overcrowded, overloaded little bus. Those who managed to catch the bus or at least secure a place on the running-board arrived in time for roll-call at nine o'clock. Women who had been shoved aside in the crush could still run up the hill and try and make the second roll-call. A second bus, however, was not provided. These women were either admitted in the second group, in which case they were happy even though it meant missing the train back, or they had to wait for the next visiting day, even if this was not for another six months. The women had to line up in front of the prison in two rows and wait until they were admitted – never mind whether it was raining or snowing, or whether the temperature stood at twenty below zero or thirty in the shade.

Once inside the great hall of the prison, they were lined up again at a distance of six feet from their menfolk. A shouted command – and an ear-splitting din broke out. Everyone had to talk at once; one could hardly understand a word. Such was the meeting of husbands and wives, mothers and sons, sisters and brothers, often after months of separation and with the prospect of further months of the same state. Afterwards the waiting began again, the brooding, the quiet hoping and the silent despair. But above all the preparation for the next visit.

There was one other sort of encounter between the prisoner and his family. Each Sunday morning trusties ran from cell to cell handing each prisoner a little packet – the photographs of his wife and children. We were permitted to keep and look at these pictures of our loved ones until two o'clock in the afternoon. Then they were collected up again. The same thing happened every Sunday in Maria Nostra. And every time the shaft of happiness burst through the steely armour of bureaucratic inhumanity.

The women would have found it easier to endure their fate had they been allowed to pursue their professions. For this, however, permission was given only rarely. Eva was fired from the Vig Theatre, where she had been employed for years as dramaturge, and for a while was out of work. She applied for permission to work as a taxi-driver. In Hungary all taxis are state-owned.

345

Permission was refused. Not only that but her driving licence was taken away from her. Then she found a temporary job in some useless, dusty archive connected with the clothing industry. There she met our old acquaintance Gábor Péter, whom Rákosi had one day had arrested, not for his actual misdeeds, of course – for in these he was Rákosi's accomplice – but on the usual sort of trumped-up charge. On his premature release the former tailor was honoured with the job of librarian to a branch of the rag trade.

Hatred and revenge were frequently associated with a quite inhuman malice. An engineer whose daughter was hanged was sent a bill for the costs of the execution. Maléter's wife applied to the Party – addressing her application to Kádár – for work of no matter what kind since she was unable to feed her family. Her request was granted: the fragile, delicate young woman was found a job – at the cemetery, as a gravedigger.

Of J.H. 57–60 I am happy to be able to report that he was a quiet prisoner. He neither raged, nor wept, nor swore, nor laid about him; he did not pester his superiors with complaints and requests, and he did himself no violence. The warders naturally found him guilty of other offences that they could barely find it in themselves to excuse. For example the simple task of arranging paillasse and blanket on his plank bed with military precision proved completely beyond him. Such a lack of dexterity was irritating in the extreme.

Probably none of those warders was too clear as to the essence of our quarrel with the victors. We all called ourselves socialists, and most of us did so sincerely. But whereas the one camp understood by socialism a hitherto unrealized, as yet unknown order of society, the other camp saw the supremacy of the 'Kucsera' class as the goal, as the realization or near-realization of socialism, and bitterly persecuted as a counter-revolutionary anyone who looked for something other than and better than the dominion of that kind of bureaucracy.

One of the older warders once asked me, 'What did you get a week as a writer?' I mentioned a figure that was by and large accurate. The man stood there, open-mouthed. 'And you had the

nerve to go on strike?' I told him we had not done it for more
money.

'What for, then?'

'For the truth. Because they wanted to make us tell the world
lies. And we didn't want to.'

The man demanded further explanations, then spent a long
time deep in thought. It was obvious he still did not understand,
but from then on he stopped finding fault with the way I made
my bed.

In many practical matters Tibor Déry was, if possible, even
more hopeless than myself. But he did possess other qualities I
envied him. He managed to exploit our somewhat ambiguous
situation, which had both police and warders slightly on the hop,
to the most skilful advantage. For them, you see, we were prime
gallows-birds who had only narrowly escaped the hangman, yet
they were not even allowed to say a rude word to us, let alone
clip us over the ear. And what kind of a prisoner was that?

Tibor declared that he suffered from claustrophobia. He told
the doctor, the prison governor, anyone who was interested.
What does claustrophobia mean, actually? That it makes a chap
nervous to be shut up. When you think about it, a prison is full
of claustrophobes. But Latin is Latin even when it is half Greek,
and while we were sharing a hospital cell in Maria Nostra Tibor
contrived to make the impossible possible. He was allowed on
account of his claustrophobia to have the window open all day.
Not even the oldest trusties could recall a similar case. The only
person who remained unmoved was Tibor himself. He was too
sorry for himself – on account of his claustrophobia.

The hospital cell having a normal-sized window, we were able,
if we were careful, to look out over the meadow adjoining the
prison. The sight of the first cow come out to grass filled me with
an unspeakable feeling of happiness.

No matter what the future may hold, I shall be grateful to
Tibor for that cow my whole life long.

Of course I was only together with Déry after our conviction,
and then only temporarily. After all we were 'accomplices' and

347

had to be kept strictly separate until our sentences were pronounced.

The AVO officers who interrogated us concentrated on one thing: they went all out to persuade us to call the Hungarian Revolution of 1956 a 'counter-revolution'. This was no empty word-game – not by any means. The new government called itself 'revolutionary'. For a few days there had even been a back door open through which the new government might have been drawn from our Revolution. This possibility was soon dropped, however, and the new government described itself as 'revolutionary' without going any deeper into the question of which revolution it was true to.

The people did not know what to make of the description. But if it could be arranged for one or two distinguished writers to accept the term 'revolutionary', the picture would become very much clearer. It would even provide the juridical basis for putting the political leaders of the 1956 Revolution – however makeshift that political leadership might have been – on trial as 'counter-revolutionaries', as 'traitors to the fatherland'. However, neither the police nor the Party succeeded in luring even one writer worth mentioning into that kind of deal. The few that did in time show a willingness to compromise were either completely without popular recognition as writers or looked down on as worthless careerists. The editor of a trivial weekly published by the Ministry of Culture, who had begun by supporting the Revolution, was the first to succumb. He cashed his reward really a bit too greedily: a house in what had once been the most elegant quarter of the capital, on the former Castle Hill.

The political puppet theatre needed puppets who would appear as writers, and it also needed one who would play the president of the Writers' Union. The part was filled by someone who in his younger years had cut a dashing enough figure but who had then become a minister under Rákosi. With tears in his eyes he promised a clean-up under the Revolution; afterwards his reactivated tear glands got him the job of president of the Writers' Union.

Real literature was silent. It had been hobbled by our arrest.

It had neither the will nor the willingness to subject itself once more to the censorship it had once succeeded in shaking off. The dictatorship sought to supplement lack of quality with a super-abundance of quantity. Whatever was easily and quickly producible, even the hitherto taboo detective novel, now came into its own.

But none of these efforts succeeded in producing a literature that was prepared to call a revolution a 'counter-revolution' and a patriot a 'criminal'.

The only instrument remaining was blind, bureaucratic terror, the tragi-crackpot puppet theatre, the eternal St Bartholomew's Day Massacre.

37

*The margrave and the cardinal – A wedding
in the condemned cell – The nightingale sings
no more – Attila's confession*

'WILL that work for us or against us?' is the question that every
prisoner in every cell whispers in his cell-mate's ear whenever
something happens or appears to be happening in the outside
world. For the most part, however, one is thrown back on one's
imagination; the seal of prison is as good as hermetic. Visually
one's world ends at the cell door; aurally it is confined to the
everyday sounds of prison life.

On only one occasion during the long months of pre-trial
detention in the AVO prison did a clearly distinguishable sound
reach us from the radios in our vicinity – extended, rhythmic
applause of the kind that is customary and indeed obligatory at
official Party events. There were two of us in the cell, a man called
Tóni and myself. Before that I had spent three months on my own.
Tóni and I had not known one another before and our cases were
not in any way connected.

'Is that going to help us?' Tóni asked in high excitement.

'I think rather the contrary,' I replied, with the experience of
thirty-seven years' Party membership behind me. 'I think we've
somehow just been sold down the river.' Explaining myself a little
more clearly, I added, 'The only people that can clap with that
kind of rhythmic precision are the Kucseras. And where there are
that many Kucseras gathered together, no good can come of
it.'

As I discovered much later, the applause had been for the
Chinese Prime Minister, Chou En-lai, then visiting Budapest.
He had just abandoned his own somewhat liberal course and

350

called for merciless reprisals against us Hungarian revolutionaries. And at that time Hungary was still greeting whatever Mao and his men said with thunderous applause.

Tóni had been prescribed aspirin, on doctor's orders. A Greek warder handed him the tablets. There were quite a few Greeks in Hungary at that time; following the Communist defeat in Greece, after the Soviet Union had decided it could not or would not give any more aid, the Eastern bloc admitted numbers of Greek refugees. Many of them went into the prison service and were particularly severe with the prisoners.

Tóni accidentally dropped the tablets, an 'act of sabotage' for which he was given three days' solitary in a dark cell with a hard bed and no food. At the end of it he was taken for interrogation. When he came back several hours later he was a changed man.

'Hey, they want to hang me.'

'You're out of your mind. Did they tell you so?'

'No, but I suddenly realized. They're after my neck.'

'But there's no reason. No pretext.'

'They need class enemies. What's a counter-revolution without class enemies? I'm a margrave. That's enough.'

Towards the end of the Second World War, Anton Margrave Pallavicini was a young lieutenant, having just completed the shortened course at the Budapest military academy. In the middle of a maize field in eastern Hungary he and his crew climbed out of their tank, raised the white flag, and went over to the Russians. The Hungarian People's Army was just then being organized, and Tóni promptly joined up.

He did so out of conviction. The young margrave found a world without aristocrats thoroughly to his liking. He dropped the historical name and formally adopted the proletarian-sounding name of Pálinkás. In the People's Army he rose to the rank of major. For a while he was adjutant to General Király, the man who commanded the revolutionary National Guard in October and November 1956 and is now a well-known military historian at a large American university. The general and his adjutant were long considered indispensable. No one could organize a military parade as smoothly as those two, and in Rákosi's time

parades played a big part. Later Pálinkás became deputy commander of a tank-training school in northern Hungary, a post he
filled until the end of 1956.

At one point it was discovered in high places that there were
too few Party members in the officer corps. Pálinkás was urged
to join the Party, which he did enthusiastically. At some subse-
quent point it was decided that the officer corps included quite
enough Party members. Pálinkás's membership was taken away
from him, and he was furthermore looked at askance as someone
who, an aristocrat by birth, had tried to insinuate himself into the
Party. He did not take his expulsion too seriously. Everyone had
his calamities; why should it not happen to him for once?,

He married a middle-class girl. The marriage went wrong and
ended in divorce. Then he married a proletarian girl. There was
every indication that this marriage too was not a happy one.
Tóni's new family lived in the suburb of Lörinc. In the house
next door lived a friendly fellow who Tóni was told was an AVO
officer. Inquiring what department the man served in, he
received at first an evasive answer and then a straight one: the
neighbour was the AVO's chief hangman. Tóni told me the story
over and over again, as one does, in prison, tell everything over
and over again.

We sat at the foot of our plank bed, facing the peep-hole,
hearing at frequent intervals the little clink as the cover was
removed, keeping our hands on our knees as laid down in the
prison regulations.

Tóni was hardly what you would call a good-looking man;
slim, pale of face, he had rapidly thinning fair hair and gaps
between his teeth. He was neither brighter nor better educated
than the average member of his generation and profession. He
was dressed in a shabby officer's uniform that had been carefully
stripped of all badges of rank. He had no cap. When he was not
talking about his early life he related the events that had got him
into prison. They centred around Cardinal Mindszenty.

Not far from the tank-training school there was a farmstead
that was out of bounds to soldiers and civilians alike. There the
cardinal, prince-primate of Esztergom, condemned to life im-

prisonment, was serving his term in the strict custody of a special detachment of the AVO.

Towards the end of October the prisoner became aware of a growing nervousness among his custodians. On 30 October there appeared unexpectedly a man whom the cardinal knew already – the head of the Office for Religious Affairs in the People's Republic of Hungary. This official, backed up by the commandant of the detachment, told the cardinal he must go with him immediately since his life was in danger there.

'In danger? From whom?' Under the influence of the general excitement Mindszenty felt somewhat stouter of heart.

'From the mob,' explained the two representatives of the dictatorship of the proletariat. Whereupon they took hold of the old man by the shoulders and, wreathed in polite smiles, proceeded to drag him from the house.

Mindszenty resisted, slipped from their grasp, and clung fast to the door-jamb. It would of course have taken no great expenditure of strength to prise the frail old man free and carry him off, but the two men were labouring under the impression that a crowd of peasants armed with scythes, picks, and other appliances was rapidly assembling outside. The AVO detachment felt – somewhat prematurely, perhaps – that it was in mortal danger. Leaving the old man where he was, they betook themselves rank and file to the tank-training school, where they begged to be disarmed and taken into protective custody. As they were handing over their weapons to the school's commanding officer, Colonel Váradi, the cardinal himself arrived, having covered the short distance on his own, and likewise asked for asylum.

I have forgotten how many officers, men, cooks, and police dogs the disarmed detachment numbered. Pálinkás took care of the cardinal, to whom he introduced himself as Pálinkás-Pallavicini. The poor fellow subsequently lashed himself with Communist self-criticism. Why in the presence of a prince of the church had he allowed his old name to escape his lips? Later his AVO inquisitors exploited the slip relentlessly during innumerable interrogations.

Colonel Váradi drove off to Budapest to report the incident and ask for orders. For one reason or another he returned without any orders, and Tóni was left to do what seemed to him best.

The crowd continued to gather around the barracks and Major Pálinkás began to grow uneasy. Since the cardinal wanted to go to Budapest, he had him get in his car beside him, ordered two armoured cars to escort them, one in front and one behind (or was it four, two in front and two behind? I forget), and set out for the capital. Near Vác they had to stop so that the prince-primate could bless the vast crowd; only then could they continue. In Budapest Tóni dropped the old man at his palace and himself went on to Parliament to report; after that he paid a brief visit to his wife and children in Lörinc.

In the early hours of 4 November the cardinal appeared at the Parliament Building, asking for asylum. Who was there on that morning ('They're back . . .') who could grant him asylum? Soon afterwards the old man was seen legging it nimbly and nervously, quite alone, clutching the skirt of his soutane, across the vast, deserted square to the building opposite – the American Embassy.

Was that all the Hungarian faithful might expect of their cardinal?

When the caterpillar-tracks had finished demolishing the revolution, Tóni began to feel a little on edge. At first no one lifted a finger against him. Then, quite casually, almost companionably, he was arrested.

When Tóni described to me how the AVO officer interrogating him had bit by bit put the fear of death into him, I knew he was telling the truth. I did what I could to convince him he was not because I was thoroughly familiar with the mental and physical anguish associated with the condition. I had had prior experience of it in Vienna, and not just through my cell-mates but at first hand too, when it had looked as if Hitler was about to march in.

The shivering, the feverish chattering of the teeth, the palpitations, the sleeplessness at night followed by fatigue and a painful stiffness the next day – it is all catching, and one has to combat it in one's cell-mate before one is infected oneself. In any case I felt really sorry for poor, lost Tóni in his threadbare officer's uniform with all the badges ripped off.

The margrave and the cardinal

I had once played a kind of guessing game called 'Bar Kochba' with my friend Szivessy – dead by this time – and now, for Tóni's benefit, I brushed up the old skills. From dawn till dusk the game went on, conducted in whispers lest the warders should hear us, and stretching our powers of invention to the limit. If I stopped for a moment he begged me to go on. For him it was literally vital to be kept distracted.

In prison one never says good-bye. The warder points a finger at someone: 'You!' And if he adds, 'With your things,' then eyes meet in a last, silent glance that does instead of a farewell.

When Tóni's trial began they separated us. Much later I learned that he was then sentenced to a year's imprisonment. At the beginning there were such judges still. But the case was not allowed to stop there. The court of appeal made good the mistake, and Anton Pallavicini, ex-margrave and ex-major of the People's Army, was sentenced to death by hanging and promptly executed.

In Maria Nostra prison there were other ex-officers – colonels, lieutenant-colonels. One might have thought that they too were among those 'class enemies' who were supposed to have caused the Revolution. In reality these officers were almost without exception Communists of long standing, and there were some who had received their training at the Frunse Academy, the top military college in the Soviet Union. It was precisely their out-standing proficiency that had landed them in Maria Nostra. They had known too much – and that from the best sources.

They took their ten- or fifteen-year or even life sentences with calm resignation. At least they were still alive. Even looking back over the past they found only one thing capable of disturbing their composure: the memory of the Soviet advisers. I had the impression that the appointment of these – as the officers in convict fatigues described them – incompetents, who not only struck them as arrogant and authoritarian but also drew a much higher salary from the Hungarian national exchequer than Hungarians of the same rank, was one of the principal reasons why many Hungarian officers looked back on those recent years with such bitter exasperation.

A year's imprisonment, converted by a higher court into the death sentence: the same thing befell the young playwright Jóska Gáli. He was a student at the Academy of Theatre and consequently a pupil of mine.

Hilda Gobbi, a popular member of the National Theatre and a Communist since pre-war times, had shortly before the Revolution switched to a small suburban theatre where every evening to thunderous applause she played the lead in a play by Jóska Gáli that constituted a sharp attack on the ruling bureaucracy. Play and performance had, in the then prevailing thaw, been officially approved by Kállai.

One day – this was some time after my arrest – two young women rang at Eva's door: Jóska's wife and one of my students.

'Jóska's sentence has been increased.'

'How much?'

'Death.'

Eva, who had sat almost motionless in the corner of her sofa for hour after hour, day after day, suddenly exploded into spontaneous, feverish activity.

'Don't the idiots realize what they're doing? The death sentence for a play? That tens of thousands have cheered and applauded?' The justice of the argument was seen by many even of those who otherwise knew nothing but the language of revenge and reprisals. Writers, actors, university professors were mobilized within the hour and began to besiege Kállai's and Kádár's ante-rooms. The woman judge who had originally sentenced Jóska to a year appealed to her superiors right up to the Minister of Justice to prevent the higher sentence from being carried out. Even the judge who had pronounced the death sentence lost his nerve – or found it for the first time? – and admitted that the AVO had coerced him into it.

Then came the BBC's afternoon broadcast from London with news of the Gáli case. All of which things combined to tip the scales in Jóska's favour.

But for a long time he had been hovering between life and

death. It was a condition he had already grown accustomed to as a child in Auschwitz, where often the only thing that saved him was the fact that at moments of the greatest danger his people hid him in the latrine.

What preoccupied him even more than the question of survival was the fact that he still wanted formally to marry the heavily pregnant young doctor who had up to now been his wife only in practice. Jóska knew that hanging had its formalities too. No one could be hung without prior medical examination. As he saw it, it was a race between the prison doctor and the registrar. Thanks to the protests of public opinion the registrar won. So did life. The lethal medical examination never took place.

The ceremony was performed in the condemned cell. It was a long time before Jóska could believe the good news that he was not going to have to die afterwards. His sentence was commuted – to fifteen years. His life was saved, and four years later there was an amnesty. His wife Vera – sentenced with him – had to serve her three-year term after the birth.

Husi was the pet name of a girl in the special section of the Budapest Reception Prison, that is to say in Staff Sergeant Németh's section. For Staff Sergeant Németh Husi was just a number; for her fellow-prisoners, however, she was a nightingale. She sang so beautifully as almost to make one forget where one was. She sang until she was forbidden to sing, and after a short silence she began to sing again. She was as lovely as an angel, even in prison garb and without make-up, although she was nothing but a fledgling streetwalker from the West Station neighbourhood. I happened to catch a glimpse of her once, though this was strictly forbidden. She was surely disappointed at seeing a middle-aged prisoner and not one of the young lads who were in the habit of scratching clumsy little love-messages for her on the wall.

Husi was for the gallows. So were most of the young lads in the cells around her. Why? Hard to say. In Husi's case, because of a photo. 30 October was the day on which, under cover of the national hatred of the AVO, the underworld too had its say for a few hours. Little whores have no objection to being photo-

357

graphed in the company of strong, cruel men occasionally. Husi
is supposed to have been recognized on one such group picture
taken on the street with a summarily executed AVO officer in the
middle; she was standing to one side, an onlooker. That was
enough for the death sentence. The sentence was pronounced
and read out to the accused. Husi went on smiling and flirting
with the warders, and soon we heard the nightingale singing
again. She had not understood. She knew the kind of punish-
ments a tart has to reckon with from time to time. The death
sentence was not among them.

One morning her voice was suddenly different. What had
happened? Had she suddenly realized what she was in for? Had
she been told that President Dobi had turned down her plea for
clemency? Or was she one of those who were not yet eighteen
and so were below the legal age for execution? Was the next day
perhaps her eighteenth birthday, and destined therefore to be her
last? She had no time to sing any more. She had quickly to explain
to all who wanted to hear as well as to all who did not just how
that business of the photograph had actually come about. She
spoke in a rapid, high-pitched voice and kept beginning all over
again: 'It was like this, you see . . . ' She was no longer herself.

Next morning Husi was hanged. Did anyone really believe in
her guilt? And what of it? Who imagined that the wheels of
historical change could be blocked by the promiscuous execution of nameless human beings? Executions simply for the sake
of quantity – which they then, after all, never admitted to the
world. A bureaucratic St Bartholomew's Day.

'Aren't you Pastor Losonczy's son?'
'That's right.'
Medium height, delicate, good-looking, cultivated, an extremely talented journalist. Burning eyes, a consuming passion,
given to every form of exaggeration. A sacred sense of mission
and with it the ability to improvise with great formal beauty –
though at the risk of letting himself be carried away by his own
improvisations.
Since our first meeting in 1945 the relationship between us had

been governed by conflicting feelings. Was the air I brought with me from Moscow foreign to the young man nurtured in the national tradition? Possibly. But at the same time I was clearly not radical enough for him. He had evidently caught a whiff of Soviet conservatism off me. Losonczy's Marxism was of an over-heated, idealistic kind. The young man remained a passionately enthusiastic Communist until his dying breath. Meanwhile he failed to notice how he came little by little under the influence of Révai, and how Révai – soon a minister – sacrificed him, his under-secretary, at the first opportunity, as soon as it seemed a useful thing to do.

Géza Losonczy landed in Rákosi's jails at around the same time as Kádár and Kállai. Following Stalin's death, in the deceptive climate of the thaw, the Writers' Union campaigned for Géza's release. When he was out again and we stood face to face, he offered me his friendship with tears in his eyes, apologizing for any injustices he might have committed against myself and others while in power.

He was without a doubt one of the men whose vocation it would have been to give a political conception to the Hungarian Revolution of 1956 under Imre Nagy's leadership. For this there was not time. There was insufficient contact between the intellectual leadership and the worker and peasant masses. It was a lack that could not be made up for at the drop of a hat.

So Géza Losonczy landed in prison a second time. In the communiqué regarding the sentence and execution of Imre Nagy, Maléter, Gimes, and Szilágyi it was stated that Géza Losonczy had died while awaiting trial. This was true. The fifth death sentence had been meant for Losonczy. But he had given the hangman the slip.

Géza was in a neighbouring cell. I gathered from scraps of conversation and various noises that someone in there was refusing to take food. Passing once in the corridor, I spotted something in an open cupboard that had not been there before – a rubber tube of the kind used for forced feeding. On another occasion I took advantage of a dent in our peep-hole cover to look out on to the landing. Géza was just being shaved, as happened once a week. He was as thin and bony as a child, with sunken cheeks, dull, lifeless eyes, and barely the strength to sit upright on the chair.

Not many days afterwards we heard the unmistakable sounds of his death agony. He was hastily disposed of. In the evening I saw one of our warders removing the now superfluous rubber tube, swearing crossly as he did so.

Before Attila Szigethy made his first suicide attempt in prison (he finally succeeded with his third) he wanted to make his confession.

Attila was not a Communist; he was one of the few men in whom I glimpsed the type of the new democratic politician. He had great faith in Kádár. He had told me so at length on 23 November 1956 when we met for the last time in the House of Folk Art. This faith Kádár appeared to reciprocate, for he sent Attila – this was already after my arrest – to represent Hungary at a congress in Sofia.

But in this case too it was not honest politicians that were wanted but prestigious delinquents. Attila was arrested in the provinces, where the old AVO methods had held their ground. Such humiliating maltreatment was more than his psyche could cope with, and from then on he thought only of death.

Tapping on the heating pipe, Attila asked for a priest. He found one in a cell some way away. First asking everyone else to stand back from the heating pipe and not listen, Attila made his confession and received absolution. It was a lengthy business because the priest did not know the morse code and they had to fall back on the long-winded prison alphabet. But they were able to finish without being caught; Attila's last wish was granted.

38

The trial – No more fabrications! – The last good-bye

THE presiding judge was a Dr Ferenc Vida, a tall, thin man of about fifty with a close-cropped, black moustache and a general appearance that, if not exactly neglected, was not exactly well-groomed either.

The four assessors were laymen, three men and one woman. The latter running to chubbiness, late thirties; one of the men nearing forty, unmistakably an AVO man, leather coat; another much the same but without the leather coat; the third an elderly man in solemn black with snow-white hair, the Party-veteran type. As film extras they would have struck one as well-chosen if somewhat stereotyped.

The assessors asked questions only rarely; the leather-coat man malicious and far from stupid, the other two men malicious but stupid, the woman not unaffected by the proceedings, prejudiced throughout against the accused but inclining occasionally to sympathy, and permanently bathed in sweat.

In appearance it all had much in common with a normal court of law, but only in appearance. From beginning to end the hearing was secret. Yet the entire trial, which went on for some fourteen days, was recorded on tape. To whom the lengthy secret was later played back was something I never discovered.

In the light of the 'socialist justice' that was being so heavily propagated in official quarters at the time, certain arrangements struck one as curious. Among other things defending counsel were not allowed to make any written notes. If they did so nevertheless they had to deposit them with the court until the next session before they could leave the room.

The presiding judge appeared to be a forthright jurist. His prime concern was at all events to dissociate himself from the impending judgement in order that it might later be seen that the sentences, wholly unjustified and indeed unjustifiable in law, had been passed, independently of the proceedings of the court, at the instance of a higher authority.

The court did not meet in any of the recognized courtrooms. A room in the AVO building was adapted for the purpose. The accused thus remained in the hands of the secret police – the same men as had interrogated them – throughout. In contrast to the trials held in Rákosi's day the accused were allowed to choose their own counsel – from a list compiled specially for the purpose. If one of the defending counsel incurred the displeasure of the court or the public prosecutor, he was either forbidden to plead in political cases in future or his practice was taken away from him for alleged 'revisionist opinions'. (This in fact happened to my counsel because he had dared at my express request to argue with court and public prosecutor.) Furthermore this court recognized no appeal. The sentence pronounced by Dr Vida was to be both irrevocable and irreparable.

In 1957 I was brought to trial with three other accused – the writers Tibor Déry, Zoltán Zelk, and Tibor Tardos.

There was no explaining why precisely these four should have been wrapped in the one bouquet. It was not even suggested that we had committed some crime together. Great pains were taken to break with the practices of Stalin's and Rákosi's courts. 'Socialist justice' was the current catchphrase. Easier said than done. In order to furnish grounds for the inhuman sentences that were politically indispensable it proved necessary after all to resort again and again to the detested judicial fabrications by means of which Rákosi had until recently wangled his victims into prison and up the gallows steps. Many victims of that tyranny had managed to survive the reign of terror and were now in positions of power. But they were not happy with it. Without lies, persecution, fabricated charges, and rigged sentences they too would have got nowhere.

Pali Susán had once been a coal-miner. When I met him his

political career had already begun. He was in the army, where he became a political officer. I was mad about that young man; I thought I had made the acquaintance of a new kind of human being. But he was only one of the new ruling class.

Young Pali Susán came to see me one day during the uprising and poured out his heart to me. He told me he was fed up with the army as a profession and wanted me to advise him what to do.

'You're a miner,' I said, trying to buck him up a bit. 'With your knowledge and with your political schooling maybe you could do even more for the mining industry than you're doing in the army.'

Pali thanked me, much moved. The report of our meeting that he then submitted to the AVO ran to eight pages. I was shown the document by Major Zentai, the investigating officer, who was busy fabricating a case of 'spreading sedition in the People's Army' on the part of the writers out of it. Apparently the line that fabricated trials were supposed to be a thing of the repudiated past had already been forgotten.

There was a further document by Pali Susán's hand. Shortly after my 'Kucsera' article had appeared I met him at a big staff college. I and a number of other writers had been invited to read from our works and discuss literature generally. The officers gave me a stormy ovation and wanted to hear 'Kucsera'. After-wards there were some questions of the usual naïve kind: could a high-up officer or even a general be a 'Kucsera' too? – that sort of thing. My answer was, 'It's something no one is proof against. Everybody has to watch himself.'

This remark too Susán saw as seditious. What I had meant, he claimed, was that the Minister of Defence and other high-ranking army officers were so many 'Kucseras'. Such a statement would have been sufficient to brand me as a counter-revolutionary and the revolution as a counter-revolution. (These activities proved useful for Susán's career, incidentally. He was appointed a member of a court martial and had occasion to contribute to the passage of numerous sentences.)

But even this evidence proved so worthless that the public prosecutor felt obliged to fall back on my appearance at a meeting in Györ a few days before the outbreak of the Revolution. Actually the Györ meeting was to have been only a routine literary discussion, but to my immense surprise I arrived to find a vast crowd assembled. That evening I began – slowcoach that I was – to realize that a storm was brewing in the land. Questions were fired at me – pointed political questions, nothing like the naïveties of the staff college – about the withdrawal of Soviet troops, the exploitation of Soviet-occupied countries, the freedom of literature, the abolition of censorship, and so on. I answered on the spur of the moment; the answers were after all in the air.

The public prosecutor called two young men as witnesses, young writers from Györ; their names were new to me. Both had been in prison for months already, had been beaten up on their arrest, and were thus expected to be particularly pliable. Yet if that court had had anything to do with justice those witnesses would have been the ruin of the prosecution. Quite independently of one another they were both unanimous in their belief that what I had done in Györ was to save an extremely precarious situation; had it not been for my outspoken answers, they said, blood would already have flowed that evening. But I, as one of the witnesses said, 'had steered the ship of the Communist Party with a steady hand'.

Asked by my defending counsel why *I* had had to steer the ship of the Communist Party and whether there had been no properly appointed helmsman present, the witness replied that the entire local Party leadership had been there to begin with but that later, when things became too hot for them, they had skedaddled to a man.

Everyone knew that the witnesses were doing themselves a lot of harm with such testimony without doing me any good. But during that time one told the truth for the truth's sake.

One heard a lot of stories in prison about Györ, its AVO, and its Party leadership. The young producer Földes had recited revolutionary poetry in the street so that the Party leadership could in the meantime slip away to safety. For this 'seditious activity' Földes was hanged. The same Party leadership is said to have escaped from the crowd by way of an engineer's office, surreptitiously knocking a hole in the back wall and slipping into a side alley. The engineer got six years' jail. The Party leadership, however, survived all these various trials and sentences.

The trial

The majority of the writers called as witnesses in our case sought and found an opportunity of somehow making clear that they identified with us accused whereas they had nothing but scorn for the court and did not regard it as a legal body. The first thing they did on entering the courtroom was to salute us with a bow. Devecseri, the translator of Homer, unambiguously and with grim Homeric humour offered the court his arse.

Not that anyone was in any doubt as to the fact that this was a life-and-death affair. And if the idea of demanding the death penalty for one or even more of us was in fact dropped, it was not through any sudden access of justice nor did it have anything to do with the worthlessness of the evidence for the prosecution. It happened under pressure of public opinion both at home and abroad.

And even though the authorities refused the composer Zoltán Kodály and the writers Gyula Illyés, Áron Tamási, László Németh (though the latter in fact did us imprisoned writers much harm with a toast he later came out with in Moscow), and others permission to speak out in our favour, their protests, tenaciously repeated, were not without effect.

In our case the voice of public opinion was clearly perceptible. Our 'Help, help, help' had found an echo. Committees were formed in many countries for the liberation of the Hungarian writers. For three years and more, up until the amnesties of 1 April 1960 and 1961, the Hungarian government and also the Soviet government were bombarded with letters of protest, petitions, and telegrams. Roosevelt's widow, Nehru, Camus, de Villefosse, Sartre, the British Labour Party leadership with Gaitskell, Bevan . . . I shall not even try and list all the prominent people who spoke up for us. What Togliatti wrote about the Hungarian Revolution and its causes the brutal stringency of Party discipline forced him in large part to take back, but nevertheless his words rang true. My old friends Arthur Koestler, Ignazio Silone, and Alfred Kantorowicz were beside me once more after years of separation, even though vast distances still did separate us geographically.

A true and dependable saviour was the PEN Club; Carver in London, Csokor in Vienna. Franz Theodor Csokor, still in his old age a tireless campaigner for truth and human dignity, came pounding a second time on my cell door, refusing to be led astray by the fact that it had once been the anti-Communists and was now the Communists that had clapped me in jail.

My articles on the freedom of literature and on 'Kucsera' were reprinted over and over again in any number of languages. François Bondy, who had been in Budapest during the uprising and managed to look me up, had taken the texts back with him to Paris. And how could I forget the BBC with its life-saving promptitude? It did its bit towards saving Jóska Gáli too.

Even so the number of the victims was horrifyingly large. When I was in the special section of the Budapest Reception Prison the condemned men used to be led past my window early in the morning to the place of execution. Often they called out their names as a last good-bye. I only understood and remarked one of them, because I had known the man well – Otto Szirmai, the radio drama producer. Another way you could tell execution mornings was from the trusties who worked as barbers. They were pale and trembly. They had just shaved those about to die.

With the prosecution in such a pickle, how important the testimony of a witness like György Máté must have been! He was the Party secretary of the Writers' Union. The court had utter confidence in him. He had presided at the meeting of 23 October at which I had been nominated to go to Party head-quarters to negotiate. He had been present at my talk with Gerö, as on countless other occasions. He could have been a mine of 'mitigating circumstances'. Many people expected him to be our salvation.

'Was the witness not present,' I asked, 'when I got a certain person to promise not to open fire on the people?'

The Party secretary turned red, then white, and finally croaked out, 'I recall no such occasion.'

A Party man you could depend on.

During the trial, which lasted two weeks or so, I shared a cell with a student named Lehel. I seem to have told him a good deal about Eva because he arrived at a pretty good picture of her character. As the trial neared its end I was busy marshalling my ideas for my summing-up. I tried out the effect of my speech on my cell-mate, as is common practice in prison. I completed my peroration; Lehel was silent and thoughtful for a while. Then he said approvingly, 'Mrs Eva will be very pleased.'

My summing-up made no appeal to justice and the law. Had I not known anyway that these had little bearing on the proceedings of the court, the fact would have been brought home to me during the hearing. I talked instead about Molière. My guilt, I said, consisted in the fact that I as a playwright had failed to learn from the fate of the great Molière. He had wanted to attack the affected piety of the 'Tartuffes' and, lo and behold, the whole church had felt itself threatened. I had wanted in my 'Kucsera' article – and writing it was accounted my offence – to criticize the bad element of officialdom. Officialdom as a whole had taken my remarks to refer to itself as a whole.

I had only one request to make of my judges. If in spite of everything the court should sentence me and I should have to stay in prison, I asked that the permission to read and write that had been granted me while I had been awaiting trial should be extended. I wanted to write a historical play. I did not of course receive an answer to my request. But for more than half of the three years and three months I was to spend in jail I was in fact allowed to read and write, and Eva was allowed to send me the necessary source material.

The sentences were: Déry, nine years; J.H., six years; the other two accused, Zelk and Tardos, three and one and a half years respectively. In Déry's and my case, complete sequestration of property as well.

The two weeks of the hearing were for us accused absolute bliss. On every second day our wives were admitted to the court-room during the recess and we were allowed to sit with them. There were occasions when we could talk almost without anyone listening in. Those days remained in our memories as a time of inexpressible happiness.

39

Mohács – A nation's soul on strike – 'For Eva'

1526 was the year in which Eva and I spent together – in thought – the next few years. Mohács – a little town in the south of Hungary. Mohács – the name Hungarians are in the habit of putting to the misfortune that has oppressed the Hungarian people for centuries. At Mohács, in 1526, Hungary suffered a crushing defeat at the hands of the Turks, losing in the process its entire army, its king, and its national independence.

And the West looked on without lifting a finger.

'Follow me!'

I picked up my jacket and followed the sergeant.

I found it strange that I had been kept on in the AVO prison after my sentence and not sent to some penitentiary to serve my term.

'Along there!'

The last part of the familiar corridor had been divided lengthwise in two with freshly-planed planks since I had last been along it. One side served for the normal corridor traffic; the other side ended in a single door – the door through which witnesses were introduced into the courtroom.

So that was why they had kept me on in the AVO jail. I was to be questioned in connection with another case. For a moment all other feelings were swept aside by the feeling of joy that I might, even if only for a matter of minutes, be seeing friends again.

'In here!'

The sergeant grasped my shoulder and pushed me forward several paces. I found myself in the middle of a cone of savagely

368

bright light with darkness all around me like the walls of a narrow tower. Gradually I made out the faces on the bench. The same Dr Vida as had presided at my own trial. Beside him the assessors. The three men were the same as had passed my own sentence; only the woman was different – thin and bespectacled. This hearing too was secret, and the improvised public gallery was empty. Déry's lawyer was also present, this time apparently defending Tildy.

'Did you in the Parliament Building on the morning of 4 November notice a certain tension between Tildy on the one hand and Dobi and Rónai on the other?'

I wondered what the judge was after. Was the image of the two marionettes – the president puppet and the minister puppet – already so tarnished that a fabrication was needed to salvage it? Was the court trying to pretend that Tildy had kept the other two back there forcibly and against their will?

'No, I noticed no tension between the three whatsoever. They were sitting and drinking tea together. Three weary, broken, totally washed-up old men.'

A flicker of satisfaction passed over Tildy's face. A sigh of relief from the defence and an irritated darkening of the presiding judge's brow showed that one could not after all play court without temporarily entering into the illusion that there must be some tie-up between evidence and judgement.

'Imre Nagy, step forward!'

The familiar figure of Imre Nagy detached itself from the dark wall of the cone of light, the rest of the accused remaining outside the bright beam and thus invisible to me. He stood there with the light full on him, emaciated, pale, calm.

'Have you any questions for the witness?'

Imre stepped closer to me. An expression of deep joy spread over his face, the joy of reunion. For a moment he appeared to have forgotten that this reunion meant good-bye for ever. A joy without hope. Our looks, the looks of two elderly men, met and embraced in the weary silence of that courtroom that knew no justice.

Behind his spectacles was the knowing look of a man who now

indeed knows everything. Our farewell needed neither words nor gestures. I found it impossible to think that in a few days' time this man would in all probability be killed in cold blood.

'Thank you,' he said – the last words I was to hear him speak – 'thank you, no questions.'

I was seized by an absurd, impassioned willingness to help. I wanted to be bombarded with questions and to be able to fire back subtle, saving answers. That foolish linking of cause and effect again.

The black edges of the bright cone of light remained impenetrable. Imre Nagy and his gentle smile vanished into the darkness.

Someone took me by the arm and pulled me out of the room, out into the corridor that smelt of freshly-planed planks.

The enormous prison van was divided into a large number of little compartments. In each of these cells, which were hardly bigger than coffins, there was just enough room to cram one man. The van had already been standing in the summer sun for several hours, soaking up heat. Anyone who was then shut into one of the little cells began by gasping for breath and soon lapsed into a state of semi-consciousness.

The AVO clearly had no further use for me and was dispatching me to the Reception Prison, special section, into the custody of Staff Sergeant Németh.

Nights spent half-awake on the unfamiliar plank bed amid the acrid smell of carbolic soap. Gaudy-gloomy pictures alternating in my tired and agitated brain. Mohács . . . Louis II, King of Hungary . . .

Not knowing whether fighting statesmen have moments too in which their childhood comes back to them, nor whether at such moments they talk with God.

The young king's prayer before the Battle of Mohács in which he was to lose both his life and Hungary's freedom: 'I want to ask you for something, Crucified One.' Later it was all to be written down in one of the little blue exercise books; but first the anguished words and sentences went quivering through my tormented brain. 'Something you do not have a grain of yourself and never did have: cunning, deceit, and adroitness . . . ' No, that is no longer the voice of a young man such as King Louis was when he prepared himself to meet a hero's death on the field of Mohács. 'You are God – get hold of them somewhere and implant them in my blundering soul so that I may be more cunning than the snake, more deceitful than the fox, and more adroit than the ape. That is what I have need of on this my most arduous day . . . '

Was I hearing my own words? Or was that the vibrant voice that had got stuck in that defective loudspeaker before the Parliament Building on 23 October? Imre Nagy's diapason that had not been able to penetrate the walls of Party headquarters? Was that the voice that at the decisive moment not even his family could hear?

Mohács. Had the disaster of Mohács really recurred? Was I, lying there on that plank bed, myself one of the fallen in the repeat performance? I knew what we lacked, we latter-day successors of the tragic heroes of 1526, the Mohács dead. I knew why Louis of Hungary came seeking me out every night in my damp prison cell, and I knew too why Imre Nagy stepped through the wall of darkness into the cone of bright light. I said for both of them the belated prayer in which I asked – I knew in vain – for what both had been so short of: cunning, deceit, and adroitness. They were straightforward, honest men, utterly without falsehood, and that was why first one and then the other must lose both Hungary and his life.

J.H. 57 walked patiently round and round in the narrow box that made it possible to exercise the prisoners alone and unseen. J.H. 58 found himself getting used to wearing a striped suit. J.H. 59 learnt how a good convict can go to sleep on any old sack of straw at any time – if only he is allowed to. And year after year, day and night, I sat in my cell and worked on my play.

Where was my Damascus, then? At what point did I turn from a Saul into a Paul – or from a Paul into a Saul? Nowhere, as I believe. And that was precisely what I had to pay for.

For decades I had walked and jogged and hurried along the same path, always the same path, the one I knew as the path of socialism. Other men, though, who called themselves the Party, abandoned that narrow way. They opted for the high road of power and dominion and they said that the high road led to socialism, to Communism.

Our sort was reviled, put in prison, and threatened with death because we had tried to continue along the path the others had abandoned.

They have failed to reach their goal and I have failed to reach my goal. The difference is that I admit the goal is unattainable. For my dreams to find their realization the world must look for a new path, a path as yet unknown.

Meanwhile the outside world was pounding ever louder at my cell door. The West could swallow neither the inhumanity nor the absurdity of this mock justice. And the rulers of Hungary were faced ever more clearly with the silent protest of the people.

There was no shouting, no demonstrating. Just a general listlessness about everyday existence that proved an uncannily effective historical and economic factor. The shrill cries of 'punishment', 'revenge', and 'reprisals' so recently on the victors' lips began to die away. They left a crop of apathy sprouting from the very soil. Factory smoke-stacks belched cheerlessness. No one took a pride in his work; no one was ashamed of his low productivity. It was a general strike of the national soul.

Another watchword had to be found. The chosen substitute was 'reconciliation'. It was thought it would sound well in Western ears too. Perhaps it would bring back something of the nation's will to work, overcome its by now chronic inappetence. A 'thaw' had to come – or something that could at a pinch be so called.

Reconciliation, thaw – amnesty.

On 1 April 1960 several hundred prisoners – including J.H. 60 – in all the prisons and penitentiaries up and down the country were handed back the civvies they had surrendered years before. With them they got a piece of paper that gave them back the freedom to walk out into the street as well as some other of the human rights they had been deprived of.

That day a small, shabby Budapest taxi waited outside the gates of Maria Nostra from noon until evening. In it sat a woman, counting the hours, indeed the minutes. J.H. 60 had not yet left the building. Was it that as a particularly dangerous prisoner he could only be set at large in isolation from the mass?

'I'm sorry to have to make you wait so long . . . '

'Don't mention it, lady. On this historic day . . . ' So said a Budapest taxi-driver on 1 April 1960.

The forecourt of the ancient prison was a blaze of light. No one wanted this particularly closely watched man vanishing into the dark. Spotlights followed him like a star crossing the stage in the grand finale.

The wide iron gate swung open. The prisoner had a sack full of books and papers, including a finished play called *Mohács*. Right up until the last moment there was a danger of someone going through the contents of the sack, in which case the play called *Mohács* would of course have been lost for ever.

Major Juhász, commanding officer of Maria Nostra, was at a loss. He had seen a great many things in his years in the prison service, and he found it impossible to take this amnesty entirely seriously. The powers that be, whose representative he rightly considered himself, had surely not carried off the victory in order subsequently to surrender it. And yet and yet . . . One ought to get in good with people who yesterday were still inmates of Maria Nostra and today were suddenly free men.

Coming to an abrupt decision, Major Juhász offered me his hand. 'No offence, comrade – we're all of us only human.' And his hand was poised for me to shake it.

Should I do so or should I refuse? The salutation of an almost unknown minor official was certainly of little importance, even if he was a god to his prisoners. How often had one shaken hands with out-and-out rogues and not given the matter a second thought? Ministers, generals, potentates of every kind.

Tomorrow was a new day and with it began a new life. Would it not anyway start off with some knave or numskull shaking one by the hand? And would a single day go by without the salaams of a dozen worthless blackguards who might all be worse than this twit of a major?

Across the threshold of the prison a new life beckoned me. Was it to be no different from the old? Should I not finally start leading a sensible existence? Did I have to go on assuming responsibility for the entire world? Had I not qualified for the right to live as men usually live? Would it not be best to call on Comrade X or Comrade Y first thing in the morning, hat in hand, and sincerely rejoice should they offer me their hands to shake, show themselves willing to forgive me my 'Kucsera', and give me a bit of reading work and the odd translation to do? Should not those handshakes and the many that might follow mark the beginning of a new kind of safe, secure private life?

Let me think of my own peace for a change, my own prosperity. Let me, I thought, take the proffered hands of all who have power over me and are prepared on the occasion of this bitter-sweet amnesty to use that power judiciously: publishers, theatre managers, ministers, Party secretaries. 'No offence, comrade . . . '

Beside the man who was waiting with growing impatience for my gesture of reconciliation there fell in invisibly all the people who had presumed to deprive me of my human rights or give those same rights back to me. 'We're all of us only human, comrade.'

As these thoughts chased one another through my brain and as Major Juhász continued to hold out an expectant hand, I unconsciously stepped past him and swung my bundle of books and manuscripts into the taxi, the blue exercise books marked 'For Eva' on top.

However I began, I knew it would be my untrustworthy travelling companion the twentieth century that would show me the way. Perhaps to the West this time? Without illusions and yet in deepest disappointment?

Was it I that pulled the car door to with a bang? The major's hand was still raised in an embarrassed salute. The window now divided the world irrevocably in two. Outside all those who knew the secret of the easy, lucrative life – at other people's expense and with other people's sweat and blood. Inside the car, which drove off immediately, two of those who knew nothing of all that and clearly had no wish to do so.

And the woman who had once been the 'girl in blue' wept for happiness. Wept for the first time since her life had become so lamentable.

Appendix

The principal dramatic works of Julius Hay

Julius Hay writes in both Hungarian and German. The German titles are given here. His plays have been translated into more than ten languages and performed in more than eighteen countries.

Das neue Paradies ('The New Paradise'), 1931. A comedy of nineteenth-century America. Motto: Utopias don't last.

Gott, Kaiser und Bauer ('God, Emperor, and Peasant'), 1932. A historical play about Sigismund, King of Hungary and Holy Roman Emperor, and John Hus, the Czech reformer whom he tried and failed to help, the point being that no emperor is as powerful as money.

Der Damm an der Theiss ('The Dam on the Tisza'), 1933. In this gentle tragedy the author raises for the first time the question that is central to his whole work – man and the earth: how do they relate to one another?

Der Barbar ('The Barbarian'), 1934. Professionalism (Pompeius) gets the better of genius (Mithridates Eupator).

Haben ('Have'), 1934–6. A Hungarian peasant tragedy on the theme of how modern capitalism deforms the soul, making murderers of women who want only to live and love. Directed by Joan Littlewood, *Haben* was performed at the Theatre Royal, Stratford East, in 1954 under the title *The Midwife*.

Der Putenhirt ('The Turkey-boy'), 1938. A tragi-comedy set in the Hungarian Lowlands. The mere fact of a landowner's being a powerful lord is responsible for his becoming the murderer of little Imre, the innocent visionary.

Appendix

Gerichtstag ('Day of Reckoning'), 1944. A German working-class tragedy set in the late Nazi period.

Die Brücke des Lebens ('The Bridge of Life'), 1950. An episode from the drama of post-war reconstruction in Budapest.

Gáspár Varrós Recht ('Fair Play for Gáspár Varró'), 1953. The truth about the Hungarian village under socialism, and the tragedy of an old man sacrificed on the altar of power.

Mohács, 1958–60. The story of the background to Hungary's terrible defeat by the Turks in 1526. 1956 was not the first time Hungary had been betrayed by the West.

Das Pferd ('The Horse'), 1961. A rollicking historical comedy about Caligula, the emperor who raised his horse to the office of consul, and about the people who let him do it. Translated by Peter Hay ('my second Peter'), *The Horse* was performed at the Oxford Playhouse in 1965.

Attilas Nächte ('Attila's Nights'), 1962. Attila and Aetius are both aware that the Battle of Catelauni will be a piece of senseless bloodshed, yet the forces of history compel them to fight it.

Appassionata, 1965. An episode from the period following the defeat of the Hungarian Revolution of 1956.

Der Grossinquisitor ('The Grand Inquisitor'), 1967. A ghost comedy about power.

Index

(*Compiled by F. D. Buck*)

379

Index

Index

Index

DATE DUE

JAN 3 1 '84			

DEMCO 38-297

Hay, Julius.
  Born 1900 : memoirs / Julius Hay ; trans.
from the original German and abridged by
J. A. Underwood. With a foreword by Arthur
Koestler. LaSalle, Ill. : Open Court, 1975.

  383 p. ; 24 cm.
  "The principal dramatic works of Julius
Hay": p. 377-[378]

  I. Title.